The Japan–U.S. Alliance

The Japan Center for International Exchange wishes to thank

The Nippon Foundation

The Japan–U.S. Alliance

New Challenges for the 21st Century

edited by
Nishihara Masashi

JCIE

Tokyo ▪ Japan Center for International Exchange ▪ *New York*

The surnames of the authors and other persons mentioned in this book are positioned according to country practice.

Copyediting by Pamela J. Noda.
Cover and typographic design by Becky Davis, EDS Inc., Editorial & Design Services.
Typesetting and production by EDS Inc.
Cover photograph © 1996 The Studio Dog/PhotoDisc, Inc.

Printed in Japan
ISBN 4-88907-034-6

Distributed worldwide outside Japan by Brookings Institution Press,
1775 Massachusetts Avenue, N.W., Washington, D.C. 20036-2188 U.S.A.

Japan Center for International Exchange
9-17 Minami Azabu 4-chome, Minato-ku, Tokyo 106 Japan

URL: http://www.jcie.or.jp

Japan Center for International Exchange, Inc. (JCIE/USA)
1251 Avenue of the Americas, New York, N.Y. 10020 U.S.A.

Contents

Foreword

SINCE its establishment in 1970, the Japan Center for International Exchange (JCIE) has conducted activities aimed at effectively meeting the changing needs of the global community and Japan. At this time of transition in international society, Japan—as a member of the group of advanced industrial nations—needs to facilitate policy-related exchange and dialogue among countries and regions. In light of the increasing diversification of its society, Japan should promote domestic debate on external relations and endeavor to forge a broad-based national consensus on external policies. Concerned people at home and overseas have pointed out, however, that Japanese activities of this sort have been handicapped, at least partially, by a very weak think-tank framework for debating and promoting policies compared with the West and other Asian countries.

With this in mind, JCIE launched the Global ThinkNet project in 1996 with the help of various foundations, including the Nippon Foundation. As one of our center's main projects, the Global ThinkNet seeks to stimulate intellectual exchange domestically as well as internationally by means of policy research and dialogue. The project is designed to construct and utilize efficiently a broad network of leading research institutes and researchers at home and overseas.

One of the Global ThinkNet's programs is the Global ThinkNet Fellows Program, which seeks to develop the human resources needed for this sort of global network. This program trains researchers to conduct policy-oriented studies on the political and economic issues facing contemporary Japan. It also seeks to encourage Japanese participation in global networks for intellectual exchange. Every year study groups of promising researchers are organized; each has its own theme and is guided by one or more senior scholars. After about a year of study, each participant submits a policy-oriented research paper in Japanese and English.

This book presents the results of one of these study groups organized among six younger Japanese political scientists on the overall theme of the Japan-U.S. alliance under the guidance of Professor Nishihara Masashi, president of the National Defense Academy. The Japan-U.S. alliance is considered to be the most important factor in the stability of East Asia. While this alliance is thought to rest on a firm foundation, it is constantly affected by domestic public opinion and politics, international events and their repercussions, tensions between other counties, and cultural outlook. In this volume, the members of the Nishihara study group examine how the differences as well as the similarities in policies between the two alliance partners toward various issues and countries may affect the solidarity of the alliance and, hence, influence the stability of the Asia Pacific region at large.

On behalf of JCIE, I wish to thank Professor Nishihara, who agreed to direct a Global ThinkNet Fellows group for a second time. (The work of his first group in 1996–1997 was published in 1998 as *Old Issues, New Responses: Japan's Foreign and Security Policy Options.*) Once again, Professor Nishihara gave close personal attention to the preparation and publication of the participants' papers, both during and after the study period. I would also like to express our profound gratitude to the Nippon Foundation for its financial support and the cooperation it has extended to us for many aspects of the Global ThinkNet.

YAMAMOTO TADASHI
President
Japan Center for International Exchange

The Japan-U.S. Alliance: Defense Cooperation and Beyond

Nishihara Masashi

THE importance of the Japan-U.S. alliance for the Asia Pacific region has been stressed since its inception in 1952. During the cold war, the alliance effectively served as a deterrent against the Soviet threat and then, in the last decade of the twentieth century, its role began to expand from home defense to regional security. As we enter the new century, the alliance appears to be assuming even greater importance than in the past.

In January 1992, Japanese Prime Minister Miyazawa Kiichi and U.S. President George Bush met in Tokyo and declared they would work together to achieve a global partnership. The two nations were to work closely on global issues such as nuclear and conventional arms proliferation, regional tensions, refugees, and drug trafficking. Both countries had, indeed, cooperated in many diplomatic and economic areas in the past, but this statement confirmed that the role of the alliance no longer needed to be confined to defense, and the two partners would accelerate their efforts in areas beyond bilateral defense cooperation.

The nations entered another stage in their bilateral relations in April 1996, when Prime Minister Hashimoto Ryūtarō and President Bill Clinton issued a joint declaration on the future alliance at the conclusion of their summit meeting in Tokyo. The nations agreed to contribute to regional security, although the Japanese role would continue to be limited. This agreement culminated in the 1999 enactment of laws that stipulate the role of Japan in coping with "situations in areas surrounding Japan that will have an important influence on the peace and security of Japan."

In recognition of the importance of these developments to bilateral relations, the Japan Center for International Exchange in the fall of 1998

9

selected six young Japanese scholars to form a study group to discuss the evolving alliance. The scholars chose related topics which included the effects of the new Guidelines for U.S.-Japan Defense Cooperation, peace and security on the Korean peninsula, Taiwan, the Association of Southeast Asian Nations (ASEAN), economic sanctions on Myanmar, and small-arms proliferation. Their common objective was to identify policy differences between Tokyo and Washington on given issues, pursue their common interests, and suggest how the alliance might be strengthened by improving bilateral arrangements or by coordinating policies. Although the group participants are well known in their chosen fields, most lack experience in writing policy-oriented papers. Group discussions that took place between September 1998 and March 1999 were, thus, most useful in helping them formulate their ideas and craft them into what would become the chapters of this book.

In this introduction I would like to summarize the major points of each chapter.

STRENGTHENING
BILATERAL DEFENSE COOPERATION

A stronger alliance obviously requires close defense cooperation. Are the new Guidelines for U.S.-Japan Defense Cooperation of 1997 likely to ensure closer defense cooperation than before? This is the major concern of the chapter by Murata Kōji, a specialist in the bilateral defense relationship. The original guidelines of 1978 had dealt primarily with how the two nations would work together in the event of an external attack on Japanese territories. The revised guidelines lay out how the two nations would cooperate in the case of contingencies in areas surrounding Japan. Murata's chapter questions how effective the new guidelines will make the alliance.

The author compares the two sets of guidelines and concludes that the revised set should contribute significantly to a stronger alliance and regional stability. However, he argues that, unless the Japanese government revises its interpretation of the Constitution and moves to adopt the right of collective self-defense in addition to that of individual self-defense, Japan's role will remain limited and ineffective, and as a result the alliance may not function as it should. The view favoring the revision of the interpretation of Article 9 of the Constitution or, indeed, the revision of Article 9 itself, is gaining currency to the extent that the Diet has recently established a Constitutional Research Council that will examine the issue.

Murata also argues against excessive legalism in interpreting the kind and scope of Japanese missions to be carried out during contingencies. The law distinguishes between rear-area support (support in non-combat areas such as Japanese air and sea ports), which Japan can legally extend to U.S. operations, and combat-area support. However, the chapter maintains that such distinctions may not be possible during actual contingencies.

The author does not advocate that Japan pursue an autonomous defense. Instead, he states that credible defense capabilities require an effective civilian control system with a stronger Diet legislative staff and a strong political will on the part of the leadership.

SECURITY ARRANGEMENTS AFTER PEACE IN KOREA

In his chapter, Michishita Narushige, a specialist on Korean security issues, considers the future of the Japan-U.S. and U.S.-South Korean alliances in a post-confrontation Korean peninsula. He argues that discussion of desirable security arrangements for a post-confrontation Korea should start now, because it would give a sense of direction and predictability for all countries concerned, and because it would put pressure on North Korea to remain engaged with the United States, Japan, and South Korea.

Michishita proposes that the U.S.-South Korea alliance be maintained in the future with a sizable U.S. military presence on the peninsula. He adds that closer coordination between the U.S.-South Korea and Japan-U.S. alliances would contribute to the stability of the peninsula and the regional environment.

This chapter presents a new perspective on debates regarding future security arrangements in Northeast Asia, as many experts in Japan tend to argue that the United States should reduce its troop presence in both South Korea and Japan, and particularly in Okinawa. The author cites five reasons for a united Korea needing to retain an alliance with the United States: reassurance, regional and global security, supporting the Japan-U.S. alliance, serving as a hedge against the rise of an aggressive China, and helping to establish an East Asian community of democratic nations.

Since Kim Dae Jung took office in Seoul in 1998, political and security relations between Seoul and Tokyo have improved remarkably. This is an encouraging sign for future trilateral security cooperation. The author encourages Washington, Seoul, and Tokyo to conduct even closer consultations.

JAPAN-U.S. POLICY COORDINATION ON TAIWAN

Tension over the Taiwan Strait is, naturally, a source of security concern for Japan, which officially recognizes the Beijing position that there is only one China, and that Taiwan is part of China. However, Tokyo has chosen to take an ambiguous stance on whether Taiwan and the Taiwan Strait are included in the "areas surrounding Japan," which the new defense guidelines describe as covered by Japan's new security role.

Nakai Yoshifumi, who works on this issue, argues that Japan should shift from an approach of strategic ambiguity to one that offers more clarity in stating Japan's commitment to the security of the Asia Pacific region. Japan should clearly express its sympathy with democratic nations, he maintains.

Nakai is concerned about the different reactions of the governments of Japan and the United States to the 1996 Taiwan Strait Crisis. Unlike the United States, Japan did not perceive the possibly grave consequences of the crisis. He also notes that, after the crisis, the United States moved to modify its stance and shifted to an engagement policy with China. He sees an acute need for Tokyo and Washington to coordinate their strategies for Taiwan.

The chapter presents three likely scenarios for Japanese and U.S. policies on the Taiwan problem. According to Nakai, a diversion scenario, in which the two nations take different, uncoordinated approaches, would likely disrupt the alliance. On the other hand, a conversion scenario, in which Japan adjusts its policies in accordance with the U.S. position, would not meet approval at home and would, thus, weaken the alliance. The only desirable scenario, he suggests, would be for the two nations to acknowledge their differences, but coordinate their policies from both near- and long-term perspectives.

CLOSER TIES BETWEEN THE ALLIANCE AND ASEAN

Japan and the United States would seem to share common security interests in Southeast Asia. Both countries would like to see viable states and regional stability for the security of sea lanes in the region. Both desire a healthy solidarity for ASEAN, as a counterbalance to the expansion of Chinese power.

Yet the two nations have adopted quite different policies toward Southeast Asia in recent years. Japan has supported the controversial government of Prime Minister Hun Sen in Cambodia in the interests of political stability, while the United States has kept its political distance. In Myanmar as well, Japan was relatively quick to relax the sanctions it had imposed after the government crackdown on democracy supporters in 1990, while U.S. sanctions remain in force.

The impact of these policy differences on the bilateral alliance is the focus of Sudō Sueo's chapter. After defining the major sources of instability in Southeast Asia as the relative shift in U.S. and Chinese power in the region and the recent economic crisis and political turmoil, Sudō proposes that Japan and the United States achieve better policy coordination in the economic, political, and security fields. He argues that the two nations should take steps to help strengthen the ASEAN Regional Forum, resolve conflicts in the South China Sea, and encourage ASEAN participation in the U.S.-sponsored RIMPAC multinational naval exercises.

Southeast Asia is a geostrategically important area for both Japan and the United States. The Sudō chapter is helpful in suggesting how the alliance may be strengthened through working more closely with ASEAN.

MYANMAR AND THE ALLIANCE

Myanmar has been a source of tension between the policies of Japan and the Unites States. Both governments imposed economic sanctions in 1990, but Japan gradually relaxed its stance on economic aid. While Washington assumes that continued sanctions and political support for democracy movement leader Aung San Suu Kyi will eventually weaken the military government and bring about democratization, Tokyo assumes that the government will last and that what is most important is to assist the people suffering from economic hardship.

Hoshino Eiichi sees Japan and the United States as pursuing the same goal of promoting democracy but employing contrasting means to achieve it. Tokyo tends to assume that an enhanced standard of living will eventually lead to political pluralism, while Washington would like to see principles of democracy established first. One reason for their contrasting positions is their varying national interests: Japan has a much greater strategic stake in Myanmar, and thus Tokyo is much more concerned than the United States about the possibility that a politically isolated Myanmar will turn to China for support.

Hoshino considers four options for policies Japan and the United States could adopt towards Myanmar: disengagement by both, partial engagement by Tokyo and disengagement by Washington (the current scenario), disengagement by Tokyo and partial engagement by Washington, and engagement by both. He proposes that the two governments practice what he refers to as conditional engagement. The conditions would include reciprocity (a spirit of self-criticism), consistency, and the use of positive sanctions to encourage democratization. He also urges that the governments weigh regional and cultural sensitivities in implementing sanctions.

This is certainly a controversial issue for the alliance. While Myanmar may be a relatively minor strategic concern for Tokyo and Washington, similar issues may be seen in relations with Vietnam, China, and North Korea. The Myanmar problem, in this sense, can be a potential source of friction that could undermine the alliance unless the two governments adopt a concerted approach, as Hoshino advocates.

COMBATING ARMS PROLIFERATION

The last chapter tackles the global issue of arms proliferation. Miyasaka Naofumi finds that Japan and the United States take different approaches to the issues of proliferation of weapons of mass destruction (WMD) and the spread of small arms and light weapons. The United States regards the spread of arms as a threat to its national security, whereas Japan tends to consider it as a global security issue. Miyasaka maintains that Japan, too, should treat the issue as a national security concern, as arms proliferated by illegitimate nonstate actors have threatened Japan's national security, and may do so again in the future. He argues that this divergence in approach can cause friction between the alliance partners.

The use of WMD by terrorists is becoming a serious issue, as shown by the sarin gas attack on the Tokyo subway system by the Aum Shinrikyō cult in 1995, the bombing of the World Trade Center in New York in 1993, and the 1995 bombing of the federal building in Oklahoma City. Miyasaka argues that, while the U.S. government has responded to WMD terrorism by adopting tough new antiterrorism laws and strengthening the role of relevant agencies such as the Federal Bureau of Investigation, Japan has been slow in setting up a legal framework to cope with the problem. Similar asymmetrical responses by the two nations can be seen with regard to the issue of small arms proliferation. The United States has entered into regional and bilateral arms control treaties, but its experience as an arms exporter and a society that allows private gun ownership has made it cognizant of the difficulty of controlling firearms. Japan, on the other hand, bans private ownership of firearms, so it tends to treat the issue from a stance of moral superiority.

With these contrasts in mind, Miyasaka proposes that the two nations conclude a comprehensive agreement allowing them to cooperate more closely to fight arms proliferation by nonstate terrorists. Their cooperation should go beyond fragmented interagency contacts, he says. He also proposes that the governments establish a top-level bilateral counter proliferation center and that they strengthen the Japan-U.S. alliance by linking their policies toward transnational threats more closely.

As these chapters demonstrate, young Japanese scholars have new perspectives on how to strengthen the Japan-U.S. alliance and where it should be headed. In May 1999, the six authors in the study group visited several distinguished American universities and think tanks and exchanged views with their counterparts there on the basis of their draft policy papers. Their discussions further helped the authors articulate the issues involved and proved to be a highly rewarding experience. In all, this has been a very successful intellectual exercise.

There are many other important security issues which the two countries should tackle, and I hope that many more young scholars will be encouraged to engage in policy debates across the Pacific. Due acknowledgement for the success of this project should go to President Yamamoto Tadashi of the Japan Center for International Exchange and his staff, including Noda Makito, Paul Stares, and Furuya Ryōta. Special thanks should also be extended to the Nippon Foundation for its generous support.

The Japan-U.S. Alliance

Do the New Guidelines Make the Japan-U.S. Alliance More Effective?

Murata Kōji

THE alliance between the United States and Japan is unique. First of all, it is a bilateral alliance between the victor and the vanquished of a major war. Psychological issues thus encumber this relationship and sometimes exacerbate the difficulties that arise. Germany and Italy, which were also vanquished in the war, joined the North Atlantic Treaty Organization, but NATO is a multilateral alliance. Understandably, relations between former enemies in a larger framework suffer from less severe tensions than an alliance of only two.

Second, while Japan and the United States, according to Mike Mansfield, the former U.S. ambassador to Japan, have the "most important bilateral relations in the world," they do not have a common historical and cultural background.

Third, and most important, the Japan-U.S. alliance, unlike NATO or the U.S.-South Korea alliance, lacks a substantive military structure. That is to say, there is no organization or procedure in place for consultation and implementation of joint military actions. The avoidance of joint military action is a common characteristic of Japan's alliances, as seen also in the Anglo-Japanese Alliance and the Tripartite Pact (Tsuchiyama 1993).

In spite of these apparent drawbacks, which could have weakened ties, the Japan-U.S. alliance has been firmly in effect since 1952.[1] It is evident that the cold war was an important impetus for the stability and durability of the alliance. None of the other cold war alliances, however, have proven to be as strong as the Japan-U.S. alliance. The U.S.-South Korea alliance, for example, has suffered from doubts about the credibility of the U.S. defense commitment (see Murata 1998). The U.S. alliance with Taiwan was terminated in 1979. And among the former Communist allies, the Sino-Soviet alliance has dissolved. What, then, explains the special nature of the Japan-U.S. alliance?

First, for both parties, the alliance has been inexpensive but beneficial, and neither side has been able to find a realistic alternative to it. It is true that Japan, especially Okinawa, has borne the burden of maintaining U.S. military facilities, but that has been a far cheaper option than fully rearming Japan. Furthermore, under U.S. military protection, Japan has enjoyed great economic prosperity in a U.S.-led Western free trade system. The alternative of Japan allying itself with the Soviet Union or the People's Republic of China has not been very attractive.

Japan lies in the strategic center of Northeast Asia, so the United States has garnered great value from maintaining its military facilities there. The relationship has thus been mutually beneficial, and in this sense it would be wrong to claim that Japan is gaining a "free ride" from the alliance (although it may have been gaining a "cheap ride"). In addition, unlike South Korea and Taiwan, Japan has not been directly confronted with an external military power. Japan therefore has functioned as a safe haven for the United States, which has not had to be concerned about being entrapped in military conflict, as Japan has had to fear being embroiled in the U.S.-Soviet rivalry.[2] Moreover, the alliance has kept Japan from joining the adversarial camp, which, given Japan's economic and technological significance, would have been very harmful to U.S. interests.

Second, the Japan-U.S. alliance has been highly complementary. Japan has provided important military bases to the United States in peacetime. In return, the United States has indicated its willingness to commit its soldiers in the event of military contingencies in Japan. In 1960, Nishimura Kumao, then director-general of the Treaties Bureau of the Ministry of Foreign Affairs, called this "cooperation between the material factor and the human factor" (1960, 59). Their relations complement each other on a more micro level, as well. For example, while the U.S. Navy deploys aircraft carriers and nuclear submarines, the Japan Maritime Self-Defense Force is qualified to work on antisubmarine and minesweeping activities.

Third, the Japan-U.S. alliance has been multifunctional. Asia has lacked confrontational military blocs on the order of NATO and the Warsaw Treaty Organization. While the Japan-U.S. alliance has not been aimed at a particular direct military threat, it has functioned to deter the Soviet military threat on a global as well as regional level (for example, on the Korean peninsula). At the same time, it has contributed to easing concerns among Asian countries about the revival of Japanese militarism. This so-called "cap on the bottle" argument in regard to U.S. ties limiting Japanese expansionism should not be overemphasized; the analogy also applies to NATO and Germany, and the U.S. forces in South Korea and Taiwan. The multifunctionality of the alliance, despite the demise of the cold war and the Soviet military threat, has now afforded it the flexibility to deal with new situations.

The Japan-U.S. alliance, however, is not ironclad. First, with the ideological conflict of the cold war over, historical legacies and cultural differences have risen to the surface, causing friction between the two nations. Second, although the Japanese and U.S. governments emphasized the seriousness of the Soviet military threat to support strengthening the alliance during the cold war era, the current argument for retaining the alliance has shifted to its multifunctional character. Third, in spite of a history of almost half a century, the Japan-U.S. alliance has lacked certain institutions, such as a joint headquarters, to hold it together. Fourth, the highly complementary character of the Japan-U.S. alliance has resulted in friction as well: Each side feels that it bears an unequally heavy burden for this alliance. Okinawa wants some of the U.S. military facilities on its soil to be removed, while the United States wants Japan to be a more active ally.

The adoption and implementation of the new Guidelines for U.S.-Japan Defense Cooperation can be of great assistance in addressing these issues. The guidelines of 1997 differ greatly from the guidelines of 1978. This chapter aims to examine the impact of the more recent guidelines on the Japan-U.S. alliance by comparing it with its predecessor. I will then recommend several policies that Japan can take to make the Japan-U.S. alliance more effective for regional security and joint decision-making. Japan should realize that its security is integral to regional security, and it should establish a clearer and more concise decision-making system with the United States under the new guidelines.

IMPLICATIONS OF THE GUIDELINES OF 1978

The U.S.-Japan Security Treaty of 1952 allowed the United States to use its troops in Japan to maintain the regional security of the Far East and to quell domestic disturbances, or "internal riots." U.S. forces in Japan could be used to contribute to the security of Japan against external military attacks, but the protection of Japan was only a possible function of the forces, not an obligation. In essence, the U.S.-Japan Security Treaty was a kind of base-leasing agreement.

When the treaty was revised in 1960, the "internal riots" clause was removed, and, based on negotiations between then-Prime Minister Kishi Nobusuke and Secretary of State Christian Herter, a clause was introduced referring to the need for "prior consultation" when necessary. The clause is conventionally interpreted to mean that Tokyo's formal approval will be sought by the United States before any major changes are effected in deployment, equipment, or use of facilities in Japan for U.S. combat purposes. "Major changes in equipment" refers to the introduction of nuclear weapons. But as Michael Armacost, former U.S. ambassador to Japan, has pointed out, this clause has always been double-edged for Japan. Although it recognizes Japan's sovereign right to be consulted about U.S. activities, such prior consultation would also, in effect, make Japan bear responsibility for U.S. military activities outside Japan proper (Armacost 1991, 81). So in fact, in the history of the Japan-U.S. alliance, the prior consultation clause has never officially been observed.

The revised security treaty states that "the parties will consult together from time to time regarding the implementation of this treaty" (Article 4), and that "each party . . . declares that it would act to meet the common danger in accordance with its constitutional provisions and processes" (Article 5). Based on Article 4, the two governments established three major forums for conducting Japan-U.S. security consultations: the Security Consultative Committee (SCC) at the ministerial level, the Security Subcommittee at the vice ministerial level, and the Security Consultative Group at the deputy vice ministerial level.[3] Nonetheless, the Japan-U.S. alliance has not fostered a standing body for consultation on joint military studies and plans, as per Article 5.

The phrase "in accordance with its constitutional provisions and processes," as far as the United States is concerned, relates to Article 1 of the U.S. Constitution, which deals with the legislative authority of Congress to declare war, and to Article 2, which defines the president as the commander-in-chief of the Armed Forces of the United States. In terms of its response formula, the U.S.-Japan Security Treaty is less clear-cut than the North Atlantic Treaty, while in terms of its scope and substance it is more extensive than the U.S.-South Korea Mutual Defense Treaty. The North Atlantic Treaty, for example, speaks of an armed attack against one as "an attack against all," rather than a "common danger," and does not have the above condition attached. Also, while the North Atlantic Treaty defines "attack" to include an attack upon armed forces, public vessels, or aircraft, the U.S.-Japan Security Treaty does not have such a firm definition.

As far as Japan is concerned, the term "provisions" implies that because Japan cannot exercise the right of collective defense, in the event of emergency Japan will act in accordance with the provisions of Article 76 of the Self-Defense Forces (SDF) Law, which states: "When the Prime Minister considers it necessary from the standpoint of defending the nation against armed aggression from the outside, he may order part or the whole of the Self-Defense Forces into operation with the consent of the Diet. However, in the event of extreme emergency, he may order the operation without the consent of the Diet" and that "When the Prime Minister has ordered the operation without the consent of the Diet, he shall promptly take action to insure the approval of the Diet." These provisions contrast with those in the U.S.-South Korea Mutual Defense Treaty, which indicate that each party "would act to meet the common danger in accordance with its constitutional processes" (Article 3).

Article 6 of the revised 1960 U.S.-Japan Security Treaty states that "for the purpose of contributing to the security of Japan and the maintenance of international peace and security in the Far East, the United States of America is granted the use by its land, air and naval forces of facilities and areas in Japan." This contrasts with the U.S.-South Korea Mutual Defense Treaty, which covers the Pacific area in principle, but in practice refers to the expectation that U.S. forces protect South Korea, which is faced with a clear military threat from North Korea. And in terms of any substantive military structure for joint U.S.-Japan military operations, none, it appears, was even on the table for discussion until the late 1970s.

As for Japan, the ruling Liberal Democratic Party (LDP) wanted to avoid any measure that could provoke the wrath of opposition parties, especially the Japan Socialist Party (JSP). The opposition had stunned the ruling party in 1963 when it heaped criticism on the SDF for the Mitsuya Study, a study of contingency measures conducted by the SDF without the government's knowledge. Since the incident, the Japanese government has shown great sensitivity toward anything that could be called "contingency studies."

In addition, Tokyo did not wish to unduly irritate the communist camp, in particular Beijing, by strengthening its military ties with Washington. As long as U.S. nuclear deterrence functioned and the Pacific was an "American lake," Japan could enjoy "free security," without taking further steps.

On the U.S. side, substantive military actions and joint military studies for the alliance seemed somewhat besides the point since, for some time after 1954, the U.S. military had viewed the SDF as little more than a large-scale constabulary. The United States took time adjusting to Japanese sovereignty once the occupation was over, and because Japan's rear-area logistical support during the Korean War had been open-ended, the United States had the impression that such support would automatically be forthcoming in future regional contingencies.[4]

To sum up, the revised 1960 U.S.-Japan Security Treaty was widely regarded as basically a base-leasing arrangement: The United States would defend Japan in return for use of bases there. As Nishimura put it, the treaty was one of "cooperation between the material factor and the human factor."

Since the late 1970s, however, Tokyo and Washington have tried to establish a substantive military structure for the alliance. After the Nixon Doctrine of 1969, which suggested U.S. military reductions in Asia, and the end of the Vietnam War, Tokyo became concerned that the United States was leaving Asia and abandoning its commitments to Japan. This concern followed on the heels of an attempt in the early 1970s by Nakasone Yasuhiro, then director-general of the Defense Agency, to forge an autonomous defense policy. The attempt failed due to public opposition and fallout from the oil shock, which prevented the government from allocating large fiscal resources to defense. It was quite logical, then, for Sakata Michita, the new director-general, to seek closer defense cooperation with the United States. At the same time, the United States, experiencing a relative decline in its economic supremacy and a domestic-oriented post-Vietnam mood, began to seek Japan's more active involvement in regional security issues.

Maruyama Kō, administrative vice minister under Sakata from 1976 to 1978, recalled: "In sum, the Security Treaty with the United States was already established. We only lacked the means to implement the treaty. In principle, it was very difficult (even for the opposition parties) to oppose introducing such a mechanism. . . . My first question when I became vice minister was how Japan's defense policy was linked with American policy . . . how, when, and where the United States would project its forces in the event of contingencies in Japan and how Japan would accept them. All of this was uncertain. Everything lacked real content" (interview in Tokyo, 12 April 1996).

The adoption of the Guidelines for U.S.-Japan Defense Cooperation in November 1978 was, therefore, a turning point for Japan-U.S. security relations. In this document, the United States explicitly pledged that it "will maintain a nuclear deterrent capability, and the forward deployments of combat-ready forces and other forces capable of reinforcing them." While "in principle, Japan by itself will repel limited, small-scale aggression. When it is difficult to repel aggression alone due to the scale, type and other factors of aggression, Japan will repel it with the cooperation of the United States." For this purpose, according to this document, the SDF "will primarily conduct defensive operations in Japanese territory and its surrounding waters and airspace" and the U.S. forces will conduct "operations to supplement functional areas which exceed the capacity of the JSDF."

The guidelines further provided for Japan-U.S. joint exercises, intelligence exchange, and joint studies on three operational dimensions: prevention of aggression against Japan, response to military attacks on Japan, and joint cooperation in case of conflict in the Far East.

The guidelines are often considered the third version of the U.S.-Japan Security Treaty. General Takashina Takehiko, then chairman of the Joint Staff Council of the SDF, pointed out that "the spirit has been put into the U.S.-Japan Security Treaty for the first time since 1960" (Taiyūkai 1980, 191). It was the first step toward creating a substantive military structure, going beyond the earlier forms of simple cooperation in the Japan-U.S. alliance.

The Soviet military buildup around Japan, which narrowed any perception gap between the United States and Japan as to their common threat, was a strong impetus to agreement on these new guidelines. Even China, which until the early 1970s had been strongly opposed to the U.S.-Japan Security Treaty, condoned U.S.-Japan defense cooperation as a deterrent to the Soviet Union.

It should be noted, however, that Tokyo's interests were practical as well. It adopted the guidelines in order to maintain a credible U.S. defense commitment to Japan on a limited defense budget. After the adoption of the guidelines, the new cold war became quite a serious issue for Japan. Tanaka Akihiko notes that "although the guidelines were not adopted for the new cold war [per se], this document provided the framework 'to fight' it" (1997, 286).

The guidelines represented the first public authorization for the SDF and the U.S. forces to train together, which, in Honolulu and Washington, led to a much closer focus on and appreciation of the capabilities of the SDF. The guidelines also offered the first political sanction for contingency studies in Japan, and, by so doing, reduced the urgency of developing a concrete bilateral plan for the defense of Japan.

The implications of the guidelines for the Japan-U.S. alliance, however, should not be overemphasized. The text noted that the guidelines were not "such as would place either Government under obligation to take legislative, budgetary or administrative measures." Nor did they establish a "coordination center" for SDF and U.S. forces, although "close mutual coordination on operations, intelligence and logistic support" was to be maintained. Further, the document neglected mention of an authorized joint operations plan.

A joint study on contingencies in Japan, roughly completed in the summer of 1981 for submission to Prime Minister Suzuki Zenkō, assumed that an enemy, the Soviet Union, would land on Hokkaido with its airborne divisions, followed by two naval divisions (*Asahi Shimbun* 2 September 1996). While this scenario exemplified the thinking behind Article 5 of the U.S.-Japan Security Treaty, it was quite unrealistic, because it was inconceivable that the Soviet Union, lacking adequate landing capabilities, would attack Japan alone. In the end, this joint study was not adopted.

A joint study on contingencies in the Far East that the United States really wanted was officially initiated in 1982. But it was never completed, because Tokyo failed to establish interagency consensus that would have allowed contingency planning to be carried out by the critical ministries, such as Foreign Affairs, Transport, Construction, and Home Affairs. The late Nishihiro Seiki, former administrative vice minister of defense, said that "it was a mistake to separate the Article 6 situation from that of Article 5, as they were inseparable in nature" (interview in Tokyo, 16 November 1995).

It took Tokyo almost twenty years to overcome the shortcomings of the guidelines of 1978.

IMPLICATIONS OF THE GUIDELINES OF 1997

After an interim report was issued in June 1997, the guidelines were finally revised in September 1997.[5] The end of the cold war provided the backdrop to the revisions as it brought the demise of the Soviet military threat, which had been the primary, though not the sole, reason for maintaining the Japan-U.S. alliance. The emergence of a nuclear crisis in North Korea in the summer of 1994 posed the first serious post–cold war security challenge for the Japan-U.S. alliance. Tokyo and Washington lacked concrete joint plans in the event of military contingencies in Korea. If a full-scale war were to erupt on the Korean peninsula, the United States estimated that as many as a million people would be killed, including 80,000 to 100,000 Americans (Oberdorfer 1997). Accordingly, the United States asked Japan to contribute a total of 1,059 items to the military effort in the event war broke out. The Hata Tsutomu cabinet prepared to submit several bills to the Diet in response to the U.S. demands (*Asahi Shimbun* 16 September 1996). While the crisis was fortunately averted by former U.S. President Jimmy Carter's visit to Pyongyang, the experience reminded the Japan-U.S. security community of the vulnerability of the alliance.

In September 1995, three American servicemen raped a twelve-year-old schoolgirl near an American base in Okinawa. This tragic event piqued the wrath and long-simmering frustration of the Okinawans, and the use of U.S. military facilities in Japan, which would be essential in the event of war on the Korean peninsula, was seriously challenged. As Joseph Nye, then assistant secretary of defense for international security affairs, recalled, "it was a shock like a typhoon" (Funabashi 1997, 328). After these incidents, the Japanese government revised the National Defense Program Outline (NDPO) to further emphasize the importance of the alliance. The revised NDPO, for example, referred to the "U.S.-Japan Security Arrangements" thirteen times, as opposed to only three times in the previous NDPO. At their April 1997 summit meeting, Prime Minister Hashimoto Ryūtarō and President Bill Clinton pledged to "continue to consult closely on defense policies and military posture, including the U.S. force structure in Japan."

The guidelines revision attempted to address the problems of a lack of alliance structure and the one-sided character of the alliance in which Japan mainly provides the material factor (military facilities) and the United States mainly provides the human factor (military personnel). The new document also defined the role of the Japan-U.S. alliance in the post–cold war era. It consists of three parts: cooperation under normal circumstances, action in response to an armed attack against Japan, and cooperation in situations in areas surrounding Japan that have an important influence on Japan's peace and security. The new guidelines also "provid[e] a general framework and policy direction for the roles and missions of the two countries and ways of cooperation and coordination, both under normal circumstances and during contingencies" ("The Guidelines for U.S.-Japan Defense Cooperation" 1997, Article 1).

The new guidelines also cover alliance objectives that were not a part of the old guidelines, including cooperation in United Nations peacekeeping activities, international humanitarian relief, and emergency relief operations. In a multipolar world, an alliance, especially one that lacks historical and cultural commonality, needs broad purposes like these, besides the purely military aims of stability and durability.

The new document clearly lays out how ship inspections are to be conducted to ensure the implementation of economic sanctions against an aggressor under the United Nations resolutions, and it specifies that search and rescue operations are to take place in noncombat areas. The two governments would cooperate in planning and coordination in evacuating Japanese and noncombatants from combat areas overseas.

While the essence of the old guidelines, at least from the Japanese perspective, concerned the response to a military attack on Japan, the core of the new guidelines relates to "a situation in areas surrounding Japan." The guidelines read as follows:

> When a situation in areas surrounding Japan is anticipated, the two Governments will intensify information and intelligence sharing and policy consultations, including efforts to reach a common assessment of the situation.
>
> The two Governments will take appropriate measures, to include preventing further deterioration of situations, in response to situations in areas surrounding Japan. . . . They will support each other as necessary in accordance with appropriate arrangements.
>
> As situations in areas surrounding Japan have an important influence on Japan's peace and security, the Self-Defense Forces will conduct such activities as intelligence gathering, surveillance and minesweeping, to protect lives and property and to ensure navigational safety. U.S. Forces will conduct operations to restore the peace and security affected by situations in areas surrounding Japan. ("Guidelines" 1997, Article 5)

The new guidelines provide for conducting bilateral defense planning and mutual cooperation planning. The latter aims "to be able to respond smoothly and effectively to situations in areas surrounding Japan" in peacetime ("Guidelines" 1997, Article 6). Planning for mutual cooperation is long overdue; it should have been promoted under the guidelines of 1978. As stated earlier, the 1978 guidelines did not provide for any authorized Japan-U.S. joint operations plan, even in the event of military contingencies in Japan. With the earlier guidelines, the two governments were not even able to finalize joint studies on contingencies in the Far East. The new document calls for joint plans not only for contingencies in Japan and the Far East but also in "situations in areas surrounding Japan."

The new guidelines also state that the parties will establish "a bilateral coordination mechanism involving relevant agencies of the two countries to coordinate respective activities in case of an armed attack against Japan and in situations in areas surrounding Japan." As with the old guidelines, the new document "will not obligate either Government to take legislative, budgetary or administrative measures." Under the new guidelines, however, "the two Governments are expected to reflect in an appropriate way the results of these efforts, based on their judgments, in their specific policies and measures" ("Guidelines" 1997, Article 2).

As Japan takes more active responsibility for regional security by preparing for Japan-U.S. joint plans and creating a substantive alliance structure, the former "cooperation between the material factor and the human factor" will become less asymmetrical. It will then be easier for the two governments to discuss realistically the possibility of reducing U.S. military facilities in Japan. It is not an accident that the decision to remove the U.S. Marine base in Futenma was made subsequent to the U.S.-Japan Joint Declaration on Security, which led to the adoption of the new guidelines.

As regards the current structural changes in Japan's defense policy, the review process of the new guidelines impacts Japan's defense policy in several ways. First, this process has promoted and institutionalized Japan-U.S. security dialogue. It took two-and-a-half years from the establishment of the Subcommittee for Defense Cooperation (SDC) to the adoption of the guidelines in 1978. The review process of the new guidelines was completed within eighteen months. And it seems that bilateral security talks are gradually becoming more institutionalized.

Second, this process influences relations between the Ministry of Foreign Affairs and the Japan Defense Agency (JDA). The JDA has long been regarded as a second-rate central agency, referred to by cynics as an "appendix" of the U.S.-Japan Security Treaty Division of the ministry. As a result of its dialogue on technical aspects and details of defense cooperation with the United States, however, the JDA seems to have become more assertive and active in defense policy making. Relations between the ministry and the JDA have changed from being essentially vertical to being more horizontal and healthier in nature.[6]

Third, the influence of uniformed officers of the SDF on defense policy making has increased. This is not as dangerous as some might fear. Officers in uniform have long felt oppressed because of the public's simplistic antiwar sentiments and the excessive supervision of the JDA's Internal Bureau. It is in everyone's interest that the SDF operate effectively. Japan's postwar democracy is strong enough to prevent the occurrence of rapid remilitarization. Moreover, as Samuel Huntington says, a highly professional military is rarely politicized (Huntington 1957).

Fourth, the integration of the three services of the SDF is now in progress through dialogue with their U.S. counterparts. Because achieving a sound Japan-U.S. security system is the precondition for Japan's defense policy, it would have been impossible to promote the integration of the three services without making clear the time, scale, and function of the U.S. forces that would come to Japan in the event of a military contingency. The adoption of the guidelines in 1978 broke new ground in this respect. The integration of the three services is further promoted under the revised guidelines.

Will the adoption of the new guidelines and these structural changes in Japan's defense policy make the Japan-U.S. alliance more effective in joint decision-making and in safeguarding regional security? Yes, but its implementation will not be problem-free. One obstacle is Japan's continuing fear of entrapment in U.S. military actions. In a November 1997 public opinion survey conducted in both Japan and the United States, 39 percent of the American respondents expected that Japan would take military actions in response to military contingencies in Korea, but only 2 percent of Japanese did (*Yomiuri Shimbun* 24 November 1997).

In fact, many Japanese still question the need to have revised the guidelines after the cold war. Taoka Shunji, a senior staff writer with the *Asahi Shimbun,* for example, contends that the current revision of the guidelines is like giving a winter coat to a girlfriend (in this case, South Korea) in spring (1997, 40).[7] But if one considers the current, still stormy situation on the Korean peninsula, one understands that a winter coat is needed every winter. It need not be the most expensive. In any case, as Aesop's Fables tell us, spring is the time to prepare for winter.

More importantly, mutual cooperation planning is not a gift to a friend. The formulation of such a plan is necessary because the peace and security of South Korea is, as many Japanese prime ministers have repeated, essential for the security of Japan. This then is not a matter for friends or neighbors, but for Japan. It should be noted as well that about 14,000 Japanese are living in South Korea. In any event, Japan would be entrapped in a military contingency on the Korean peninsula even without the new guidelines. The new guidelines seek to prevent a contingency from occurring there and to limit its damage should it occur.

A large part of the difficulty of implementing the new guidelines lies in the fact that while Japan and the United States are allies, Japan and South Korea are not. They share an unfortunate history, and sentiment toward each other is not warm. In other words, although Japan may be able to help the United States in the event of military contingencies on the Korean peninsula, it cannot help South Korea directly. As far as international and domestic situations allow, therefore, Japan must promote policy coordination among the three countries on this issue.

As will be discussed later, collective self-defense issues complicate the argument over the new guidelines. In order to conform to the current interpretation of Article 9 of the Constitution, the Japanese government has developed highly technical arguments in its deliberation of guidelines-related bills in the Diet, especially the bill on "situations in areas surrounding Japan." The Cabinet Legislation Bureau has played a critical role in these arguments (Tani 1999).

It would not be wise to overemphasize military contingencies on the Korean peninsula as justification for the new guidelines. The Japan-U.S. alliance is multifunctional in nature. The Soviet military threat was strongly emphasized during the cold war era, but now that it is over, it would be best to reemphasize the multifunctional nature of the alliance.

Nevertheless, the multifunctional character of the alliance itself raises another problem: Taiwan. The implied secondary target of the new guidelines, after the situation in Korea, concerns Taiwan. Yet Beijing strongly opposes the inclusion of Taiwan when describing "a situation in areas surrounding Japan." Because the review process of the guidelines was initiated so soon after the crisis over the Taiwan Strait in March 1996, China became suspicious about the intentions of the United States and Japan.

China's negative reaction to the new guidelines has caused friction among Japanese. While Secretary-General of the LDP Katō Kōichi indicated in July 1997 that the Taiwan Strait was not included within the "areas surrounding Japan," Chief Cabinet Secretary Kajiyama Seiroku asserted that Taiwan would be "naturally covered" under the Security Treaty in the event of conflict between China and Taiwan. During his visit to China in September 1997, Prime Minister Hashimoto therefore felt compelled to reassure China that "no specific areas are being discussed" with regard to "situations in areas surrounding Japan" (Heiwa Anzenhoshō Kenkyūsho 1999, 175–176).

In response to China's strong expression of concern, the new guidelines state that the meaning of the phrase is "not geographical, but situational" and that "the two governments will make every effort, including diplomatic efforts, to prevent such situations from occurring." But even after adoption of the new guidelines, the Treaties Bureau of the Ministry of Foreign Affairs complicated things further by insisting that the phrase "areas surrounding

Japan" corresponded with what was referred to as the Far East in the U.S.-Japan Security Treaty (Tani 1999).

The guidelines-related bills were submitted to the Diet in April 1998, and were passed by the Diet in May 1999. How can the abovementioned problems be overcome to make the Japan-U.S. alliance more effective?

FURTHER TASKS

As the late Professor Kōsaka Masataka wisely pointed out, there is no universal measure for achieving national security (Kōsaka and Momoi 1973). Each country must pursue its national security according to its own conditions. In the Pacific War Japan was the loser, but its actions in the war have never been forgotten by its neighbors. Japan also happens to be a far greater economic power than its neighbors (a circumstance quite different from Germany, whose neighbors are more or less developed countries). Japan is a densely populated, geographically small island country, whose prosperity depends on international trade. Given these conditions, Japan need not, and should not, pursue an autonomous defense as what is referred to as a "normal country."

The Japan-U.S. alliance will remain asymmetrical and complementary. No country in the world can make a fully symmetrical alliance with the United States. Once the military tension on the Korean peninsula decreases, however, a reduction in the U.S. forces in Japan, especially of the Marines in Okinawa, can be seriously considered (see, for example, Mochizuki 1997). It will then be time for the alliance to go beyond "cooperation between the material factor and the human factor." We must prepare for this step by implementing the new guidelines effectively.

The collective defense issue remains the major obstacle to promoting further Japan-U.S. defense cooperation for regional security. Japan is a member of the United Nations, and is now seeking a permanent seat on the UN Security Council. The right of a collective defense is recognized as indigenous to every sovereignty under the UN Charter, but according to the Japanese government the Japanese Constitution disallows the government from exercising that right. The government has been reluctant to move from that position.

The concept of collective defense, however, changes in the context of the international system. When the Japanese Constitution was adopted, the cold war was the dominant feature of the international system. Thus, the concept of collective defense was interpreted as implying the right of joint military action to defeat, eliminate, and even destroy an aggressor. In the post–cold war era, however, this definition does not necessarily apply. Collective defense could instead be understood as referring to the obligation to conduct joint military action to prevent military conflicts and to limit damage should they occur. In this sense, as Inoguchi Kuniko says, the concept of collective defense can now be viewed as collective crisis management (Inoguchi 1997). The Japanese Constitution does not contemplate such a notion, and therefore does not prohibit it. Even the concept of "out-of-area" in NATO is expanding in the post–cold war era.

Okazaki Hisahiko, former Japanese ambassador to Thailand, has said: "The correct interpretation would be: 'Yes, we have the right of collective self-defense. However, the spirit of the Constitution dictates that we should act with the utmost prudence in exercising it.' This simple statement would resolve all problems concerning this issue" (*Daily Yomiuri* 29 March 1999).

In reality, it may take time for Japanese to change their interpretation of the right of collective defense. To advocate a new interpretation would be politically risky for a Japanese coalition government. Even under the current interpretation, however, Japan could do a great deal to implement the new guidelines. Former General Shikata Toshiyuki, for example, argues that the following activities lie in a gray zone of what may be possible under the current interpretation: (a) noncombat activities exclusively for protecting the lives of Japanese citizens in forward areas with the relevant country's permission; (b) noncombat activities exclusively for humanitarian aims in forward areas with the relevant country's permission; (c) activities supporting UN forces in rear areas (for example, maintenance and supply); and (d) activities supporting multinational forces under UN resolutions in rear areas (for example, maintenance and supply) (Shikata 1999).

Further discussions on the collective defense issue are needed. But until the issue is resolved, this should not be an excuse for Japan to avoid regional security responsibilities in the post–cold war era. The Diet should establish a Constitutional Research Committee as soon as possible.

Japan should not indulge in overly legalistic arguments concerning military contingencies. By nature, contingencies are unpredictable, the result of "friction," in von Clausewitz's term, and we cannot regulate all of them by legal measures. Too many legalistic arguments will stifle wider public understanding and support of the guidelines.

Some have argued that it is impossible to make a clear distinction between rear areas and active combat areas and that Japan might be entrapped in belligerency by rear area support to the United States (see, for example,

Kobayashi and Nishizawa 1999). This is a variation of the old fear of entrapment. No alliance can be made without risk. Even if Japan does not become involved in military operations, an aggressor might regard Japan as an enemy. Under the current constitutional interpretation, Japan must refrain from conducting active combat operations, but it is difficult, if not impossible, to make a clear distinction between rear and active combat areas. Yet this ambiguous situation is far better than either having no regulations or excessive regulations. It is unrealistic to expect perfection in reference to military contingencies. In addition, although Japan could in some cases supply munitions as well as noncombat goods to the U.S. forces in rear areas, that does not mean that it would do so in all cases. That would fall into the realm of political judgment.

Diet arguments over ship inspections on the high seas have been very complicated. Ozawa Ichirō, leader of the Liberal Party, says that since the new guidelines are within the framework of the U.S.-Japan Security Treaty, UN resolutions are not required for ship inspection. The U.S.-Japan Security Treaty is a bilateral treaty, however. A flag country will be more agreeable to ship inspection under UN resolutions. Others say that ship inspection is impossible without compulsory measures. Nevertheless, not all ships will agree to inspection on the high seas under UN resolutions. In the case of economic sanctions against Iraq in 1990, UN forces fired a warning shot at an Iraqi merchant ship, albeit only once. The minimal use of weapons exclusively for self-defense should be, of course, permitted. Ship inspections were not covered by recent guideline-related legislation, but this omission can be rectified. It is clear that further discussion is needed before establishing the rules of engagement for the SDF.

Some Japanese are concerned about the temporary use of a limited number of civilian ports and airports by U.S. forces in a military contingency.[8] Regarding the use of airports and ports for noncombat evacuation operations or for supplying noncombat materials such as food, water, and medicine, local governments should cooperate with the U.S. forces as much as possible. It is impossible, however, for the Japanese government to specify all of the possible uses for civilian airports and ports before concrete contingency plans are made. In short, we have to overcome the temptation to regulate in advance all activities that might be called for in contingencies.

China will continue to be critical of the new guidelines, especially the allusion to "situations in areas surrounding Japan." It is up to Beijing and, to a lesser extent, Taipei, whether Taiwan is to be included in the interpretation of this phrase. Inasmuch as Beijing respects regional stability, it does not have to worry about Japan-U.S. defense cooperation. It bears noting that the Taiwan Strait is considered international waters, and that the Senkaku Islands, which China claims to be a part of Taiwan, are also quite legitimately claimed by Japan. At the same time, Tokyo and Washington should not encourage Taipei to pursue its goal of independence. Beijing is not likely to abandon the option of military action against Taipei to prevent that from happening. While it is highly unlikely, supposing that Taipei did declare its independence, and supposing that China brought limited military action against Taiwan, there would be little that Japan could do under the new guidelines. Whether or not Taiwan is to be included in "situations in areas surrounding Japan" is, therefore, not a matter that can be determined in advance by Tokyo alone. In this sense, the concept of "situations in areas surrounding Japan" is literally situational. It should also be noted that Japan's strategic ambiguity could complicate China's (and Taiwan's) strategic calculations and make them more cautious of taking assertive and unilateral actions.

The U.S. and Japanese governments should reinstate both prior and regular consultation provisions. As mentioned earlier, the prior consultation clause has never been exercised. Furthermore, the Japanese government has taken the position that it will not propose prior consultation to the U.S. government and that the content of such consultation need not be reported to the Diet. As Japan is willing to take more active roles in the Japan-U.S. alliance, however, this position should be revised. Also, although the two governments meet regularly for consultation, especially at the senior officials' level, given the importance of daily communication between the allies, a standing consultative body at the working level would be more effective. The establishment of such a body would be helpful in cultivating and educating security specialists on both sides as well.

Finally, given changing civil-military relations in Japan, the mechanisms for civilian control over the military need to be rethought. It is important to avoid unnecessary anxieties in neighboring countries about the revival of Japanese militarism, but maintaining a professional defense apparatus within the country does not constitute a threat to others. On the contrary, it is more dangerous to ignore Japan's defense establishment and, as a consequence, to abandon control over it.

In the event of future "situations in areas surrounding Japan," the government should submit a follow-up report or request prior consent of the Diet regarding the activities of the SDF. Article 76 of the SDF Law could be a model for this: In the case of an extreme emergency, the prime minister could order the SDF to act without prior consent of the Diet, but would be required to obtain the consent soon after, within a given time period. Japan needs to satisfy both the need for readiness and the democratic process. In order to secure prompt judgment by the prime minister, the roles of the Prime Minister's Office and the Security Council of Japan, including senior SDF advisors and the chairman of the Joint Staff Council, should be given greater latitude. Also, the role and function of the chairmanship of the Joint Staff Council should be clarified and strengthened. It might be that the Diet will refuse consent and that the SDF will have to suspend its activities. Although that would seem unlikely, if it should happen, then, in democratic Japan, it must be accepted.

The Diet should strengthen its legislative staff. As of 1998, the House of Representatives had a research staff of only 278, and the House of Councillors only 178. The Research and Legislative Reference Bureau of the National Diet Library had fewer than 100 research staff members, who are obliged to cover all policy issues from defense to education. In the United States, as of 1997, the House of Representatives had 1,276 committee staff members, and the Senate 1,216. Staff at the Congressional Research Service of the Library of Congress number 747, half of whom are research specialists (Shiroyama, Suzuki, and Hosono 1999). Without substantial research capabilities, the Diet cannot make sound judgments on defense policy, either in peacetime or in crisis.

In implementing the revised guidelines, Tokyo and Washington need to keep in mind that the new guidelines constitute only "guidance." An alliance is not based on a piece of paper. Whatever perfect guidelines and laws we make in peacetime will not work in a crisis without strong political will and sound judgment. As Okamoto Yukio speculates, so far "we have a security alliance that works fine in peace but which will fail the most likely tests of war" (Stokes and Shinn 1998, 1). It is our political will and judgment that are now being seriously tested.

NOTES

1. The U.S.-Japan Security Treaty was signed in 1951 and implemented in 1952.

2. "Entrapment" refers to being dragged into a conflict over an ally's interests that one does not share, or shares only partially (Snyder 1984, 467).

3. As for the SCC, U.S. members were upgraded from the ambassador to Japan and the commander-in-chief of the U.S. Pacific Command to the secretaries of state and defense in December 1990.

4. This observation is from Michael Green, senior fellow at the Council on Foreign Relations.

5. For a review of the process from the time the interim report was made public to the adoption of the new guidelines, see Heiwa Anzenhoshō Kenkyūsho (1999, 60–66).

6. The scandal over the Central Procurement Office—in which in 1998 charges of bribery and breaches of trust led to the resignation of the defense minister, reorganization of the procurement office, and conviction of the office's former director-general for bribery—will, in the short-term, harm the prestige and credibility of the JDA. This scandal clearly shows that the JDA has a new face as a policy-making agency and an old face as a procurement agency.

7. Taoka asked four questions about the guidelines. First, why must Japan justify its intentions to South Korea by revising the guidelines? Second, will U.S. forces help Japan rescue Japanese citizens in South Korea in the event of a contingency? Third, is there any guarantee that the scope of "areas surrounding Japan" will not be arbitrarily expanded by the United States? And fourth, are there any legal grounds to carry out inspections and minesweeping outside of Japanese territory?

8. During the review process of the guidelines, the United States reportedly asked about the possible use of such airports as Shin-Chitose, Kansai, Fukuoka, and Nagasaki, and such ports as Tomakomai, Hakodate, Niigata, Kobe, Hakata, and Naha (*Asahi Shimbun* 29 August 1997).

BIBLIOGRAPHY

Armacost, Michael H. 1991. *Friends or Rivals? The Insider's Account of U.S.-Japan Relations*. New York: Columbia University Press.

Funabashi Yōichi. 1997. *Dōmei hyōryū* (Alliance adrift). Tokyo: Iwanami Shoten.

"The Guidelines for U.S.-Japan Defense Cooperation." 23 September 1997. <http://www.osk.threewebnet.or.jp/-btree/catch/yuji/doc/NGui_E.htm> 1999.

Heiwa Anzenhoshō Kenkyūsho (Research Institute for Peace and Security), ed. 1999. *Ajia no anzenhoshō 1998–1999* (Asian security 1998–1999). Tokyo: Asagumo Shimbunsha.

Huntington, Samuel P. 1957. *The Soldier and the State: The Theory and Politics of Civil-Military Relations*. Cambridge, Mass.: Harvard University Press.

Inoguchi Kuniko. 1997. Comment at the International Symposium and Lectures on "A Nuclear-Weapon-Free Zone in Northeast Asia and the Role of Japan." Hiroshima (29 July).

Kobayashi Hideyuki and Nishizawa Masaru. 1999. *Chōmeikaiyaku de yomitoku Nichibei shi gaidorain* (Reading the new Guidelines for U.S.-Japan Defense Cooperation: An extremely clear translation). Tokyo: Nihon Hyōronsha.

Kōsaka Masataka and Momoi Makoto, eds. 1973. *Takyokuka jidai no senryaku*

(Strategy in the multipolar era). Tokyo: Nihon Kokusai Mondai Kenkyūsho (Japan Center for International Affairs).

Mochizuki, Mike, ed. 1997. *Toward a True Alliance: Restructuring U.S.-Japan Security Relations.* Washington, D.C.: Brookings Institution Press.

Murata Kōji. 1998. *Daitōryō no zasetsu: Kātā seiken no zaikanbeigun tettai seisaku* (Downfall of a president: The Carter administration's policy to withdraw U.S. forces from South Korea). Tokyo: Yūhikaku.

Nishimura Kumao. 1960. *Kaiteiban nichibei anzenhoshō taiseiron* (On the U.S.-Japan security system). Revised edition. Tokyo: Jiji Press.

Oberdorfer, Don. 1997. *Two Koreas: A Contemporary History.* Reading, Mass.: Addison-Wesley.

Shikata Toshiyuki. 1999. "Nichibei bōei kyōryoku no tameno shishin kaitei no keii" (The process of revising the Guidelines for U.S.-Japan Defense Cooperation). In Gaikō Seisaku Kettei Yōin Kenkyūkai (Study Group on Foreign Policy-Making Factors), ed. *Nihon no gaikō seisaku kettei yōin* (Japan's foreign policy-making factors). Tokyo: PHP Kenkyūsho.

Shiroyama Hideaki, Suzuki Hiroshi, and Hosono Sukehiro, eds. 1999. *Chūō kanchō no seisaku kettei katei* (Decision-making process in central agencies). Tokyo: Chūō Daigaku Shuppankai.

Snyder, Glenn. 1984. "The Security Dilemma in Alliance Politics." *World Politics,* no. 36 (July).

Stokes, Bruce, and James Shinn. 1998. *The Tests of War and the Strains of Peace: The U.S.-Japan Security Relationship.* New York: Council on Foreign Relations.

Taiyūkai, ed. 1980. *Hachijūnendai kiki no shinario to taiō* (The scenario and response to crisis in the 1980s). Tokyo: Taiyūkai.

Tanaka Akihiko. 1997. *Anzenhoshō: Sengo gojyūnen no mosaku* (National security: The search for it in the 50 years since World War II). Tokyo: Yomiuri Shimbun.

Tani Katsuhiro. 1999. "Nichibei bōei kyōryoku no tameno shishin no sakutei katei to shibirian kontorōru no kyōka" (The decision-making process of the Guidelines for U.S.-Japan Defense Cooperation and the reinforcement of civilian control). *Meijo Hōgaku* 48(3): 107–109.

Taoka Shunji. 1997. "Gaidorainzu ni yottsu no gimon" (Four questions on the guidelines). *Ronza* 3(9): 40.

Tsuchiyama Jitsurō. 1993. "Araiansu jirenma to Nihon no dōmei gaikō: Nichibei dōmei no owari?" (The alliance dilemma and Japan's alliance diplomacy: The end of the Japan-U.S. alliance?). *Leviathan,* no. 13: 51–58.

Security Arrangements after Peace in Korea

Michishita Narushige

THE revised Guidelines for U.S.-Japan Defense Cooperation (or the new guidelines), signed in September 1997, delineate an appropriate response by Japan and the United States to contingencies, particularly "in situations in areas surrounding Japan" (Defense Agency 1998, 374). Of foremost concern is the Korean peninsula, which may face situations such as the imposition of economic sanctions on North Korea, the collapse of the North Korean regime, or invasion from the North. Preparations for such short-term contingencies are well under way; what are now being discussed are operational issues of how to implement what the two countries have agreed on. With the issue of how to respond to the contingencies largely settled, it is not premature for Japan, the United States, and South Korea to look further into the future at a situation in which the North Korean threat no longer exists.

The current North Korean threat could disappear if any of three events were to occur, namely, the North Korean regime collapses and is replaced by a peace-loving government, the North Korean armed forces are destroyed in a military conflict, or peaceful coexistence is firmly established between the North and the South. Any of these events would drastically alter the strategic environment and all countries concerned would be forced to reassess their respective military postures and alignments. Japan and South Korea, in particular, would face the task of reassessing and possibly reconfiguring their alliance relationships with the United States.

In this chapter, an attempt is made to provide a blueprint for the Japan-U.S. and U.S.-South Korea alliances should the North Korean threat disappear. Even should peace prevail on the Korean peninsula, neither of the alliances would lose their relevance.[1] Rather, it seems that they would become more like one integrated entity. While transforming these alliances into a formal trilateral alliance would not only be politically unsustainable but also strategically counterproductive, it would be quite possible and desirable for the three partners to work more closely and continue to maintain peace and stability in the region.

In this chapter, the relationships among the major powers, namely, Japan, the United States, and China, are assumed to be amicable, or at least nonconfrontational, while the inherent difficulties are acknowledged. This assumption is based on the current strategic environment in the region. Rather than post-unification issues, ways to deal with the post-confrontation situation have been addressed.[2] Post-confrontation Korea is assumed to be either unified or in transition from division to unification.[3]

UNDERLYING FACTORS

Several factors underlie this discussion. First, it is impossible to predict when change in Korea will take place, be it the creation of a truly peaceful coexistence between North and South Korea, the collapse of North Korea, armed conflict, or Korean unification. History suggests that major changes can come suddenly and dramatically, as seen in the fall of the Berlin Wall, the end of communism in Eastern Europe, and the disappearance of the Soviet Empire. However, the North Korean regime, some contend, is much stronger internally as well as externally—and, thus, far more stable—than is widely believed. Recent developments have suggested that there is some validity to this claim. For example, internally, Kim Jong Il formally assumed the highest post in the government, the North Korean leadership was reshuffled in his favor, and potential political dissidents were purged. Externally, North Korea demonstrated its impressive military capabilities with a 1998 test launch of a three-phased ballistic missile over Japan. In addition, it is conducting diplomatic negotiations with the United States, among others, while neighboring countries, including South Korea, agree that, for the moment, peaceful coexistence may be a wiser tack to take than early unification.[4]

It is no less true, however, that the situation in North Korea has deteriorated terribly in recent years and prospects for reversing the tide are not very bright. Since 1990, the North Korean economy has experienced negative growth,[5] the shortage of food has worsened (UN Food and Agriculture Organization [FAO] and UN World Food Program [WFP] 1998), and the number of defectors has increased rapidly.[6] Various sources contend that between 400,000 and two million people have died of starvation or malnutrition.[7] Meteorological misfortune accounted for part of this, but the primary cause is structural: The difficulties that beset North Korea are the result of an inefficient economic policy. Even with outside help, it seems likely that the North Korean economy will not become fully self-sustaining. If North Korea does collapse, there will have been ample warning, although the implications for unification remain uncertain (Tenet 1999).

The second factor underlying this discussion is that, once the North Korean threat disappears—as this chapter assumes, in time, it will—South Korea can be expected to play a leading role in shaping the future of the Korean peninsula. When this occurs, the United States and Japan will be offered an invaluable opportunity.

South Korea has enjoyed an alliance with the United States since 1954. Politically, the United States and South Korea share democratic values and institutions. And with the election of opposition leader Kim Dae Jung as president in February 1998, South Korea experienced its first peaceful transition of presidential power from a ruling to an opposition party.[8] Economically, the United States is both the largest trading partner and largest export market for South Korea which, in turn, is the United States' seventh-largest trading partner, fifth-largest export market, and fourth-largest market for agricultural products.[9] Socially, a large number of the South Korean elite have been educated or have lived in the United States. Finally, the United States and South Korea have long maintained a close strategic partnership. The U.S.-South Korea Combined Forces Command binds the two countries' armed forces, allowing the U.S. Forces Korea and South Korean forces to operate alongside one another, much in the way that North Atlantic Treaty Organization (NATO) forces work together.

Japan and South Korea have had their occasional difficulties, but since the normalization of diplomatic relations in 1965, they have gradually deepened their bilateral relationship on both the political and economic fronts. They share similar political and economic systems based on democratic values and a free market economy. Japan is the second-largest trading partner of South Korea, which is Japan's fourth-largest trading partner (Ministry of Finance 1998). Both are non–nuclear weapon states. Their security cooperation, based to a large degree on the alliance each enjoys with the United States, has developed substantially since the early 1990s (Defense Agency 1997, 86–87; Michishita 1997; and Park 1998). Japan and South Korea could be characterized as quasi allies.

Were Korean unification to occur, it seems possible, and even probable, that Chinese influence in Korea would grow dramatically. However, it is inconceivable that China's influence will supersede the U.S.-South Korea or Japan-South Korea relationship in the foreseeable future. It was only in 1992 that South Korea and China normalized diplomatic relations, and while the United States and, to a lesser extent, Japan are open-minded about Korea's unification, China seems to have a vested interest in the status quo (Wang 1998). In view of this, for South Korea to maintain a close relationship with the United States and Japan would seem a logical choice. In other words, the United States and Japan are in a good position to maintain close ties with South Korea even after the North Korean threat recedes.

The third consideration to be borne in mind here is that, once the North Korean threat disappears, the level of forward-deployed U.S. forces in East Asia seems certain to be reduced. Pressure from Japan and South Korea as well as from the U.S. public would make troop reductions, if not withdrawal, inevitable.[10] But how large a reduction and under what terms? When asked in August 1998 if the current level of 100,000 U.S. troops would be maintained, U.S. Ambassador to Japan Thomas Foley replied that were the confrontation on the Korean peninsula resolved, it would be appropriate to review the U.S. forces' deployment in Asia Pacific (*Mainichi Shimbun* 20 August 1998). U.S. Ambassador to South Korea Stephen Bosworth said in March 1999 that the United States could reassess the U.S. troop presence in South Korea were threats posed by North Korea reduced (*Korea Times* 25 March 1999).

Finally, with the rise of China, the balance of power within the region has shifted and will continue to do so. Although the World Bank's estimate of annual growth averaging 7 percent until the year 2020 may be overly optimistic, China should continue to grow quite rapidly (World Bank 1997).[11] The Organization for Economic Cooperation and Development (OECD) has estimated China's gross domestic product (GDP) growth rate at somewhere between 5.6 percent and 8.0 percent during the years from 1995 to 2020, while Japan's annual growth rate is estimated to be between 1.9 percent and 2.7 percent (Organization for Economic Cooperation and Development 1997, 92). WEFA estimated in 1996 that China's GDP in 2020 will have surpassed that of Japan.[12]

The Japanese economy seems to have reached a plateau. The era of rapid economic growth has ended, and a phase of slow, sustained growth has set in. Japan is an aging country. Lower employment levels are expected to have a negative impact on GDP after 2000 (OECD 1997, 62), with the population declining after 2007. The Ministry of Labor has estimated that the labor force will start to shrink in the year 2005, and that by 2020 the number of workers will be reduced to 64 million from the 1999 level of 68 million. A more pessimistic estimate suggests a decline in the Japanese labor force by more than 6 million by 2020. In addition, the burden of sustaining the elderly will be a drag on the economy, and it seems unlikely that the annual growth rate will exceed 2 percent by 2010 (Iwamoto 1999; and Kuninori 1999).[13]

In a 1996 report, the Korea Development Institute (KDI) suggests that after the year 2000, South Korea will be entering a low-growth phase of economic development. Compared to an average of 7 percent to 8 percent growth in the 1980s and 1990s, the expected growth rate for the 2000–2010 period is 5.5 percent, and for the 2010–2020 period 4.0 percent (Korea Development Institute 1996). After its economic crisis of 1997, however, it is not certain whether South Korea can even achieve these diminished expectations.

North Korea poses yet another obstacle to South Korea's recovery and success. As long as North Korea exists, South Korea must devote much of its resources to defense, yet once the North-South confrontation is resolved, South Korea will have to finance the reconstruction of North Korea and the rehabilitation of its economy. Of the three Northeast Asian nations, it would seem that China will gain the most, at least in terms of relative economic strength.

THE U.S.-SOUTH KOREA ALLIANCE AFTER PEACE ON THE KOREAN PENINSULA

It is widely accepted both that after the North Korean threat disappears, the Japan-U.S. alliance is likely to continue and U.S. forces in Japan will not be withdrawn; and that the same may not hold true for the U.S.-South Korea alliance and U.S. forces in South Korea. The basis of the U.S.-South Korea alliance has been deterrence or, in the event this fails, defense against North Korean aggression.[14] Thus, it is widely believed, should the reasons for the alliance cease to exist, the U.S.-South Korea alliance could be dissolved.

However, dissolution of this alliance would be precipitous and unwise. The objectives of the alliance would necessarily change, but its relevance and importance would remain for five main reasons. It provides reassurance as well as regional and global security, allows for Japan–South Korea burden sharing, serves as a hedge against the rise of China as an aggressive power, and serves, together with the Japan-U.S. alliance, as a foundation for the East Asian community of democratic nations.

REASSURANCE

The main reason for maintaining a post-confrontation alliance is reassurance.[15] The U.S.-South Korea alliance, together with the Japan-U.S. alliance, would contribute to stable relations in the region, particularly between Japan and South Korea, South Korea and China, and Japan and China.

These countries are currently embarked upon various trust- and security-building measures in order to eliminate mutual misperceptions and misunderstandings. There have been personnel exchanges, an increase in the availability of information, and bilateral/multilateral forums for discussion. Even China, once a reluctant participant, is now an active member in the ASEAN Regional Forum (ARF) and other bilateral/multilateral security exchange programs.

Mutual mistrust among these countries is deep-rooted, however, and is expected to linger for some time. History will not go away. It is fair to point out that, to some extent, South Korea and China find it to their benefit, diplomatically, to raise this issue, but there is substance to their sentiments. In fact, Japan's history is one critical reason why South Korea and China remain concerned about the remilitarization of Japan.[16]

In 1998, Japan and South Korea agreed that South Korea would gradually open its doors to Japanese popular culture, including music, drama, and movies. Security ties have grown, and there have been visits by the respective defense ministers, student exchanges, port calls, and joint search-and-rescue training (Defense Agency 1998). Genuine trust has yet to be attained, however, and mutual reservations exist concerning future, if not current, policy.[17]

Some Japanese policymakers have expressed the fear that South Korea or a unified Korea might become hostile to Japan once the North Korean threat is gone. This fear has been fueled by the fact that talk about Japanese remilitarization quickly spread in South Korea in the early 1990s, when it was perceived that the North Korean threat was dwindling and unification was just around the corner.[18]

Undoubtedly, policymakers in South Korea have worried that Japan might, in the future, dominate Korea militarily with its vast industrial base and technological superiority. The Japanese economy is roughly ten times the size of South Korea's, and its defense expenditure is three times as large (International Institute for Strategic Studies 1998, 183, 187). The Japanese population is three times that of South Korea, and twice as large as that if the two Koreas combined. In terms of defense, Japan is far more advanced in aviation, rocket, and space technologies. Indeed, apart from the United States, Japan is the only country with multimission Aegis-equipped destroyers, the most powerful surface ships ever built. The great South Korean fear is Japanese aggression, should the United States effectively unleash Japan by withdrawing U.S. forces from East Asia.[19]

For reasons grounded in history and domestic politics, anti-Japanese sentiment in South Korea and anti-Korean sentiment in Japan cannot be easily dismissed. In a way, anti-Japanese sentiment in Korean domestic politics might take on an even larger dimension once anticommunism becomes obsolete as a tool for political mobilization. The territorial dispute over Takeshima Island (known as Tokdo Island in Korean) remains a potential source of tension. However well-intentioned the majority in both countries, those sentiments provide an easy means of exploitation for political purposes by a small group.

The U.S. presence in both Japan and South Korea plays an important role in dampening the potential for tension arising between the two countries (O'Hanlon 1998; Armacost and Pyle 1999). By maintaining armed forces in both countries, the United States would be making two clear points: that it is committed to the security of the countries, and that confrontation between the two countries will not be tolerated.

A South Korea that is secure and anchored to the alliance is good not only for the relationship between Japan and South Korea, but also for the relationship between South Korea and China. Ronald D. Asmus, Richard L. Kugler, and F. Stephen Larrabee contend that, "A secure Poland is likely to be less anti-Russian and more interested in cooperation and bridge-building than an insecure Poland again caught in the old geopolitical dilemma between Germany and Russia" (1995, 20–21). By the same logic, a secure South Korea is likely to be less anti-Chinese and more interested in cooperation and bridge-building than an insecure South Korea caught in the old geopolitical dilemma between Japan and China. Although China is likely to oppose a continued U.S. military presence in South Korea after the North Korean threat disappears, China would in fact benefit from it.

A U.S. presence in a unified Korea would encourage the Koreans and Chinese to exercise caution. The fact that a unified Korea would not be maintaining a huge military force would be conducive to China's interest as well. If a unified Korea maintained the smallest possible force, China would not have to answer with a large military force of its own. China would then be able to use the saved resources for more constructive purposes like economic development. There are, to be sure, potential sources of tension between Korea and China that might erupt once Korea is unified. China, for example, might want to stifle growing Korean influence in the northeast province, home to more than one million Chinese of Korean origin.[20] Or border disputes might arise again.[21] But, with U.S. forces present in the united Korea, Korea and China would be inclined to moderate their behavior lest conflict escalate into a U.S.-China confrontation that no one would want.

Korea would also benefit in that its need to build an independent defense capability would be dramatically reduced. This is important since, even without the North Korean threat, South Korea would feel the need to defend its borders and contribute to stability in the region, and this need would be magnified were the Korean peninsula united. Although a confrontation between a united Korea and China is not inevitable, Korea's concern would be natural, given the size of China and its military potential.

A U.S. presence in Korea would, moreover, prevent tension from arising between Japan and China. In the Sino-Japanese War—Japan's first major modern-day war—influence over Korea was the issue at stake. Although the world has since changed and a Sino-Japanese confrontation in Korea is not likely to be repeated, Japan and China are certain to feel uneasy should the United States exit the region.[22] Wang has written that toward the end of the cold war, China began to "gradually and quietly accept and even like the U.S.-ROK alliance for its utility in stabilizing the Korean Peninsula and constraining the Japanese," although the story might be somewhat different were Korea unified (1997, 11).

Should the United States leave Korea without sufficient reassurance, Korea might be tempted to play Japan and China off against each other in order to enhance its position. Korean strategists in favor of a nonaligned Korea tend to advocate this kind of manipulative diplomacy. Yet, while the tactic may serve to maximize short-term benefits for Korea, it would probably complicate the relationship between Japan and China, destabilizing the region.

Finally, the presence of U.S. forces would prevent Korea from developing a nuclear capacity, other weapons of mass destruction (WMD), and an offensive capability, including medium- to long-range ballistic missiles.[23] Reassured of the U.S. commitment, Korea would feel much less need for WMD. The nuclear deterrent provided by the United States is indispensable, but without the maintenance of U.S. forces in Korea, such a nuclear guarantee would ring hollow. The U.S. presence would, again, clearly help prevent tensions from arising between Japan and Korea, between Korea and China, and between Japan and China.

As South Korean President Kim Dae Jung has said, "The U.S. forces stationed on the Korean Peninsula and in Japan are decisive to the maintenance of peace and the balance of power, not only on the Peninsula but also in Northeast Asia. By the same token, the U.S. forces in Europe are an indispensable factor for the peace and stability of all of Europe" (Kim Dae Jung 1998). Despite the words "balance of power," Kim's remark sounds more like reassurance than conflictive balance of power.[24]

REGIONAL AND GLOBAL SECURITY

A second reason for maintaining a post-confrontation U.S.-South Korea alliance is the role it would play in regional and, possibly, global security. The fourth (1998) in the East Asian Strategy Report (EASR) series, entitled *The United States Security Strategy for the East Asia–Pacific Region 1998* states:

> The bilateral alliance and U.S. military presence will continue to contribute to the residual defense needs of Korea and assist in the integration of the two Koreas as appropriate. Beyond the Peninsula, instability and uncertainty are likely to persist in the Asia-Pacific region, with heavy concentrations of military force, including nuclear arsenals, unresolved territorial disputes and historical tensions, and the proliferation of weapons of mass destruction and their means of delivery serving as sources of instability. After reconciliation and, ultimately, reunification, the United States and Korea will remain deeply committed to mitigating such regional sources of instability.
>
> Also, in keeping with the growing global role of the ROK [Republic of Korea], the United States and ROK will continue to share a worldwide commitment to peaceful conflict resolution, arms control and nonproliferation, right of access to international sea, air and space, and promotion of democratic and free market practices. The bilateral security alliance and overseas presence of U.S. military forces will continue to serve as important instruments for achieving these common objectives over the long term (Department of Defense 1998, 62–63).

Until now, the U.S.-South Korea alliance has been geared toward coping with the North Korean threat. The U.S. forces in South Korea have never been used for extrapeninsular missions. However, once the North Korean threat disappears, these forces could be used not only for Korean security, but also for regional or possibly global missions. In particular, the U.S. Air Force deployed in Korea could easily be sent to other parts of Asia Pacific, especially were it not possible to quickly utilize the U.S. Air Force in Japan. In addition, it has been suggested that the U.S. forces in Korea could undertake such nontraditional missions as counterterrorism and peacekeeping operations (O'Hanlon 1998).

Korean forces could be used for extrapeninsular missions as well, if Korea so decided, as South Korean forces were sent to Vietnam to fight alongside U.S. forces in the Vietnam War. Although it may not be desirable today for Korean forces to engage in combat missions overseas, it would certainly be possible for Korean forces to join humanitarian operations or counterterrorism missions. As a member of the United Nations, Korea could participate in UN peacekeeping operations[25] and other security missions with a UN mandate, something which South Korean public opinion has strongly supported.[26]

The United States and South Korea have long experience working together under a combined command. Several thousand South Koreans are employed as the Korean Augmentation to the U.S. Army (KATUSA). Fluent in English, they serve as communication channels between U.S. and South Korean forces. Even after the North Korean threat disappears, U.S. and Korean forces could work together, turning their attention to, for example, the sea lines of communication (SLOC) they have in common. The protection of SLOC would be no small accomplishment. They could also undertake other missions such as humanitarian relief, peacekeeping, hostage rescue, noncombatant evacuation operations, and counterpiracy and counterterrorism efforts.[27] In a February 1999 opinion poll, 82.1 percent of the South Korean respondents agreed that one of the objectives of the U.S.-South Korea alliance was to maintain security in East Asia (*Wolgan Joongang* April 1999); the abovementioned activities would support this objective.

An increased Korean role in the alliance, once the North Korean threat is over, would be appropriate for two reasons. One, it would change the relationship from being an alliance of dependence by Korea to being a partnership. Two, it might ease Chinese concerns. Wang says that Chinese People's Liberation Army officers have suggested that "changes in such a direction would benefit the region and the Peninsula, since a greater Korean say in the U.S.-ROK alliance may result in a less likely American threat" (Wang 1997, 17).

Finally, the U.S.-South Korea alliance could look forward to working closely with the Japan-U.S. alliance in various international security missions. Experience obtained from participation in the U.S.-sponsored Rim of the Pacific (RIMPAC) exercises in past years would become a useful basis for such combined activities. Combined operations for the three countries would eliminate duplication and thus make economic sense as well. And as long as the United States continued to play the leading role, increased military roles by Japan and Korea would probably be accepted by other regional actors.

Continued security cooperation between the United States and Korea would have another positive effect in the region, and possibly beyond: It would symbolize the fact that even without a clear and imminent threat, countries with two very different cultures could work closely together. As O'Hanlon points out, the Japan-U.S. and U.S.-South Korea security relationships are the "principal intercultural and interethnic security unions in the world today" (1998, 9).

BURDEN-SHARING BETWEEN JAPAN AND SOUTH KOREA

The third reason for maintaining a post-confrontation U.S.-South Korea alliance is its contribution to the long-term stability of the Japan-U.S. alliance. Given domestic politics and public perceptions in both Japan and South Korea, it seems that one bilateral alliance can be well maintained only if both exist at the same time (Armacost and Pyle 1999).

U.S. forces in Japan and South Korea have played a critical role in preserving peace and stability in the region, but it has not been without political, economic, and social cost to Japan and South Korea. Safety and noise are two major problems that Japanese must face, particularly in Komatsu, Yokota, Atsugi, and Kadena, where there are bases in urban areas. The rape of a Japanese schoolgirl by U.S. servicemen in September 1995, however exceptional the case may have been, symbolized the disquieting aspects of the U.S. presence in Japanese society. Okinawa, where the rape took place, hosts about 75 percent of the U.S. bases and facilities in Japan. U.S. bases occupy about 10 percent of Okinawa prefecture, or about 18 percent of the main Okinawa island (Defense Agency 1998).

U.S. bases are a concern to South Koreans as well (Nam 1998, 14). While problems pertaining to the bases are not as politically serious in South Korea, owners of the land leased to the U.S. forces are not compensated as well as are their Japanese counterparts. Furthermore, there have been cases where landlords were prevented from disposing of their property and the bases acted to hinder city planning.

In addition, both Japan and Korea incur financial costs by contributing to the stationing of U.S. forces in their countries. In fiscal year 1997, Japan provided US$6 billion dollars in host-nation support (HNS), an amount equal to 10 percent of its defense budget, while South Korea spent US$363 million (Ministry of National Defense 1999, 228).

Finally, accommodating foreign troops is not without political complications. U.S. forces initially played the role of occupier in Japan, and this history lingers, whereas they arrived in South Korea as liberators in 1945 and 1950. Regardless of the historical differences, leaders of both Japan and South Korea have to convince their people that the benefits of accommodating U.S. forces supercede the costs. This would be more difficult if there were no tangible threat.

But if either alliance were abolished, it would become politically problematic justifying the other. What sophisticated strategic thinkers may say about this may matter less than the sentiments of ordinary citizens. Moreover, for one country to sustain a much heavier burden than the other over a long period of time creates problems. Of course, it would be impossible for Japan and Korea to share the burden equally simply because of differences in geostrategic position, population, geography, and size of economy. The perception of fairness is critical, but burden is largely a matter of subjective judgment. Once the clear and present danger posed by North Korea disappears, the Japan-U.S. and U.S.-South Korea alliances would have a better chance of survival if they were maintained with a meaningful presence of U.S. forces in both countries.[28]

HEDGE AGAINST THE RISE OF AN AGGRESSIVE CHINA

The fourth reason for maintaining a post-confrontation U.S.-South Korea alliance is the hedge it provides against the rise of China as an aggressive power.[29] An aggressive China does not necessarily mean that China would start a major war, but it could suggest the threat or the use of force for limited expansionist purposes or could put hostile strategic pressure on neighboring countries.[30] There are three primary sources of concern regarding China.[31] First, China has in the past two decades repeatedly exercised force, albeit in a limited manner, to enhance its position in East Asia. In 1988, China clashed with Vietnam over ownership of the Spratly Islands. In 1992, China enacted a territorial waters law that unilaterally designated the Senkaku Islands, Spratly Islands, and Paracel Island as part of its territory. In 1995, China was found to have stationed armed vessels at, and built structures on, Mischief Reef, ownership of which was claimed by both China and the Philippines. Then in 1996, China threatened Taiwan by launching missiles that overflew it. China, many fear, has been trying to expand its sphere of influence by declaring its ownership of disputed land as a fait accompli.[32]

In the 1990s, China's defense budget grew by more than 10 percent annually, and even this figure does not take into account some defense-related expenditures listed as non–defense budget items. China is modernizing its strategic nuclear force by developing three new solid-fuel ballistic missiles, a new generation of nuclear-powered submarines, and multiple warheads (Jones et al. 1998, 55).

A second reason for concern is that Chinese political reform has lagged behind economic reform and, at this point, it seems likely that Chinese politics will in time undergo a period of instability. While democratic peace theorists contend that fully democratic countries do not fight each other, they note that nations are actually more likely to go to war in the period of democratization (Doyle 1996; Russett 1996a; Russett 1996b; and Owen 1996). According to this theory, in the ten years following democratization, nations are twice as likely to go to war as are autocratic countries. Moreover, great powers tend to become expansionist when they democratize. Two cases in point are the Weimar Republic and Japan in the interwar period (Snyder 1991; Kupchan 1994; and Mansfield and Snyder 1995). China would likely become quite unstable during such a transitional period, and even Chinese leaders themselves might not be able to prevent the country from heading down this road in the course of democratization.

Finally, China's economic strength is rapidly growing. As discussed earlier, the Chinese economy is expected to eventually surpass the economies of Japan and Korea. With China's position in the world thus enhanced, China seems certain to demand greater international status.

For these reasons, as one security expert points out, a favorable strategic outlook would be a balance of power in which "China stands alone, though respected and unthreatened, and the United States leads a coalition of regional powers as a hedge against possible threats from China" (Rozman 1998, 132). This would not require the maintenance of a force level sufficient to deal with an aggressive China, but the infrastructure and minimum necessary base force upon which a larger force could be built quickly. If undertaken in a sophisticated manner, such an approach would also have the effect of discouraging those Chinese leaders who would otherwise try to use military force to achieve their own ends. Together with the Japan-U.S. alliance, the U.S.-South Korea alliance and the continued presence of U.S. forces in Korea, though at a lower force level, would be the most appropriate mechanisms to cope with any potential Chinese threat.

A bonus effect of the U.S. presence in Korea would be that China would feel less free to concentrate its armed forces in the southern region and to conduct offensive operations in the Taiwan Strait or in the South China Sea.[33] Obviously, it would be best if constructive engagement succeeds and China becomes a full member of the international community. Under such circumstances, peace and stability would prevail in East Asia; this, in turn, appears to be a precondition for China's continued growth. Deepening interdependence and interaction with other countries seem to be moderating Chinese behavior in the international arena. Chinese leaders are learning that aggressive foreign policy invites negative reactions from countries and international organizations, the cooperation and support of which are essential to China's economic development. Japan, the United States, and South Korea must make their utmost effort to create a strategic environment in which China will be encouraged to pursue its goal of becoming a great nation not by military effort, but by peaceful means.

EAST ASIAN COMMUNITY
OF DEMOCRATIC NATIONS

The fifth and final reason for maintaining a post-confrontation U.S.-South Korea alliance is that it can serve as a foundation, in combination with the Japan-U.S. alliance, for the East Asian community of democratic nations.[34]

The United States can function as an honest broker in East Asia because of the credibility of its political system.[35] Similarly, China is regarded with suspicion in East Asia because its political system lacks credibility, i.e., it is a laggard in terms of political development. In the foreseeable future, among the four countries discussed here—Japan, the United States, South Korea, and China—the United States seems likely to remain the most stable and trustworthy. The long history of American democracy has become an important source of its credibility, and the transparency of American decision-making processes assures its predictability, even with a drastic policy change. Of course, this is not to say that the United States will never resort to force, but if it does, more often than not it will probably do so for legitimate reasons.

Comparatively speaking, the political systems of Japan, South Korea, and China are less widely trusted. Japan is regarded as the most institutionalized democracy in Asia, and its democratic tradition dates back to the early twentieth century. Yet, Japan has demonstrated an inability to respond quickly and effectively to a changing environment.[36] Despite the often-voiced public outcry for change, Japan has failed to undertake fundamental political reform. In its defense policy, a large gap remains between its declared policy and actual policy.

Democracy seems to have taken root in South Korea, and its democratic transition has made the country a model for other democratizing countries. However, here again seeds of uncertainty remain. The South Korean government has long relied on opposition to communism to maintain internal cohesion. Once the North Korean threat is gone, what will take its place? Bracken says, "As anticommunism wanes, nationalism is the most likely replacement" (1998, 420). If nationalism serves as a positive force in unifying a historically divided nation, fine, but there is concern that anti-Japanese or anti-American sentiment could also arise. It would be worrisome if the leaders of Korea were tempted to use anti-Japanese sentiment as a means of marshaling popular support and facilitating national unity.

In China, dramatic socioeconomic change is ongoing. The Chinese Communist Party is still in charge, but socioeconomic change might, in the near future, bring on the demise of its ideology. Any political transition is likely to cause at least some instability. In the early 1990s, the Chinese leadership was apparently agitating nationalist sentiment in order to mobilize political support and unify the country. Territorial claims on the Spratly, Paracel, and Senkaku islands, made partly for such purposes, have posed a serious threat to its neighbors.

Although they differ in degree, a lack of transparency undercuts the credibility and predictability of the policies of China, Japan, and South Korea. This uncertainty makes political reform and improvement in democratic institutions in these countries key to achieving security in East Asia. A continued U.S. presence would provide the stability indispensable to such reform. Maintaining the two bilateral alliances could help further democratic reform in the region.

In November 1998, South Korean President Kim Dae Jung and U.S. President Bill Clinton announced an agreement to create a democracy forum, which would seek measures to foster both democracy and a market economy in Asia. Led by the U.S. National Endowment for Democracy and the Korean Sejong Institute, the forum would bring together young leaders from the region ("Opening Remarks" 1998), and the program would be further strengthened were Japan to join in the effort.

The importance of each of the five reasons for having a post-confrontation U.S.-South Korea alliance will necessarily vary according to the situation. However, what is important is that these different reasons, if put together, will certainly bring us to the conclusion that the maintenance of the U.S.-South Korea alliance is a good idea.

TOWARD SYMMETRICAL ALLIANCES

In post-confrontation Asia, the U.S.-South Korea alliance could be expected to function similarly to the Japan-U.S. alliance.[37] Until now, the primary objective of the U.S.-South Korea alliance has been to deter North Korean aggression. U.S. ground forces deployed to the north of Seoul serve as a tripwire. If North Korea attacks the South, it would be attacking the U.S. forces as well. Because of the constancy of this threat, U.S. forces in South Korea have been unavailable for missions outside the Korean peninsula.[38]

In contrast, the Japan-U.S. alliance is multifaceted and complex in nature. During the cold war, the primary objective, supposedly, was to deter the military threat of the Soviet Union against Japan; in actuality, other sometimes more important interests were pursued. The security of South Korea was one. In 1969, Prime Minister Satō Eisaku declared that the security of South Korea was essential to the security of Japan, tacitly affirming that Korea was a major focus of interest of the Japan-U.S alliance (Kashima Heiwa Kenkyūsho 1984, 880; Lee 1985). This fact was reconfirmed by the new defense guidelines formulated in 1997.

During the Vietnam War, Japan served as an indispensable base for the U.S. war effort and helped provide medical treatment for casualties. During the 1980s, Japan's significant defense buildup helped to contain the Soviet threat worldwide. During the Persian Gulf War, a contingent of U.S. forces in Japan was sent to the Middle East.

Once the North Korean threat is gone, the U.S.-Korea alliance might be restructured so as to make it more multifunctional as well. Such a U.S.-Korea alliance could contribute, as noted earlier, to such objectives as reassurance, regional and global security, and the expansion of democratic institutions.

Currently the U.S.-South Korea alliance is self-concerned, contributing little tangibly to the security of Japan, while the Japan-U.S. alliance has a direct and crucial impact on the strategic equation on the Korean peninsula. But should functions other than deterrence against North Korea become more important, the relationship between the two alliances would become more complementary. Historically, South Korea has worried that the United States might abandon it. In fact, it was so concerned in the 1970s that it attempted to produce its own nuclear weapons. This was not a fear that Japan shared, largely due to the difference in the way its alliance has functioned. Should the two alliances become more complementary, the Koreans would not have to worry too much about being abandoned.

FUTURE ALLIANCE STRUCTURE

A New Alliance for the Next Century, published jointly by the Rand Corporation and the Korea Institute for Defense Analyses (KIDA), provides a useful definition of an alliance. According to the report, in order for a relationship to be an alliance, it must involve: one, a strategic concept defining the shared obligations of alliance partners; two, a defense strategy that specifies the roles and responsibilities of each partner; three, an agreement on the types and levels of forces required to implement a common defense strategy; and four, a range of more specialized agreements on command relations, base agreements, and burden-sharing (Pollack and Young et al. 1995).

Based on this definition, the future structure of the two alliances would be hard to determine now. A restructured alliance would require that the military and defense bureaucratic leadership, based on general principles formulated by the highest political authorities, formulate specific force structure, disposition, roles and missions, command and control arrangements, and other specifics.

The current official U.S. policy is to maintain 100,000 troops in Asia Pacific. Other things being constant, the force level would likely be reduced after the disappearance of the North Korean threat. The important question would then be how to strike a balance among the alliance members' different policy objectives, and how to assign roles and missions to Japan's Self-Defense Forces (SDF), U.S. forces, and Korean forces. It seems likely that U.S. forces would play a primary combat role in a regional and global context, while Japanese and Korean forces would play a secondary role in such operations. However, Japanese and Korean forces would have to provide deterrence and defense capabilities for their own territories, with U.S. forces supplementing such missions. Japanese and Korean forces would be expected to take on larger burdens in fulfilling various security roles in the region.

BUILDING A CONSENSUS

It now appears likely that the U.S. forces in South Korea will remain even after the disappearance of the North Korean threat. The United States and South Korea have agreed publicly that the forces must be maintained. The EASR series for 1998 also states that: "The United States welcomes the public statements of ROK President Kim Dae-Jung affirming the value of the bilateral alliance and the U.S. military presence even after reunification of the Korean peninsula. The U.S. strongly agrees that our alliance and military presence will continue to support stability both on the Korean peninsula and throughout the region after North Korea is no longer a threat" (Department of Defense 1998, 62).

The question then is how a consensus might be achieved with regard to the future of the two alliances. In order to arrive at a fair and sustainable agreement, it is imperative to look for an appropriate framework, to initiate discussions at the right time, and to implement the agreement effectively. What would be the appropriate framework for such a discussion? Should the parties conduct bilateral, trilateral, or multilateral discussions? The decision is important because the two alliances have several different faces, and each framework has its strengths as well as drawbacks.

A bilateral framework could rely on some well-established institutions to address specific issues. The Security Consultative Committee (SCC), the Security Sub-committee, the Security Consultative Group, the Sub-committee for Defense Cooperation (SDC), the Japan-U.S. Joint Committee, and the Bilateral Planning Committee (BPC) are major forums for the Japan-U.S. alliance (Defense Agency 1998, 188). The U.S.-South Korea alliance includes the Security Consultative Meeting (SCM), the Military Committee Meeting (MCM), the Policy Review Subcommittee (PRS), and the Security Cooperation Committee (SCC) as part of its security dialogue (Ministry of National Defense 1999, 127–131). However, these institutions are based on bilateral relationships and do not effectively deal with the broader issues of redefining the two bilateral alliances as part of a whole.

Formally, the two alliances are two separate entities, with no security arrangement to tie Japan and South Korea. In reality, however, the two alliances frequently work together, with the United States as a hub. A trilateral framework is ideal for discussing how to redefine the two alliances and assign roles and missions. Such a framework would represent the interests of the three nations more fairly, and precedence does exist in a trilateral framework designed originally to discuss issues concerning North Korea. Not listening to other regional players runs the risk of offending them, however, and this would be particularly true regarding China.

Finally, a multilateral framework would be inclusive and thus well-suited to incorporating different points of view and to resolving differences among countries in the region. Such a framework would reflect the fact that the Japan-U.S. alliance has regional and sometimes global implications, and that the U.S.-South Korea alliance will become more regionally and globally oriented absent the North Korean threat. The weakness of a multilateral framework, however, is that because of the wide range of diverging interests, such a framework would likely invite never-ending discussions with no constructive results. Alliance relationships, by nature, touch on vital national interests of the member countries. Therefore, it would no doubt be unacceptable to Japan, the United States, and South Korea to allow a multilateral forum to have a strong say in matters that concerned their respective vital interests.

The best result would probably be attained by carefully mixing the three different frameworks so that they would complement each other according to need and context. That said, the trilateral framework would most likely be used to initiate the discussion and make crucial decisions with regard to the future of the two alliances. There are two reasons for this. First, in redefining the alliance relationships, the national interests of the member countries would, and must, be of utmost importance. The trilateral framework best accommodates this diversity of interests.[39] Second, since China is committed to maintaining the status quo—the North Korean regime— it would be impossible for the Chinese to initiate discussions of a world without North Korea.

The multilateral framework could serve as a means for the three countries to inform their neighbors of the progress of discussion and for their neighbors to make their views known. Just as Japan kept South Korea and China abreast of the progress of the revised defense guidelines, Japan, the United States, and South Korea should do their best to explain to their neighbors the progress of their policy-making.

In the final stage of the restructuring process, the bilateral framework probably would matter most. Theoretically, it is possible that the Japan-U.S. alliance and the U.S.-South Korea alliance could be combined, but that would be politically unsustainable in Japan and South Korea, and it might lead China to assume that the three countries have joined in a sinister, anti-Chinese coalition. The two bilateral alliances had better remain separate, with the administrative organizations of each alliance working to implement agreements made in the trilateral forum.

MOBILIZING DOMESTIC SUPPORT

One of the most challenging tasks that the leaders of Japan, the United States, and South Korea face is to persuade their people to understand and support maintenance of these alliance relationships after peace on the Korean peninsula. The old days of the clear "global Soviet threat" and fear of "North Korean Red monsters" will be gone. Reassurance, regional/global security roles, burden sharing, hedging, and the idea of a democratic community are complex and abstract concepts to sell to the general public.

So it is good news that people are quite supportive of both alliance relationships. In an opinion poll conducted in 1997, about 70 percent of Japanese respondents and 50 percent of American respondents expressed the hope that Japan and the United States would remain allies into the twenty-first century. Fifty percent of the Japanese and 53 percent of the American respondents said that U.S. forces deployed in the Pacific should be maintained at the current level (*Yomiuri Shimbun* 24 November 1997). In an opinion poll conducted in South Korea in 1999, an overwhelming 89.1 percent of the respondents agreed that the U.S.-South Korea alliance must be maintained after unification. In the same poll, 57.2 percent supported keeping U.S. forces in Korea after unification, while 39.5 percent said the level of forces must be reduced. The most popular response when asked about the post-unification alliance relationship was that "the U.S.-South Korea alliance should be maintained with a reduced number of U.S. forces in Korea" (*Wolgan Joongang* April 1999, 245).[40]

ENGAGING CHINA

The policies described above must be accompanied by an engagement policy toward China, or China may regard the alliances as pursuing a containment policy, thereby exacerbating the security situation.

Carpenter writes that the "challenge for China is to fully assume its place among the global great powers in a manner that contributes to the overall peace and stability of Asia and the Pacific" (1998, 2). This is a difficult task. For China, a continued strong U.S.-South Korea alliance may be a less-than-desirable future scenario, but it might be wrong to assume that China would oppose it outright. The voices coming out of China are not monolithic. In fact, there have been signs of flexibility. According to interviews conducted by American scholars Garrett and Glaser, Chinese officials have allowed that "permitting foreign troops to be stationed on its soil is a nation's sovereign right" and that "China would not interfere with a decision by Seoul to permit a continued U.S. force presence" (1997, 87).

A Chinese expert, a researcher from the China Institute of International Strategic Studies, has stated that the continued U.S. military presence in Korea after unification is a good idea. He notes that U.S. forces would "serve as a buffer, a reassurance" against any armed animosity between Japan and Korea, although China would probably oppose "the redeployment of U.S. forces to the northern part of Korea close to the Chinese border" (Garrett and Glaser 1997, 87).

If this is the case, there are at least two options the alliance partners can take. First, the United States and South Korea could agree not to redeploy U.S. forces to the north of the military demarcation line once Korea is unified. They could also agree to reduce the number of troops deployed in Korea concomitant with a reduction of U.S. forces in Japan, which would bring the number of American troops in the region to below 100,000. These reductions would be substantive in the sense that the removal of the North Korean threat would have been taken into account. And they would be symbolic in the sense that the reduction in number of troops would not necessarily mean reduction in capability.[41]

It is pointed out that "counting heads" is "an eighteenth century measure of military power" and that the magic number 100,000 does not necessarily represent military capability in the modern world (Vickers and Kosiak 1997, 17). Yet, that troop level has been widely seen as being necessary for deterrence. If North Korea, correctly or incorrectly, viewed reduction in the number of troops as a sign of a reduced U.S. commitment, that would undercut the effectiveness of deterrence. Once the North Korean threat disappears, however, the fixation on 100,000 actually offers a diplomatic opportunity. If maintaining this level has symbolic meaning, reducing it would also have symbolic meaning, and this could be useful in persuading China to accept maintaining U.S. forces in Korea and the U.S.-South Korea alliance (Bracken 1998, 422).

Second, a consultative and cooperative security link, similar to the NATO-Russia Permanent Joint Council, could be created between the two alliances and China. The link in Europe has been established in order to address the concern that NATO expansion might antagonize Russia (North Atlantic Treaty Organization 1997). It has worked at promoting transparency and confidence building; fostering cooperation; and encouraging constructive Russian participation in the European security system. It would be a good idea for Japan and the United States and the United States and South Korea to separately conclude such agreements with China.

CONCLUSION

Discussion about the future of these alliances should start soon. Establishing a broad design for the alliances will provide a sense of direction and predictability for the countries involved. Although it is impossible and inappropriate to draw a detailed picture of force levels or disposition, countries can easily become suspicious of others' intentions if they lack generally shared expectations for the future.

The occurrence of a drastic event like the collapse of North Korea would precipitate all kinds of domestic pressure, international tension, and mutual suspicion. If that happens, it would be extremely difficult to agree on issues that are contentious at the best of times.

The ongoing existence of the North Korean threat provides the parties with a practical political basis to discuss issues of trilateral concern. Meetings among Japan, the United States, and South Korea, originally set up to discuss the North Korean nuclear issue, have been regularized, and high-level officials frequently meet to discuss not only North Korean issues but also other security issues of concern. This trilateral cooperation, now at an unprecedented level, should be expanded further while these common interests prevail.

Certainly, discussion of the future may have some negative short-term consequences. If, for example, North Korea misjudges and believes that the United States is trying to reduce its commitment to the South, it might then try to exploit the situation for diplomatic purposes by proposing an arms control dialogue. Or South Korea might believe that the United States is backing out and taking a more equidistant policy toward the North and the South. Others might believe that Japan, the United States, and South Korea expect the collapse of North Korea soon, which would be problematic since the United States and South Korea are pursuing an engagement policy toward North Korea. Japan, the United States, and South Korea must take care to strike a balance between short-term and long-term policy imperatives.

Discussion about the post-confrontation world would, if conducted in a well-calculated and coordinated manner, put reasonable pressure on North Korea. Engagement is a double-edged sword. With positive incentives, it is designed to build confidence and to encourage political and economic reform. However, because it is a policy employing positive incentives only, North Korea might well become complacent and even more reluctant to undertake reforms. A carrot works well only when combined with a stick. Discussion of the disappearance of the North Korean threat, which by implication suggests possible change in the leadership, is a warning that if North Koreans insist on the development of WMD and military-diplomatic brinkmanship, neighboring countries might decide that the collapse of North Korea should become their policy objective.

It is anticipated that political difficulties and bureaucratic inertia will hinder the initiation of the process suggested in this chapter. However, the oft-quoted dictum, "if it ain't broke, don't fix it," should not be adopted. Alliances must be reordered to keep up with the environment in which they operate. In order to keep the two alliances in good shape and ensure that they survive major changes in the strategic environment, efforts must begin now.

An abridged version of this chapter was published as "Alliances After Peace in Korea" in *Survival,* vol. 41, no. 3 (Autumn 1999), pp. 68–83.

NOTES

1. A flaw in the forward-looking book *Toward A True Alliance: Restructuring U.S.-Japan Security Relations* (Mochizuki 1997) is that it fails to pay enough attention to the U.S.-South Korea alliance when it talks about the Japan-U.S. alliance; another report that looks to the future, *A New Alliance for the Next Century: The Future of U.S.-Korean Security Cooperation* (Pollack et al. 1995), fails to take the Japan-U.S. alliance into account when it looks at the U.S.-South Korea alliance.

2. For a detailed discussion on how to cope with the unification process, see Lho (1997).

3. Why division under peaceful coexistence would not last long is discussed in Michishita (1998, 11–12).

4. The reasons for North Korea being more durable than many observers believe are elaborated in Noland (1997). South Korea swung back to a peaceful coexistence policy with the North under the Kim Dae Jung administration. Toward the end of his presidency, Kim Young Sam pursued a policy for unification (see chapters 14 and 15 in Oberdorfer 1997).

5. The Bank of Korea reported that, in 1997, the North Korean economy contracted 6.8 percent to a nominal gross domestic product of US$17.7 billion. In particular, manufacturing shrank 16.8 percent and construction 9.9 percent,

though the service industry grew 1.1 percent ("Gross Domestic Product of North Korea" [1999]).

6. The number of recorded defectors rose from three in 1993 to eighty-six in 1997 and seventy-two in 1998 (Ministry of Unification 1999, 126). A report published by South Korea's National Assembly states that there were about 90 defectors from North Korea who were former members of the North Korean government or party, although the report does not identify them. According to this report, the number of defectors started to increase drastically in 1994. In addition, there were 2,000 to 3,000 people living in China and Russia who had fled from North Korea (*Kyodo tsūshin nyūsu sokuhō* 18 September 1998).

7. Lee Jong Chan, former head of South Korea's National Intelligence Service, estimated the death toll in North Korea since 1995 at 400,000 (*Korea Herald* June 1993, 3 and 7). A high-ranking North Korean defector, Hwang Jang Yop, contends that he was informed of 500,000 deaths in 1995 and about one million deaths in 1996 (Hwang 1999, 335). Seoul's Korea Institute for National Unification estimates that in North Korea, 500,000 to 800,000 people have died every year since 1996 (Korea Institute for National Unification 1999). Also, *Rodong Sinmun,* the North Korean Workers' Party organ, reported on April 22, 1999, that Kim Jong Il had said he approved of developing artificial satellites knowing that this would deny North Korean people food and better living standards.

8. The United States took specific note of this point in an official document (White House 1998, 42).

9. Statistics by the Institute of Developing Economies are available at the Institute of Developing Economies (1999) and Sutter (1998, 2).

10. For an argument against maintaining U.S. forces in Korea, see Bandow (1992, 1996, and 1998).

11. The Chinese version of the future vision depicted in Xin (1998, as reported in the *Mainichi Shimbun,* 18 June 1998) is more optimistic than its counterparts. The Chinese economy is expected to see an average annual growth rate of 7 percent until 2020. Its gross domestic product will surpass that of Germany in 2005 and of Japan in 2025; and it will be equal to that of the United States in 2041.

12. In 2020, China's GDP is expected to be US$12,278 billion, Japan's US$11,281 billion, South Korea's US$4,081 billion, and that of the United States US$26,908 billion (WEFA 1995, 1996, quoted in Korea Development Institute 1996, 12).

13. Leading Japanese university scholars agree that "diplomacy based on economic strength" as seen in the past cannot be sustained over the medium to long term and that other resources available for Japanese diplomacy must be explored (Inoguchi et al. 1999).

14. For discussion on the U.S.-South Korea alliance, see Tucker (1998), Ahn (1998), and Murata (1998b).

15. Michael Howard wrote that what NATO provided the European allies with was "the kind of reassurance a child needs from its parents or an invalid from

his doctors against dangers which, however remote, cannot be entirely discounted" (1983, 248). Ronald D. Asmus, Richard L. Kugler, and F. Stephen Larrabee (1995) contend that reassurance is one of the important ingredients of NATO expansion.

16. For a Chinese perspective on Japan, see Whiting (1989).

17. For Korea's concern vis-à-vis Japan, see Kil (1998, 288–290). For an analysis of misunderstandings between the two countries, see Michishita (1997).

18. Major articles to this effect include Chung (1990); Shin Yong Ha (1991); Youn Jung-Suk (1991); Auh (1993); and Kim (1995).

19. In a February 1999 opinion poll conducted jointly by *Joongang Ilbo* and the Rand Corporation in South Korea, 70.6 percent of the respondents agreed that one of the objectives of the U.S.-South Korea alliance was to prevent Japan from becoming a military superpower (*Wolgan Joongang* April 1999, 246). Also, see Shin Yong Ha (1991).

20. In a Korea Institute for National Understanding (KINU) opinion poll, conducted among experts in South Korea and the United States, 12.5 percent of respondents answered that it was "highly likely" that the Korean-Chinese living near the border would become a source of tension between Korea and China; 57.5 percent said the possibility was "medium" (Ok and Kim 1997, 127).

21. Such a situation would be avoided if Korea were aligned with either the United States or China. Were Korea aligned with China, the reason is obvious. Were Korea aligned with the United States, Washington would try to prevent Korea from making any attempt to expand into Chinese territory or increase its influence in China, out of fear that such an attempt might escalate into direct confrontation between the United States and China. Cho warns against the possible emergence of the contention that a unified Korea must recover territory it previously lost in China. Such a contention would become a cause of conflict with China (Cho 1997). In the KINU opinion poll, 10.0 percent of respondents answered that it was "highly likely" that the rearrangement of the northern border would become a diplomatic issue; 17.5 percent said the possibility for this was "medium" (Ok and Kim 1997, 126).

22. Brzezinski claims that "a reunified Korea without U.S. troops on its soil would be quite likely to gravitate first toward a form of neutrality between China and Japan and then gradually—driven in part by residual but still intense anti-Japanese feelings—toward a Chinese sphere of either politically more assertive influence or somewhat more delicate deference" (1997, 190).

23. In a February 1999 opinion poll, 85.4 percent of South Korean respondents said that the country must go nuclear if the U.S.-South Korea alliance collapsed; 75.7 percent said that nuclear capability would be necessary to check great powers in Asia after unification. Only 15.0 percent said that South Korea must never possess nuclear weapons (*Wolgan Joongang* April 1999).

24. Howard claims that, while the effectiveness of deterrence in Europe was hard to determine, it was clear that "reassurance had worked" (1983, 248).

25. To date, South Korean forces have been engaged in UN peacekeeping

operations in Western Sahara, India and Pakistan, and Georgia (Ministry of National Defense 1999).

26. In a February 1999 opinion poll, 84.7 percent of the respondents answered positively when asked whether they believed South Korean forces should be used to protect sea lanes vital to Korean security, 83.3 percent supported the participation of South Korean forces in multinational forces with a UN mandate, and 62.9 percent supported using South Korean forces to protect sources of energy in the Middle East (*Wolgan Joongang* April 1999, 245).

27. These missions have been suggested as future roles that Japan could play (Mochizuki and O'Hanlon 1998).

28. Robert Dujarric, a research fellow in the national securities department of the Hudson Institute, has contended that Japan, the United States, and South Korea can enhance the level of burden-sharing by reverse basing. It would be good for military efficiency if Japan and South Korea could keep some forces in the continental United States for training purposes, because it is difficult to find good training grounds in Japan or South Korea due to space limitations, and because it would be possible to convince Japanese and Korean citizens that it is a balanced relationship (Dujarric 2000, 98).

29. In a February 1999 opinion poll, 52.8 percent of South Korean respondents agreed that one of the objectives of the U.S.-South Korea alliance was to deter China from building up its military power (*Wolgan Joongang* April 1999). Deterrence and geostrategic hedge were other ingredients of NATO expansion. See Asmus, Kugler, and Larrabee (1995, 11).

30. This is particularly important since asymmetry is becoming one of the most important characteristics of modern wars (Freedman 1998).

31. Robert R. Ross (1997) points out that there were three major factors that motivated Chinese leaders' behavior: territorial ambitions; domestic political instability; and desire for recognition as a regional power.

32. Of course, China may not be solely responsible for all its apparent aggression. As regards Taiwan, the objective of the Chinese action was more defensive than meets the eye. China was not alone in challenging the status quo in cross-strait relations: At the time of the crisis, Taiwan had embarked on a proactive course of "pragmatic diplomacy" that impinged on China's traditional claim of Taiwan as an integral part of China.

33. Of course, this would create some stress in the relationship between the United States and Korea, which would be concerned about becoming entangled in the conflicts in the Taiwan Strait or in the South China Sea. This possibility was clearly seen during the Taiwan Strait Crisis, when South Korea declared that the mutual defense treaty with the United States did not cover contingencies there (Carpenter 1998, 13). However, the U.S. military presence in Korea would have a deterrent effect on China in other areas even without actual use of it. Therefore, the United States would be able to deter Chinese aggression without complicating its relations with South Korea.

34. Another benefit of keeping U.S. forces forward-deployed is that it would enable high-ranking U.S. uniformed officers to obtain in-depth knowledge and understanding about host nations (Dujarric 2000, 94–95). Also, see O'Hanlon (1998–1999, 83).

35. This issue has already been pointed out by the U.S. Department of Defense. Its 1995 report claims: "The United States has the capability, credibility, and even-handedness to play the 'honest broker' among nervous neighbors, historical enemies, and potential antagonists" (Department of Defense 1995, 23).

36. For a balanced account of Japanese politics, see Richardson (1997). Richardson claims that political power in Japan is fragmented and conflictive.

37. For comparison between the two alliances, see Murata (1998a).

38. The United States contemplated using U.S. forces in South Korea in the Vietnam War. However, in order to maintain deterrent capability on the Korean peninsula, South Korean forces were dispatched to Vietnam instead.

39. There is one important difference between German unification and Korean unification. While East Germany was dominated by the Soviets, North Korea is not subject to any foreign dominance.

40. In the KINU poll, 15.0 percent of the expert respondents answered that it was "highly likely" that the U.S.-Korea alliance would be strengthened after the unification; 60.0 percent said the possibility was "medium" (Ok and Kim 1997, 127).

41. Revolution in Military Affairs (RMA) is expected to have two major effects on alliance relations. One is that the need for forward-deployed forces would be reduced. The other is that the United States would still be capable of providing its allies with the same level of protection even if forward-deployed forces are reduced or withdrawn. However, it is unlikely that forward deployment would become "much less" important (O'Hanlon 1998–1999, 72–85).

BIBLIOGRAPHY

Ahn Byung Joon. 1998. "The Origins and Evolution of the Korean-American Alliance: A Korean Perspective." Discussion papers. California: Asia/Pacific Research Center, Institute for International Studies, Stanford University.

Armacost, Michael H., and Kenneth B. Pyle. 1999. "Japan and the Unification of Korea: Challenges for U.S. Policy Coordination." *NBR Analysis* 10 (1). Seattle: The National Bureau of Asian Research.

Asmus, Ronald D., Richard L. Kugler, and F. Stephen Larrabee. 1995. "NATO Expansion: The Next Steps." *Survival* 37 (1): 7–33.

Auh Soo Young. 1993. "Ilbonui kunsa taegukhwa chungch'aegul uryohamyo" (Worrying militarization policy of Japan). *Hanil Journal* 23 (1): 81–94.

Bandow, Doug. 1992. *The U.S.-South Korean Alliance: Time for a Change.* New Brunswick, N.J.: Transaction Publishers.

———. 1996. *Tripwire: Korea and U.S. Foreign Policy in a Changed World*. Washington, D.C.: Cato Institute.

———. 1998. "America's Obsolete Korean Commitment." *Orbis* 42 (4): 605–617.

Bracken, Paul. 1998. "How to Think about Korean Unification." *Orbis* 42 (3): 409–422.

Brzezinski, Zbigniew. 1997. *The Grand Chessboard: American Primacy and Its Geostrategic Imperatives*. New York: Basic Books.

Carpenter, Ted Galen. 1998. "Managing a Great Power Relationship: The United States, China and East Asian Security." *The Journal of Strategic Studies* 21 (1): 1–20.

Cho Ji Youn. 1997. *T'ongilkwa kanghan kundae: ku chulryakkwa ridosip* (Unification and strong military: Its strategy and leadership). Seoul: Heng Lim Chulpan.

Chung Ku Chong. 1990. "Ch'olcho yon'gu: Ilbon Chauidae" (In-depth research: Japan's Self-Defense Force). *Shin Dong-a* (December): 384–401.

Defense Agency, Japan. 1997. *Defense of Japan 1997*. Tokyo: Defense Agency.

———. 1998. *Defense of Japan 1998*. Tokyo: Defense Agency.

Department of Defense, Office of International Security Affairs, United States. 1995. *United States Security Strategy for the East Asia–Pacific Region*. Washington, D.C.: Department of Defense.

Department of Defense, Office of International Security Affairs, United States. 1998. *The United States Security Strategy for the East Asia–Pacific Region 1998*. Washington, D.C.: Department of Defense. <http://www.defenselink.mil/pubs/easr98/> (21 May 1999).

Doyle, Michael W. 1996. "Kant, Liberal Legacies, and Foreign Affairs." In Michael E. Brown, Sean M. Lynn-Jones, and Steven E. Miller, eds. *Debating the Democratic Peace*. Cambridge, Mass.: The MIT Press.

Dujarric, Robert. 2000. *Korean Unification and After: The Challenge for U.S. Strategy*. Indianapolis, Ind.: Hudson Institute.

Freedman, Lawrence. 1998. "The Revolution in Strategic Affairs." Adelphi Paper 318. London: International Institute for Strategic Studies.

Gaddis, John Lewis. 1974. "Was the Truman Doctrine a Real Turning Point?" *Foreign Affairs* 52 (2): 386–402.

Garrett, Banning, and Bonnie Glaser. 1997. "China's Pragmatic Posture toward the Korean Peninsula." *The Korean Journal of Defense Analysis* 9 (2): 63–91.

"Gross Domestic Product of North Korea." 1999. <http://www.bok.or.kr/cgi-bin/nph-hwp2html/data/eng8/UP/nkgdp.hwp.19980617163252> (21 May).

Hiramatsu Shigeo. 1998. *Chūgoku no gunjiryoku* (Chinese military power). Tokyo: Bungei Shunjū.

Howard, Michael. 1983. *The Causes of Wars*. Second edition. Cambridge, Mass.: Harvard University Press.

Hwang Jang Yop. 1999. *Kin Shōnichi e no sensen fukoku* (Declaration of war on Kim Jong Il). Tokyo: Bungei Shunjū.

Inoguchi Takashi et al. 1999. "Charenji 2001: 21 seiki ni muketa Nihon gaikō no kadai" (Challenge 2001: Agenda for Japanese diplomacy into the 21st century). A proposal paper submitted to the Ministry of Foreign Affairs (6 January). <http://www.mofa.go.jp/mofaj/gaiko/hoka/teigen/index.html> (21 May 1999).

Institute of Developing Economies. 1999. "Kuni, chiiki betsu bōeki" (Trade statistics by country and region). <http://www.ide.go.jp/Japanese/Material/h42h40.html> (21 May 1999).

International Institute for Strategic Studies. 1998. *Military Balance 1998/99*. Oxford: Oxford University Press.

Iwamoto Yasushi. 1999. "Nihon no senzai seichōryoku (1)" (Japanese growth potential [1]). *Nihon Keizai Shimbun* (25 January).

Jones, Rodney W. et al. 1998. *Tracking Nuclear Proliferation: A Guide in Maps and Charts, 1998.* Washington, D.C.: Carnegie Endowment for International Peace.

Kashima Heiwa Kenkyūsho, ed. 1984. "Joint Comminiqué between U.S. President Richard M. Nixon and Japanese Prime Minister Satō Eisaku 21 November 1969." In *Nihon gaikō shuyō bunsho/nenpyō* (Basic documents on Japanese foreign relations), vol. 2.

Kil Soong Hoom. 1998. *Hyondae Ilbon chungch'iron* (Politics of modern Japan). Seoul: Seoul University Press.

Kim Dae Jung. 1998. Address to the 54th Commencement Exercises of the Korea Military Academy. Seoul (16 March). <http://www.bluehouse.go.kr/engpdown/031717485480316-1.html> (21 May 1999).

Kim Kyung Min. 1995. *Ilboni irosonda: Segaenun Ilbonui kunsaryogul anunga* (Japan arises: Does the world know Japanese military strength?). Seoul: Koryo-won.

Korea Development Institute. 1996. "21 segi Hanguk kyungjeui uisang" (Prospects of the Korean economy in the 21st century). Seoul: Korea Development Institute.

Korea Institute for National Unification. 1999. *White Paper on Human Rights in North Korea 1999*. Seoul: Korea Institute for National Unification.

Kuninori Morio. 1999. "Nihon no senzai seichōryoku (2)" (Japanese growth potential [2]). *Nihon Keizai Shimbun* (26 January).

Kupchan, Charles A. 1994. *The Vulnerability of Empire*. Ithaca: Cornell University Press.

Lee Chong-Sik. 1985. *Japan and Korea: The Political Dimension*. Stanford, Calif.: Hoover Institution Press.

Lho Kyongsoo. 1997. "The Endgame in Korea: From 'Softlanding' to Reunification." Occasional Paper No. 122. Berlin: Berlin Ostasiatisches Seminar, Freie Universität.

Mansfield, Edward, and Jack Snyder. 1995. "Democratization and the Danger of War." *International Security* 20 (1): 5–38.

Michishita Narushige. 1997. "The Japan-ROK Security Relationship and Korean Unification." In *Hanbando t'ongil ul hyanghayo: Chongch'aek kwa kukche hwangyong* (Toward Korean unification: Policy and international environment). Seoul: Minjok T'ongil Yongu Won.

————. 1998. "Regional Aspects of Korean Reunification: Focusing on Strategic Issues." A paper prepared for the EU Policy Seminar, North Korean Scenarios and EU Responses (1998–2003). Brussels (13 October).

Ministry of Finance, Japan. 1998. "Ōkurashō bōeki tōkei" (Ministry of Finance trade statistics). <http://www.mof.go.jp/trade-st/199828c.htm> (21 May 1999).

Ministry of National Defense, South Korea. 1999. *Defense White Paper 1999*. Seoul: Ministry of National Defense.

Ministry of Unification, South Korea. 1999. *Unification White Paper 1998*. Seoul: Ministry of Unification.

Mochizuki, Mike, ed. 1997. *Toward A True Alliance: Restructuring U.S.-Japan Security Relations*. Washington, D.C.: Brookings Institution.

Mochizuki, Mike, and Michael O'Hanlon. 1998. "A Liberal Vision for the U.S.-Japanese Alliance." *Survival* 40 (2): 127–134.

Murata Kōji. 1998a. *Daitōryō no zasetsu: Kātā seiken no zaikan beigun tettai seisaku* (Downfall of a president: The Carter administration's policy to withdraw U.S. forces from South Korea). Tokyo: Yūhikaku.

————. 1998b. "The Origins and Evolution of the Korean-American Alliance: A Japanese Perspective." Discussion papers. California: Asia/Pacific Research Center, Institute for International Studies, Stanford University.

Nam Chang Hee. 1998. "Miil dongmaengui yokhwal hwaktaewa 21segi Hanmi donmaengui panghyangsung" (Expansion of roles of U.S.-Japan alliance and the direction of the ROK-U.S. alliance in the twenty-first century). *Dong-so Youn-gu* 19 (1): 5–24.

Noland, Marcus. 1997. "Why North Korea Will Muddle Through." *Foreign Affairs* 76 (4): 105–118.

North Atlantic Treaty Organization. 1997. "Founding Act on Mutual Relations, Cooperation and Security between NATO and the Russian Federation" (27 May). <http://www.nato.int/docu/basictxt/fndact-a.htm> (21 May 1999).

Oberdorfer, Don. 1997. *Two Koreas: A Contemporary History*. Reading, Mass.: Addison-Wesley.

O'Hanlon, Michael. 1998. "Keep US Forces in Korea after Reunification." *The Korean Journal of Defense Analysis* 10 (1): 5–19.

————. 1998–1999. "Can High Technology Bring U.S. Troops Home?" *Foreign Policy* 113 (Winter): 72–86.

Ok Tae-hwan and Kim Soo-am. 1997. *T'ongil Hangugui uisang* (Features of a unified Korea). Seoul: Minjok T'ongil Yongu Won.

"Opening Remarks." 1998. Joint Press Conference after ROK-US Summit. Seoul, South Korea (21 November). <http://www.kocis.go.kr/StateVisit/usa/conference/6-11.html> (21 May 1999).

Organization for Economic Cooperation and Development. 1997. *The World in 2020: Towards a New Global Age*. Paris: OECD Publications.

Owen, John M. 1996. "How Liberalism Produces Democratic Peace." In Michael E. Brown, Sean M. Lynn-Jones, and Steven E. Miller, eds. *Debating the Democratic Peace.* Cambridge, Mass.: The MIT Press.

Park Hahnkyu. 1998. "Between Caution and Cooperation: The ROK-Japan Security Relationship in the Post-Cold War Period." *The Korean Journal of Defense Analysis* 10 (1): 95–120.

Pollack, Jonathan D., and Young Koo Cha et al. 1995. *A New Alliance for the Next Century: The Future of U.S.-Korean Security Cooperation.* Santa Monica: Rand Corporation.

Richardson, Bradley. 1997. *Japanese Democracy: Power, Coordination, and Performance.* New Haven: Yale University Press.

Ross, Robert R. 1997. "Beijing as a Conservative Power." *Foreign Affairs* 76 (2): 33–44.

Rozman, Gilbert. 1998. "The Great Power Balance in Northeast Asia." *Orbis* 42 (1): 130–142.

Russett, Bruce. 1996a. "The Fact of Democratic Peace." In Michael E. Brown, Sean M. Lynn-Jones, and Steven E. Miller, eds. *Debating the Democratic Peace.* Cambridge, Mass.: The MIT Press.

———. 1996b. "The Democratic Peace—And Yet it Moves." In Michael E. Brown, Sean M. Lynn-Jones, and Steven E. Miller, eds. *Debating the Democratic Peace.* Cambridge, Mass.: The MIT Press.

Shin Yong Ha. 1991. "Hanguk T'ongilul panghaehanun Ilbon sin kunguk chuui" (Japanese neo-militarism that inhibits Korean unification). *Shin Dong-A* (February): 132–150.

Snyder, Jack. 1991. *Myths of Empire: Domestic Politics and International Ambition.* Ithaca, N.Y.: Cornell University Press.

Sutter, Robert G. 1998. "Korea: U.S.-South Korean Relations." CRS Issue Brief. IB97047 (updated July 20).

Tenet, George J. 1999. "Statement of the Director of Central Intelligence George J. Tenet as Prepared for Delivery Before the Senate Armed Services Committee Hearing on Current and Projected National Security Threats" (2 February). <http://www.odci.gov/cia/public_affairs/speeches/ps020299.html> (21 May 1999).

Tucker, Nancy Bernkopf. 1998. "The Origins and Evolution of the Korean-American Alliance: An American Perspective." Discussion papers. California: Asia/Pacific Research Center, Institute for International Studies, Stanford University.

UN Food and Agriculture Organization and UN World Food Program. 1998. "UN Food Agencies Say North Korea Still Needs Substantial Food Assistance despite Improved Harvest; Cite Need for Economic Reform and Increased Aid to Agriculture." Press release (13 November). <http://www.wfp.org/prelease/981113.html> (21 May 1999).

UN World Food Program. 1998. "Nutritional Survey Confirms Serious

Malnutrition in North Korea." Press release (18 November). <http://www.wfp.org/prelease/981118.html (21 May 1999).

Vickers, Michael G., and Steven M. Kosiak. 1997. *The Quadrennial Defense Review: An Assessment.* Washington, D.C.: Center for Strategic and Budgetary Assessments.

Wang Fei-Ling. 1997. *Tacit Acceptance and Watchful Eyes: Beijing's Views about the U.S.-ROK Alliance.* Carlisle Barracks, Penn.: Strategic Studies Institute, U.S. Army War College.

———. 1998. "China and Korean Unification: A Policy for Status Quo." *Korea and World Affairs* 22 (2): 177–198.

WEFA. 1995. *World Economic Outlook.* 20-Year Extension (March). Eddystone, Penn.: WEFA. <http://www.wefa.com>.

———. 1996. *World Economic Outlook* (February). Eddystone, Penn.: WEFA <http://www.wefa.com>.

The White House. 1998. *A National Security Strategy for a New Century* (October).

Whiting, Allen. 1989. *China Eyes Japan.* Berkeley, Calif.: University of California Press.

World Bank. 1997. *China 2020: Development Challenges in the New Century.* Washington, D.C.: World Bank.

Xin Zhang, ed. 1998. *Yu 2049 nian de zhongguo duihua* (Dialogue with China in 2049). 5 vols. Beijing: Zhongguo Jingji Chubanshe.

Youn Jung-Suk. 1991. "Ilbonun Hangukui kasangchoki toelkosinga" (Is Japan going to become a potential enemy of Korea?). *Wolgan Chosun* (May): 234–239.

Policy Coordination on Taiwan

Nakai Yoshifumi

THE face-off between Chinese and U.S. forces near Taiwan in March 1996, the so-called Taiwan Strait Crisis, shattered the peaceful complacence of Asian nations. The crisis demonstrated that post–cold war turbulence could also occur in Asia, bringing with it the potential for causing damage to both the economies and political stability of the region. The crisis also demonstrated how the policies of Japan and the United States toward Taiwan could differ, and how they would be likely to diverge further. It suggested that this policy divergence, if unresolved, could seriously erode the foundations of the U.S.-Japan Security Treaty and jeopardize the security of Taiwan as well as, eventually, that of Japan and the Asia Pacific region.

This chapter examines the causes of policy divergence and argues that there is a need for policy coordination between Japan and the United States with respect to Taiwan. In order to cooperate, both sides need to clarify their differences. They need to be clear about their goals and interests, and at the same time, they need to understand their expectations and limitations. The Taiwan Strait Crisis was a wake-up call, an indication of how future events in this area may test both the credibility of Japan-U.S. security cooperation as well as Japan's own commitment to the security of the Asia Pacific region.

No one can afford to discount the complexity of the Taiwan problem. Both Japan and the United States have stated repeatedly that they would adhere to a "one China" policy. Although the Chinese official press often accuses foreign nations of "ruffling China's feathers" or "playing with fire," no country does so intentionally. All the nations in Asia Pacific benefit tremendously from peaceful China-Taiwan relations, and no one should tolerate China's unilateral military aggression toward Taiwan. Policy co-ordination as well as diplomacy are needed to prevent such a scenario from recurring.

This chapter has four sections. The first section reviews the impact of the 1996 Taiwan Strait Crisis on Japan-U.S. relations, discussing how and why the reactions of Japan and the United States differed so greatly, although they faced a common threat. Changing perceptions of threat, the declining credibility of the alliance, and domestic politics all contributed to widening the gap between Japan and the United States in their response to the crisis.[1]

The second section traces the policy divergence between Japan and the United States after the 1996 crisis. Both countries' policies are examined with respect to three aspects of the Taiwan problem: democracy, independence, and the defense of Taiwan and the arms race in the region.

The third section analyzes the implications of the Taiwan issue for the Japan-U.S. alliance. The argument is made that policy divergence must be controlled in order to prevent the foundations of the alliance from deteriorating. Common ground is identified, where Japan and the United States can work together to deal constructively with the Taiwan issue.

The last section elaborates on ways that policy coordination can be translated into practice in the two countries' handling of the Taiwan problem.

JAPAN-U.S. RELATIONS

THE TAIWAN STRAIT CRISIS

In March 1996, Chinese and U.S. troops faced off near Taiwan. There was no exchange of fire, no casualties were sustained by the United States, nor was there direct contact between the two forces. But this was the first military confrontation between the two countries in many years. The last incident had occurred in 1958, when China bombed two small islands near Fujian province, causing the United States to dispatch seven aircraft carriers to the region.

In 1996, it was not bombing but missile tests and large-scale military exercises that provoked the U.S. reaction. The sequence of events was as follows:

On March 5, the first day of China's annual National People's Congress, the People's Liberation Army (PLA) announced that it would conduct surface-to-surface missile tests in international waters near Taiwan from March 8 to March 15. The exercise, with the Chinese code name Strait 961, was carried out in three stages: missile-firing tests; joint navy and air force exercises; and joint exercises of the navy, air force, and army. The schedule and the content of Strait 961 provided a clear indication, despite China's denial, of Beijing's intention to influence Taiwan's first direct presidential election, which was scheduled to take place on March 23.

On March 8, the first day of the exercise, China's nuclear rocket force, the Second Artillery Division, fired three M-9 ballistic missiles from its land base across the Taiwan Strait. A fourth was fired on March 13. The missiles landed in the sea lanes adjacent to Taiwan's two principal seaports, Keelung in the north and Kaohsiung in the south.[2] In mid-March, the exercise proceeded to the second stage, an air-and-sea superiority campaign in the southern part of the strait. The PLA mobilized submarines, destroyers, and Russian-built SU-27 fighters, and they tested various types of missiles—air-to-air, land-to-air, surface-to-air, and surface-to-surface. The third stage of Strait 961, joint exercises of the amphibious forces of the navy, army, and air force, began on March 18. They gathered on Haitan, an island close to Taiwan, and secured a beachhead in an assault exercise.

In response to these events, the United States dispatched two aircraft carriers with combat-ready battle groups to Taiwan on March 9. On the same day, the Chinese *People's Daily* and the *PLA Daily* published a joint editorial titled "Lee Teng-hui's Plot for 'Taiwan Independence' Is a Most Dangerous Act." On March 11, Foreign Minister Qian Qichen condemned the United States for dispatching aircraft carriers to Taiwan. On March 13, the PLA representative reported that the Guangzhou and Nanjing military districts had joined forces in a new Southeast battle district. On March 16, another militant joint editorial, "People's Army Calls for Unity of the Motherland," appeared in major Chinese official newspapers. On March 19, the U.S. House of Representatives passed by an overwhelming majority of votes a resolution for the defense of Taiwan. Two days later, the Chinese Ministry of Foreign Affairs spokesman strongly condemned the U.S. act, and on March 22, China postponed its defense minister's visit to the United States.

The turning point of the crisis came on March 23, when Lee Teng-hui was elected president of Taiwan by 54 percent of the popular vote. It was an overwhelming victory for Lee, proving that China's intimidation had not discredited him. After the election, China suddenly dropped the year-long national media campaign against Lee, which had begun after his visit to the United States in June 1995 (Shibuya 1996). On the day of the election, the New China News Agency simply reported that a "change in the method of electing the leader of the Taiwan district" had been completed. Despite this change, a Chinese official of the Taiwan Affairs Office commented, "Taiwan remains a part of China." On March 24, Secretary-General of the United Nations Boutros Boutros-Ghali visited China and, to China's relief, denied the possibility of Taiwan being admitted to the UN. On March 25, China declared that the final stage of the joint exercise had been completed.

The passing of the crisis became public when several top Chinese leaders went on foreign trips in late March. President Jiang Zemin, meeting with the U.S. Senate Foreign Affairs Committee on April 3, confirmed the Chinese position that its confrontation with the United States had ended, saying that the "rain has stopped and fine weather is here," alluding to China-U.S. relations. On April 6, former President George Bush visited Beijing to begin discussions with Jiang and Premier Li Peng. China-U.S. talks on intellectual property rights began in Beijing on the same day.

THE U.S. RESPONSE

An article by Barton Gellman suggests two reasons for the prompt, resolute U.S. response to the Chinese military exercises in the Taiwan Strait (Gellman 1998). First, the United States believed that China had escalated its intimidation of Taiwan to a dangerous degree. In February 1996, the U.S. Office of Naval Intelligence reported that China had begun to shift missiles, heavy equipment, and several brigades—about 10,000 troops—to Fujian province on the coast. According to Gellman, Chairman of the Joint Chiefs of Staff John Shalikashvili had ruled out the possibility of a full-scale Chinese invasion of Taiwan in a meeting at the Pentagon in early March, but the United States remained uncertain about what steps China might take.

Second, the United States believed that China might use nuclear weapons against the United States were it to feel unduly threatened, a possibility outlined in a classified report by former Assistant Secretary of Defense Charles Freeman Jr. In January 1996, Freeman visited Beijing to discuss the Taiwan issue with top Chinese military officials. Once back in Washington, he reported that what he had been told by one of the officials he had met, Lieutenant General Xiong Guangkai, carried an implied nuclear threat against the United States. According to Freeman, whose report was leaked to the *New York Times,* Lieutenant General Xiong had said something to the effect that: "In the 1950s, you threatened China with nuclear strikes three times. You could do that because we couldn't hit back. Now we can. So you're not going to threaten us again because, in the end, you care a lot more about Los Angeles than you do about Taipei.[3]

There could be at least four other factors contributing to the U.S. decision to mobilize its firepower in the Taiwan region.

- The failure of diplomacy in controlling damage caused by President Lee's June 1995 visit. Distrust of the top Chinese leaders and China's foreign ministry by the U.S. State Department at that time seemed too deep to overcome. In July 1995, the White House sent its trusted messenger Henry Kissinger to Beijing, where he met Premier Li and Foreign Minister Qian Qichen. But in the United States, the arrest of American-born Chinese human rights activist Harry Wu in western China attracted as much attention as the Taiwan issue. House Speaker Newt Gingrich criticized the Kissinger mission as an unnecessary concession and advocated the resumption of immediate and full diplomatic relations with Taiwan. The meeting between Qian and Secretary of State Warren Christopher in Brunei, on the occasion of the ASEAN Regional Forum (ARF) in August, failed to produce a tangible agreement.

- China's move to seek closer ties with Russia. The year 1995 happened to be the fiftieth anniversary of the end of World War II, and in the summer there was a massive national campaign commemorating the "Great Victory of the Proletariat over the Fascist Forces." Russian President Boris Yeltsin visited Beijing in April 1996. The result was the jointly signed Beijing Declaration, which stressed the strategic partnership between the two countries. The Yeltsin delegation brought with it eleven newly purchased SU-27 jet fighters, and another eleven arrived in China the next day.

- China's strident campaign against Taiwan. The *People's Daily* and other official Chinese press published various articles around this time criticizing the Taiwan government and President Lee. Some were provocative, predicting a clash over the Taiwan Strait and emphasizing China's resolute attitude against any attempt to divide the homeland. Some simply defamed Lee and his family, alluding to him as a spy and conspirator, and used a variety of ugly expressions. This not-so-subtle campaign offended the American public, who had welcomed Lee as a freedom fighter a year earlier.

- Frustration felt by congressmen and others in the U.S. government over issues pending with China. To Congress, the arrest of activist

Wu in July 1995 epitomized the lack of improvement in China's human rights record. First Lady Hillary Clinton participated in the UN World Conference on Women in Beijing in September, but the Chinese press ignored her speech. China and the U.S. Trade Representative (USTR) agreed in February to protect U.S. intellectual property rights (IPR), but many congressmen voiced doubts over China's promises to implement the agreement. China conducted two nuclear tests in 1995 and declared it would test again in 1996 before signing the Comprehensive Test Ban Treaty (CTBT).

■ Unity among the top U.S. policymakers. China's firing of missiles in March 1996 elicited a united response from U.S. agencies, particularly the Department of Defense and the State Department. On March 7 (U.S. time), after U.S. reconnaissance had monitored China's firing of M-9 missiles, Secretary of Defense William Perry, Secretary of State Christopher, and National Security Advisor Anthony Lake met for dinner at the State Department and announced to their guest, Chinese Vice-Foreign Minister Liu Huaqiu, that "grave consequences" would ensue should Chinese weapons strike Taiwan (Gellman 1998). President Clinton's decision to authorize the buildup of naval force in the region came promptly thereafter. Admiral Joseph Prueher ordered his U.S. Pacific Command to form a crisis action team to coordinate intelligence and air-and-sea operations around the clock. On March 11, Christopher announced that a U.S. battle group was heading to Taiwan. On March 13, a Department of Defense spokesman reported that a statement had been received from China, saying it had no intention of attacking Taiwan.

THE JAPANESE RESPONSE

Japan, on the surface, seemed to be discounting the seriousness of the crisis. On March 6, the chief of the Asian Affairs Bureau of the Ministry of Foreign Affairs summoned the councilor of the Chinese Embassy in Tokyo to express Japanese concern over China's plan for missile tests near Taiwan. The Maritime Safety Agency dispatched a patrol ship to Okinawa, near the exercise zone. On March 13, a foreign ministry official explained in the House of Councillors that since U.S. naval forces were conducting regular exercises near Taiwan, there was no need for prior consultation, as is required procedure in the event of a contingency. Foreign Minister Ikeda Yukihiko expressed Japan's concern again on March 31, when Chinese Foreign Minister Qian visited Japan after the crisis. Those were about the only overt actions the Japanese government took regarding the Taiwan Strait Crisis.

Behind the scenes, however, Prime Minister Hashimoto Ryūtarō held a series of urgent meetings and set up a contingency plan, comprising a strategy for the evacuation of Japanese residents in Taiwan, an emergency plan for Japanese immigrants there, coastal safety measures, and rear-area support for the U.S. armed forces (Funabashi 1997, 422–423). The Japanese Defense Agency closely monitored the Chinese exercises and missile tests. Hashimoto also requested real-time information on the Chinese exercises, including satellite launches, from the United States. U.S. Ambassador to Japan Walter Mondale relayed Hashimoto's request to the White House, and soon the Prime Minister's Office was ankle deep in dispatches.

So why the low-key response by Japan? For one thing, although the United States used bases in Japan for the deployment of forces to the Taiwan region—Yokosuka for the navy battle group and Okinawa for the marines—the Japanese public was little aware of this. The prefectural government of Okinawa, normally a vocal critic of the central government, said little about the crisis. The government realized that to recognize the crisis as a threat to Japan's security might have required it to clear a psychological hurdle, in that this would have raised questions about Japan's commitment to U.S. military operations.[4]

There are five main reasons that Japan downplayed the crisis:

- Inexperience and inertia. It was only in the 1990s that Japan had begun to clearly address the fundamental question of how to defend peace against real threats of war. Japanese leaders found the issue extremely difficult to face; since they had never pondered this possibility, they almost panicked in dealing with the crisis (Kuriyama 1997, 16–17).
- Prime Minister Hashimoto was preoccupied with other issues. The year 1996 began with many unresolved matters carried over from the previous year. Taiwanese President Lee's visit to the United States got little attention in Japan because at that time Japan was confronting the United States over trade issues, and castigating France and China over nuclear testing. In September 1995, three U.S. Marines raped a Japanese schoolgirl in Okinawa. The event dominated Japanese politics for the rest of the year, in part because it strengthened the demand of the Okinawa prefectural government for a reduction in the U.S. forces in Okinawa, which serve as the linchpin of the U.S.-Japan security alliance.

Until he took over as prime minister from Murayama Tomiichi in January, Hashimoto, then minister of international trade, had been negotiating a comprehensive trade agreement with the USTR. The two countries' differences had brought them to the brink of a trade war. In early March right before the crisis, Hashimoto, who was in Bangkok for a meeting of Asian and European leaders, held separate talks with Chinese Prime Minister Li and Korean President Kim Young Sam.

■ Japan's perception of the threat was different from that of the United States. Japan did not regard the possibility of nuclear attack by China as seriously as did some American leaders, for two reasons. One reason is that Japan felt a more urgent and direct threat from North Korea, which had been a source of great tension in 1994, when it defied the international nuclear regime. From that period on, North Korea dominated Japan's security policy agenda and left little room for consideration of regional threats from China or Taiwan.

The other reason is that China's nuclear tests irritated Japan much more than its conduct near the Taiwan Strait. The two underground tests China conducted in 1995 were badly timed. The first test took place on May 15, about ten days after Prime Minister Murayama's official visit to China. During the visit, in his meeting with President Jiang, Murayama had given an official apology for the atrocities Japan had visited upon China in the past. Murayama had also promised that he would work to convince the Diet to issue a resolution admitting to Japan's "invasion" of China. When China conducted a second test on August 17, two days after the anniversary of Japan's surrender in World War II, Japan reacted promptly by suspending its yen grant program to China.[5]

■ Japan's security policy priorities lay in Okinawa, not in Taiwan. The rape of a schoolgirl in Okinawa on September 4, 1995, drastically changed Japanese perceptions about the costs to the nation of the U.S.-Japan Security Treaty. With its wartime history and high concentration of U.S. bases, Okinawa embodies many of the controversial aspects of the U.S.-Japan Security Treaty.

The Taiwan crisis had both negative and positive implications for Okinawa and the bilateral alliance. First, the crisis helped Japanese and U.S. lawmakers negotiate new agreements regarding Okinawa and, more broadly, the U.S.-Japan Security Treaty. The crisis occurred at the right time—before President Clinton's planned April visit to

Japan, where he was to sign the Common Agenda on the U.S.-Japan Security Treaty. Japan, by that time, was beginning to realize its potential security risks. The face-off in the Taiwan Strait had shown quite clearly that post–cold war disturbances could happen in Asia in areas other than the Korean peninsula. The crisis helped both Japan and the United States enlarge the focus of their negotiations from narrow, domestic issues concerning U.S. bases in Okinawa to broader cooperation for security in Asia (Akiyama et al. 1996).

Second, the crisis spotlighted the strategic importance of U.S. bases in Okinawa, and, more broadly, U.S. forward deployment in East Asia. However, the attention this point received in Japan was quite different from what it got in the United States. Okinawa's importance was widely assumed in the United States.[6] Among the Japanese, however, the strategic importance of Okinawa was barely recognized, if at all. The Okinawa prefectural government showed almost no interest in the Taiwan Strait Crisis, discounting the role that Okinawa actually played in it.[7]

Political calculations were probably at work, however, in both Okinawa and Tokyo. The Okinawa government might have worried that the crisis would have an adverse effect on the return of the U.S. bases. After all, the Futenma Air Station, which the United States had agreed to return to Okinawa, belonged to the marines, and the marines in Okinawa were preparing for possible military operations during the crisis. But this kind of thinking could also have led the Japanese government to discount or diminish the domestic impact of conflict in Asia. The result could have been a dangerous spiral in which the United States, annoyed by Japan's inaction, exaggerated or dramatized the impact of Asian conflict in order to motivate Japan to support U.S. military activity.

▪ Ideological divisions. In Japan, the common ideological division between socialism and capitalism is complicated by the broad spectrum of popular attitudes toward socialism, from communists, socialists, and social-democrats to liberal-democrats and rightists. In addition, there is a range of pro-China and pro-Taiwan stances, as well as pro-U.S. and anti-U.S. views. The Taiwan Strait Crisis, which was not serious enough to overcome the varying ideological divisions, served to highlight the antipathies. Some Japanese today deny the value of the U.S.-Japan Security Treaty (Tsuru 1996), others advocate its reform, still others accept it with qualifications, and some support it in full. No opinion seems to have a clear majority backing, however, and it is likely that Japan will remain this way for a while.

There is a tendency in Japan to discount the implications of the Taiwan Strait Crisis for Asia's overall security. An article by former Prime Minister Hosokawa Morihiro (1998), for example, argues that Japan no longer needs U.S. forces stationed in Okinawa, or anywhere in Japan. He narrowly defines the purpose of the security treaty as being solely for Japan's defense, thereby paying little heed to the U.S. stance that "U.S. alliances in the region have long served as the cornerstone of regional security" (Department of Defense 1998, 19). A recent book compiled by prosocialist scholars opposes any revision of the 1960 security treaty (Yamauchi 1999, 1–2). As suggested by the book's subtitle, "Now Ask Again for the Choice of Peace," the authors advocate Japan's neutrality without relying on armed forces. They charge that the 1997 Guidelines for U.S.-Japan Defense Cooperation are unconstitutional, and argue that Japan's defense commitment should be restricted to within its national boundaries.

THREE ASPECTS OF THE TAIWAN PROBLEM AND CURRENT JAPANESE AND U.S. POLICIES

This section addresses three aspects of the Taiwan problem: democracy, independence, and the defense of Taiwan and its influence on the arms race in the region. The impact the Taiwan Strait Crisis had on Japan was different from that on the United States, and in its aftermath, Japan and the United States have diverged further in their handling of key aspects of the issue.

DEMOCRACY

The United States regarded Lee's victory in Taiwan's first popular presidential election as a triumph of democracy, especially since the election was conducted in a basically democratic manner. The Taiwan campaign—the decision to dispatch a U.S. battle group to Taiwan—was in line with the traditional idealpolitik thinking of American foreign policy, which tends to view events according to the simple dichotomy of freedom versus tyranny (Talbott 1996, 49).

Japan's reaction to Taiwan's democratization, on the other hand, was more cautious. Its colonial occupation of Taiwan, its surrender of sovereignty over Taiwan to China at the end of World War II, and the 1972 Joint Declaration, which avowed that there is only "one China," made the picture more complex for Japan, preventing the government from viewing the situation simply in terms of good versus bad.[8] Instead of focusing on democracy in Taiwan, Japan has chosen to encourage the country's economic integration into the Asia Pacific region. That strategy seemed to be working well, and by the time China and Taiwan agreed to meet for talks in Singapore in April 1993, cross-strait trade and direct investment from Taiwan had reached an unprecedented high level.[9]

Democratization of Taiwan, however, destroyed the congenial spirit of cross-strait communication. In 1992, not long before the April 1993 cross-strait meeting, Taiwan held an election for the national legislature in which the Democratic Progressive Party (DPP), which was for the first time allowed to field candidates, won 32 percent of the seats. The DPP had vocally advocated that the government issue an immediate declaration of independence. With this feeling gaining public support in Taiwan, the Taiwan delegation to the Singapore meeting decided to refuse to discuss reunification based on the Chinese framework of "one country, two systems." Taiwan's sovereignty, the delegation claimed, belonged to the Republic of China. Taiwan began to speak out boldly to the international community: We have democracy, a strong economy, and a population of 21 million; we deserve some respect.

The November 1997 local-level elections marked another landmark in Taiwan's democratization. The DPP, the largest opposition party, won handily, surpassing the popular vote of the ruling Nationalist Party. The previous local election in 1993 had been close, but the Nationalists had retained a majority with 48 percent of the vote versus 41 percent for the DPP. In 1997, the order was reversed, with the Nationalists claiming a 42 percent share and the DPP 43 percent. One reason for the DPP victory might have been the decision to modify its platform at the party conference in spring 1997. The new platform no longer advocated immediate independence, but proclaimed the desire to seek independence as an "historic" goal. This slight but important modification brought the DPP's position on independence closer to that of the Nationalists.

The change in Taiwan's domestic politics was a shock to China, the United States, and Japan. Democracy brought independence with it. To China, the victory of the DPP meant that its threats had backfired. Since the 1996 crisis, the independence movement in Taiwan, though more moderate, had become stronger. The rise of the DPP also meant that the Communist Party's traditional channel of communication with the Nationalists would not be sufficient.

To the United States, the new political climate in Taiwan was a mixed blessing. Democracy had created an open, more liberal society. At the same time, however, it encouraged division and the urge for independence, two destabilizing factors. The situation was especially complicated for Japan because the DPP was mainly composed of native Taiwanese who tended to favor closer ties with Japan.

INDEPENDENCE

China's official position, that it would resort to military force if Taiwan declared independence, remains unchanged. President Jiang's political report at the 15th Party Congress in September 1997—and, more recently, in a joint statement by Jiang and Foreign Minister Qian regarding Taiwan in January 1998—reiterated this official position. Nonofficial sources, often the origin of differing views, also closely toe the official line. Liu Ji, vice president of the Chinese Academy of Social Science, wrote in an article, "The day Taiwan declares independence will be the day that war is declared" (Liu 1998,10).

Chinese Premier Zhu Rongji endorsed Liu's assessment at the official press conference of the National People's Congress in March 2000. The Congress ended just three days before Taiwan's presidential election. Premier Zhu pointed his finger in the air and shouted, "The people of Taiwan are standing at a very critical historical juncture, so let me give advice to all the people of Taiwan: Do not act just on impulse, otherwise you will regret it very much and it will be too late to repent" (*Daily Yomiuri* 17 March 2000). Apparently, the majority of Taiwan voters did not take his advice. Whether they will repent their choice of President Chen Shuibian remains to be seen.

After the election, the United States proceeded to modify its stance on Taiwan's independence. It started not only engaging China but also discouraging Taiwan from pursuing independence. This sudden and major policy shift made it appear as if the United States had abandoned idealpolitik in favor of realpolitik. In contrast, Japan behaved as if nothing had happened. It continued to engage both Taiwan and China economically, and seemed to be hoping that the independence issue would simply go away. As it had with the Taiwan Strait Crisis, the United States resorted to action and a policy change, Japan to inaction and a minor amendment of its policy.

The dual targets of engaging China and discouraging Taiwan's independence became the dominant theme of U.S. foreign policy after the crisis. First, the United States restored high-level contact and missions with China. Secret meetings during the crisis between National Security Adviser Lake and his Chinese counterpart Liu Huaqiu not only cleared the air but helped conceive a U.S.-Chinese policy agenda. The two nations followed up with a series of diplomatic and military contacts in 1996 and 1997.[10]

Second, President Clinton himself expressed renewed interest in engaging China. In contrast to his first administration, Clinton took a conciliatory approach at the start of his second term. The United States and China reached agreement in February 1997 on U.S. textile exports to China. In March 1997, Vice President Al Gore, who had referred to the Chinese leaders as butchers in Beijing during the 1992 presidential campaign, visited Beijing and confirmed that President Jiang would visit the United States in November.

On October 31, 1997, China and the United States issued a joint statement, in which their respective presidents agreed to build a "constructive strategic partnership." The joint statement contained nine "baskets of cooperation." To China, however, the most important accomplishment of Jiang's U.S. visit was gaining confirmation of the U.S. government's official position regarding Taiwan.[11] According to the statement, "The United States reiterates that it adheres to its 'one China' policy and the principles set forth in the three Sino-U.S. joint communiqués."[12]

Third, in the wake of the DPP's surprising November 1997 victory, the United States took great pains to persuade Taiwan not to seek independence, at least for the time being, and to resume cross-strait talks. In 1998, former officials of the first Clinton administration, former Assistant Secretary of Defense Joseph Nye, former Defense Secretary Perry, and former National Security Adviser Lake, made consecutive visits to Taiwan and delivered a clear message: "Forget independence, or we won't support you." They also advocated the resumption of cross-strait talks, which had been suspended since Lee's visit to the United States in 1995.

Nye's visit to Taiwan in January 1998 provided the most straightforward expression of the U.S. policy shift. He proposed that Taiwan maintain "strategic clarity and tactical ambiguity" for its defense. He also recommended that the United States, China, and Taiwan agree to a series of steps and assurances. First, the United States would not recognize Taiwan if it declared independence, and at the same time, the United States would try to persuade China to abandon the military option against Taiwan. Second, China would give Taiwan greater room for international activity and allow it broader self-rule than Hong Kong. Third, Taiwan would not seek independence but would strengthen cross-strait talks and economic exchanges (Ihara 1998, 142–143).

Japan refrained from any show of support for Taiwan's independence, so China felt no need to raise the issue with Japan after the crisis. China, however, harbored deep suspicions as to Japan's hidden support for President Lee, whose close association with Japan is undeniable: He grew up speaking Japanese and spent most of his college years in Japan. Lee's interview with Japanese novelist Shiba Ryōtarō, published in a popular Japanese magazine in May 1994, angered China greatly. In the interview, Lee mentioned that his role as the leader of Taiwan was just like that of Moses in the Exodus.[13] China took this remark to be a show of Lee's not-so-hidden intention to seek independence. In October 1994, China prevented Lee from attending the opening ceremony of the Hiroshima Asian Games by threatening a boycott. After his visit to the United States, Lee's next goal was joining the November 1995 Asia-Pacific Economic Cooperation (APEC) meeting in Osaka. Japan had to persuade him not to come.[14]

The flare-up of the territorial dispute in summer 1996 over the Senkaku Islands, where China's claim conflicts with Japanese possession, added confusion to the already complicated China-Taiwan-Japan trilateral relations. When a group of Japanese right-wingers built a makeshift lighthouse on an uninhabited Senkaku island in July 1996, pro-China groups in both Hong Kong and Taiwan reacted violently. They chartered boats and tried to land on the islands. One Hong Kong resident died in an accident during the protest, but Lee refused to play up this incident because he knew that pro-China, anti-independence groups in Taiwan were behind the demonstration (Watari 1998). China condemned Japan as being hegemonic, but refrained from using the incident to incite a major national campaign against Japan, probably because it believed that to do so would draw Japan and Taiwan closer together.

As regards independence, the most significant change after the dispute was Taiwan's modification of its stance. Gone was the demand for immediate independence. Public support for the DPP declined sharply in the December 1998 election for the national legislature. DPP legislative candidates could only gain an average of about 30 percent support, and the party lost the mayoralty of the capital, Taipei. Jianguodang, a splinter group that advocated the immediate declaration of independence, won only a few seats in the legislative assembly. The election results indicated that an overwhelming majority of voters, across party lines, supported the status quo.

In 1999, the center of gravity appeared to be slightly to the left of center in the Nationalist Party, headed by Lee, who sought neither immediate independence nor unification.[15]

China's threat could have played a part in this change. But a more important change took place in the perception of independence among the general public in Taiwan. To a majority of Taiwan citizens, independence was no longer a realistic option. Nor was unification. In a summer 1998 public poll, conducted by a pro-unification group, roughly 75 percent of the respondents rejected unification, stating that the gap in lifestyles across the strait was too wide to bridge. Roughly 94 percent agreed with President Lee's statement that twenty-one million Taiwan residents, not the Chinese Communist Party, should decide the fate of Taiwan (*Eurasian Studies Newsletter*, October 1998).

Lin Bizhao, a member of President Lee's brain trust, elaborated on Taiwan's interpretation of independence. Intentionally avoiding the term independence, he proposed synchronizing Taiwan's practical diplomacy, which sought wider international recognition, with its policy toward China. Lin accepted the concept of "one China" as a common ground for cross-strait dialogue, admitting that doing so was probably a precondition for beginning such talks. However, he said, the definition of "one China" should be left to each government, to guarantee that the most practical method by which this might be achieved would be chosen. One could say the guiding principle of Lin's proposal was "one China, different interpretations" (Lin 1999,11).

Lin has advocated a moderate policy toward China, which should encourage cross-strait trade and communication. Taiwan must initiate "gradual, not radical" reform of its policies toward China, he has said, in order to avoid discordance between old policies and new. In the past, Lin has acknowledged, there was a serious split in Taiwan about how to handle its China policy, with some daring to provoke China. But a consensus started forming in 1997, he has said, based on support across the strait for divided rule and gradual, not rapid, unification (Lin 1999).

THE DEFENSE OF TAIWAN AND THE ARMS RACE IN THE REGION

The Taiwan Strait Crisis proved the importance of the U.S. military presence in Asia. Quick deployment of the U.S. armed forces in the area offset the Chinese military threat against Taiwan. The crisis, however, also revealed the vulnerability of the present security arrangement in three ways.

First, since Taiwan's security largely hinges on U.S. support, as outlined in the Taiwan Relations Act, one wonders about the depth of the U.S. commitment to the defense of Taiwan. It was the unilateral response of the United States that provided the practical protection against the Chinese threat this time. Would the United States do the same thing if Taiwan declared independence?

Second, the crisis revealed the weaknesses in Taiwan's defense system, particularly the lack of surface-to-surface missiles to deter a Chinese missile attack. Taiwan's geographical and economic vulnerability against sustained and massive aggression from China is well documented (Hiramatsu 1999, 84–111). Taiwan has been upgrading its air and surface weapons systems but, if the 1996 crisis is any indication, China would be likely to begin an assault with a massive missile attack on major military targets in Taiwan. Taipei lacks the capability to deter such an attack.

Third, the international commitment to the defense of Taiwan is uncertain, and Asia Pacific has no regional system of collective defense like NATO. Action by the United Nations would be impossible as long as China holds a seat on the Standing Committee of the Security Council. The ARF provides a regional forum for confidence-building measures (CBM), but it lacks a mechanism for countering aggression in the event of a conflict. So, for Taiwan, the most important bilateral alliance for providing prompt and effective support in the event of a contingency is the U.S.-Japan Security Treaty.

After the crisis, it became clear that China could pose an "asymmetrical threat"[16] against Taiwan. The U.S. action during the crisis also made it clear that if Chinese missiles hit Taiwan, there would be U.S. retaliation. To avoid such a confrontation, the United States began to press Taiwan, as discussed above, not to declare independence. It is clear that if the new Taiwan regime did declare independence, the United States would not guarantee that it would continue to act in Taiwan's defense. Therefore, to help guarantee that a practical defense scheme was in place, the United States began to consider installing a theater missile defense (TMD) system in Taiwan.

Japan, meanwhile, has not stood completely idle. In April 1996, Prime Minister Hashimoto and President Clinton signed the U.S.-Japan Joint Declaration on Security, a rare demonstration of Japanese initiative in promoting Japan-U.S. security cooperation. It took the 1996 Taiwan Strait Crisis, together with North Korea's defiance and a base-related incident in Okinawa, to produce this "reconfirmation" of the U.S.-Japan Security Treaty. Japan began to "behave like a real ally" (Akiyama et al. 1996, 25) in declaring its commitment to the security of Asia Pacific.

For Taiwan, the most significant aspect of the agreement was Japan's commitment to cooperate with the United States in contingencies outside Japan. Article 5 Section (b) of the joint declaration states: "The two leaders agreed on the necessity to promote bilateral policy coordination, including studies on bilateral cooperation in dealing with situations that may emerge in the areas surrounding Japan and which will have an important influence on the peace and security of Japan" (*Gaikō Fōramu*, Special edition, 1996).

To support this commitment in a more concrete manner, Japan and the United States agreed to initiate a review of the 1978 Guidelines for U.S.-Japan Defense Cooperation, and they reached agreement on new guidelines in September 1997. These guidelines are twice as long as the 1978 guidelines and devote about ten times more text to describing what security cooperation would entail "in the event of an emergency in areas surrounding Japan (*shūhen jitai*)." The "emergency in areas surrounding Japan" is not defined by geography but by situation, and clearly the guidelines were revised to reinforce Japan-U.S. security cooperation in the Asia Pacific region, possibly including the Taiwan Strait.

The new guidelines guarantee U.S. forces the use not only of U.S. bases in Japan but also of public airports and ports. Japan would provide rear-area support to U.S. forces, and such support could take place in international waters and air zones surrounding Japan. Japan and the United States would cooperate closely in the collection and exchange of defense-related information, centered on the "situation in the Asia-Pacific region."

The U.S.-Japan Acquisition and Cross-Servicing Agreement (ACSA) that the two countries originally signed in April 1996 covered two joint activities: military exercises and UN peacekeeping operations. In April 1998, then-Foreign Minister Obuchi Keizō and U.S. Secretary of State Madeleine Albright signed a proposal to include a third category pertaining to the event of an emergency in areas surrounding Japan. Later, as prime minister, Obuchi indicated a desire to extend the ACSA to include a fourth situation, a direct military attack on Japan (*Daily Yomiuri* 1 April 1999).

Although the new guidelines and ACSA advanced prospects for Japan-U.S. security cooperation, Japan and the United States are showing signs of divergence in three areas related to the defense of Taiwan, namely, China's allegations that conspirators are behind moves for Taiwanese independence; the role of Japan outside of its territory; and installation of a TMD system in Taiwan. All three are closely related to China's opposition to Japan-U.S. security cooperation. And, since China fears that such cooperation may serve to bolster Taiwan, China is likely to try to widen the gap between the Japanese and U.S. positions at every possible opportunity.

China has put forth a conspiracy theory as its argument for retaining a military option against Taiwan. President Jiang's policy report to the 15th Party Congress in September 1997 confirmed China's intention not to abandon a military option against Taiwan, stating that "some foreign powers want to intervene in China's internal affairs and plot the independence of Taiwan." This theory still represents the official Chinese position. In early 1998, both Vice Premier Qian and Defense Secretary Chi repeated the same point, making it appear that the foreign ministry and the army were in full accord.

Despite hard-line Chinese official statements, China shows some signs of relaxing its claim that the United States is conspiring with Taiwan. Wang Daohan, the Chinese representative at the cross-strait talks, visited the United States before Jiang's formal visit and never referred to a foreign conspiracy. In Shanghai in February 1998, with representatives from the United States and China present, he chaired a semi-official meeting to prepare for Jiang's visit to the United States. In an article published in January 1998, Liu Ji, a close associate of Jiang, treated conspiracy with Taiwan not as a major theme but as a policy option of the United States. The likelihood that the United States would conspire with Taiwan to achieve independence is not strong, according to Liu, because such a move would lead inevitably to war between China and the United States, which neither side could easily win (Liu 1998, 9–10).

Increasingly, China is targeting Japan with this conspiracy theory, its suspicions bolstered by President Lee's close association with Japan. China has come to believe that Japan has territorial ambitions concerning Taiwan and would intervene in Taiwan's affairs in order to expand its influence in Asia Pacific. When the dispute over the Senkaku Islands suddenly surfaced in July 1996, after Japanese right-wingers built a makeshift lighthouse and claimed Japanese sovereignty over the islands, the Chinese government exercised some restraint and the issue was contained. The incident did show, however, that Japan and the United States have quite different issues to settle with China over Taiwan. President Jiang, just before he participated in the ceremony returning Hong Kong to China, remarked that there were "worrisome powers in Japan opposing friendship" (*Chūgoku sōran* 1998, 754).

China also suspects Japan's military ambitions. China highlighted Japan's involvement when it televised President Clinton's speech from the deck of the aircraft carrier *Independence* right after it returned to Yokosuka, a U.S. naval base near Tokyo, following service in the Taiwan Strait Crisis.[17] When the interim report about the new guidelines was released in the summer of 1997, China's foreign ministry and defense department both suggested that Japan take a "cautious" attitude toward military cooperation with the United States.

The Chinese defense white paper of July 1998 is openly critical of the U.S.-Japan Security Treaty. "Some country," it claims, is still clinging to a cold war mentality, rarely hesitating to use force against sovereign nations. The white paper implies that reinforcement of the Japan-U.S. military alliance must be opposed because it serves as a mechanism for military threats and intervention and because it runs against the general trend of the times. The inclusion of the Taiwan Strait, whether directly or indirectly, in the areas of security cooperation covered by the military alliance would, the white paper contends, constitute a violation of China's sovereignty and intervention in Chinese internal affairs (Hiramatsu 1998, 19).

China's criticism of expanding Japan-U.S. defense cooperation beyond Japanese territory, the second area in which Japanese and U.S. policies diverge, has been directed mainly toward Japan. The 1978 guidelines simply defined the area for defense as "the Far East" and said the content of the cooperation was to be "studied." However, it is commonly accepted by Japan and the United States that the Far East includes Taiwan as well as the Korean peninsula. When the revision of the guidelines entered its final stages in early 1997, China vehemently objected to the inclusion of Taiwan in the "areas surrounding Japan." This point became the focus of contention between Japan and China in the fall of 1997.

In its arguments against Japan's actions, China intentionally confused the issue by interchangeably addressing concerns over the Taiwan Strait, which is international waters, and Taiwan, which is part of China. The United States, with its actions toward Taiwan governed by the Taiwan Relations Act, did not distinguish between the two, but Japan sent confusing messages about this to China. In July 1997, Katō Kōichi, secretary-general of the Liberal Democratic Party (LDP), visited China and explained that the new guidelines did not consider China to be a potential enemy. A month later, Kajiyama Seiroku, chief cabinet secretary of the Hashimoto cabinet, declared to the contrary that the area of Japan-U.S. defense cooperation naturally included the Taiwan Strait, which was a view shared by many members of the ruling party.

China responded vehemently to Japan's inclusion of the Taiwan Strait in the scheme. The Chinese Ministry of Foreign Affairs spoke of "deep regret" and demanded an official explanation from the Japanese government. The *People's Daily* published a series of special editorials condemning Kaji-yama's "dangerous speech" and the "serious situation damaging Chinese-Japanese relations" (*Chūgoku sōran* 1998, 759). It was left to Prime Minister Hashimoto to settle the dispute when he visited China in September. He explained to Prime Minister Li that the new guidelines were not aimed at a specific country or area. Li withheld his acceptance of the explanation, stressing that China would not tolerate the inclusion of Taiwan in the new guidelines.

The third area of Japan-U.S. policy divergence on Taiwan emerged when Taiwan and the United States began considering the installation of a TMD system in Taiwan. To Japan, the system is designed strictly to counter the threat from North Korea. One month after North Korea had fired a Taepodong missile through Japanese air space into the Pacific on August 31, 1998, Japan and the United States agreed to proceed on joint research for TMD. In October, the Japanese government appropriated ¥1 billion for the project, amid strong doubts about the system's reliability and costs.

Japan and the United States may yet diverge further on the issue of a TMD system in Taiwan, as well as the prospect of a cross-strait arms race, for despite China's harassment, Taiwan has shown its willingness to catch up militarily.[18]

Countries in Asia Pacific have been amassing modern arms for years, and the region is now the world's second-largest arms export market. A European expert on NATO has observed that many East Asian procurement plans have remained resilient despite the recent regional financial crisis. Like Brunei and Singapore, Taiwan has not been significantly affected by the crisis (Umbach 1998).

The spiraling military buildup on both sides of the strait constitutes a serious challenge to the peace and stability of the region. Taiwan has a diverse plan to modernize its forces and deep pockets to support it. In a few years, Taiwan may be a formidable military force. Its current modernization drive includes the development of modern conventional submarines; delivery of 150 F-16s, sixty Mirage 2000-5s, and 130 locally produced Ching-Kuo fighters; development of modern missiles; and procurement of naval vessels and patrol craft.

China can be expected to counter Taiwan's military modernization with its own modernization and deployment measures. The firing of surface-to-surface, nuclear-capable missiles during the crisis demonstrated China's growing prowess. A U.S. military source indicated that China had deployed between 150 and 200 M-9 and M-11 missiles in the southern region since the crisis (*Daily Yomiuri* 12 February 1999). Premier Zhu repeatedly denied the report during his trip to the United States in April 1999. A Japanese researcher observed that Taiwan's rapid modernization drive over the previous few years had forced China to display its military capability in the Taiwan Strait Crisis (Hiramatsu 1997). And according to one Chinese account, China's military exercises in 1995 were triggered by a series of military exercises conducted by Taiwan's armed forces from 1994 to 1996, during which Taiwan showed off its newly acquired equipment (Si 1998, 747).[19]

Given this arms race display, Japan is not likely to show much interest in installing a TMD system in Taiwan. Japan's concerns are focused on the North Korean threat, and Japan is reluctant to add to its many issues of contention with China. Japan's reluctance is likely to conflict with the more proactive stance of Taiwan and the United States, but it may be up to the other two parties to find a balance. The U.S. defense industry has a large stake in the military modernization of Taiwan, as seen in the sale of F-16s. However, if the U.S. government can exercise self-restraint as regards the lucrative arms business, it can prevent the arms race from becoming a major source of conflict.

In the meantime, Taiwan seems to be taking up a more realistic defense posture. Lin, for example, has proposed that Taiwan lay out its national policies in terms of "comprehensive security" (1999, 9). Lin acknowledges that the post–cold war international environment has generally favored Taiwan, but asserts that Taiwan has a right to expect an indirect guarantee of its security from the international community, which supports human rights and democratization. In terms of national defense, however, Lin argues for self-reliance because Taiwan is not part of any military alliance (the Taiwan Relations Act of the United States is not an international treaty).

Lin's proposal for self-reliance in defense does not imply an arms race across the strait. Quite to the contrary: According to Lin, the defense posture of Taiwan should be that of "minimum defense which is designed for preventing China from using force in the strait area" (1999, 9). Taiwan's defense forces should consist of counterattack forces, which would not provoke an enemy's attack but would repel it. He notes that China's diplomatic offensive, which had the effect of isolating Taiwan, has increased China's links with the global community. China's growing contact with the international community could, in turn, help constrain China from taking unilateral action against Taiwan.

THE TAIWAN PROBLEM AND THE JAPAN-U.S. ALLIANCE

The Taiwan Strait Crisis raised a series of practical questions for U.S. and Japanese policymakers to consider: To what extent could U.S. military actions be regarded as being in defense of Japan? What kind of support does the United States expect from Japan? What kind of support does Japan consider constitutional and what would it be willing to provide? How can the crisis be interpreted according to the language of the U.S.-Japan Security Treaty?

In connection with their future policies regarding Taiwan, there are three possible scenarios.

DIVERGENCE SCENARIO

Japan and the United States continue to disagree about the Chinese threat and the prospects for Taiwan's independence. Japan, meanwhile, discounts the Chinese threat and hopes Taiwan and China reach an accord through dialogue. Basically, Japan tries to shield itself from trouble. The United States feels the Chinese threat is real and urges Taiwan to be ready for the worst. Although the United States considers the defense of Taiwan to be a burden, it concludes that there is no alternative but to intervene should China attack Taiwan.

In this scenario, Japan and the United States would take a completely different stance as to the defense of Taiwan. Japan would likely leave the defense of Taiwan solely to the United States, and would be only minimally involved, at best. The United States would probably rely on limited air strikes against China. Full support would be difficult to achieve because of domestic opposition to risking U.S. lives. The United States would be inclined to advocate installing a TMD system in Taiwan.

This scenario has shortcomings in terms of concept and in practice. The defense of Taiwan would be difficult in practice without support from Japan. Until the unlikely event that TMD can provide a reliable shield against Chinese missiles, U.S. forces would have to rely on conventional forces that use U.S. bases in Japan, including all the bases in Okinawa. Were the confrontation prolonged, this support would become even more important. Nevertheless, the very idea of the United States fighting alone in a war with China is nearly unthinkable. Would it be worth the U.S. casualties or, in the worst case, a nuclear confrontation? U.S. lawmakers and citizens would find it difficult to understand why the United States would, alone, be defending Taiwan. Their puzzlement would be justified, because Japan and all the countries of Asia Pacific share a vital interest in maintaining peace in the region.

This divergence scenario, if unchecked, would lead to the collapse of the U.S.-Japan Security Treaty. The United States would not hesitate to blame Japan, as Tokyo's inaction would have hurt the credibility of the alliance (Walt 1997, 160). Trust in Japan as an ally would be lost, as a result of which the bilateral security treaty would be unlikely to function. Japan would be left in a more dangerous world, as a non-aligned but isolated country.

CONVERGENCE SCENARIO

In this scenario, Japan and the United States achieve complete convergence in their policies and actions. When they believe a threat from China is imminent, they act jointly. Japan provides whatever assistance possible within the limits of its constitution. If the constitution places too great a constraint on joint military action, the government takes pains to revise it or change the most recent interpretation. The Self-Defense Forces (SDF) engages in rear-support activities during such a conflict, which might develop into a full-scale confrontation. Missiles will fly, and there will be military and civilian casualties. However, Japan's participation in semi-military operations in Asia Pacific means that the U.S.-Japan Security Treaty becomes a balanced military alliance.

This scenario might be ideal for the defense of Taiwan. There would be no logistical problems defending Taiwan, and the bases in Okinawa and elsewhere in Japan would be fully utilized. With this comprehensive defense shield, Taiwan would be likely to declare independence. That would be a step forward for democracy in Asia Pacific, as the United States, Japan, and Taiwan share common democratic values.

Unfortunately, the scenario also has substantial deficiencies that render it an unrealistic option. First, Japan would be even further aligned with the American camp, a stance which would be most unpopular, especially with the cold war over.[20] Second, there would be strong domestic opposition to revising the constitution, although recent polls show increasing public support for amendment.[21] It is quite unlikely that Japan would go so far as to revise its constitution merely to allow it to help defend Taiwan or make the United States happy.

Of far more substance, however, is the matter of China's reaction to this convergence scenario. China would abandon any overtures for engagement with the United States and Japan, and would probably renew its ties with Russia and non-aligned nations such as India and Pakistan. China might choose to close its doors again, as it did during the Cultural Revolution, to try to keep its national integrity intact. China's leadership would adopt an aggressively militant policy, which would make the Asia Pacific region far more dangerous.

COORDINATION SCENARIO

This is an eclectic and compromising approach. In contrast to the convergence scenario, this approach begins with a presumption of differences. Japan and the United States understand that their policies regarding Taiwan differ because their relations with Taipei differ historically, they have different legal frameworks for military action, and their domestic politics differ. Japan tends to emphasize continuity and stability by supporting the status quo in its relations with Taiwan and China, while the United States prefers unilateral action, which sometimes works but often causes confusion and inconsistency (*Economist* 20 March 1999).

This approach depends on policy coordination to succeed. First, Japan and the United States must continue to implement an engagement policy with China and Taiwan. It is important that China is engaged in discussions and international activities and treaties to promote a larger sense of mutual dependence and responsibility. Meanwhile, Taiwan should not be left in international isolation. Second, Japan and the United States must coordinate their policies regarding defense and security in Asia Pacific. Regarding Taiwan, Japan and the United States share vital interests in protecting peace in the region. Any violation of, or challenge to, peace should be subject to a coordinated response.

Although this approach is the most realistic option, it too has shortcomings. For it to work, both Japan and the United States would first have to modify their present approach toward China and Taiwan. Japan would have to become more involved in defense and security matters, and the United States would have to refrain from unilateral action and excessive devotion to idealpolitik.[22] Any change in policy orientation would be likely to face local opposition. Policy coordination is extremely difficult when policies are confusing and inconsistent. Japan and the United States need to share a clear mid-term goal, even as their routes to the goal differ.

The U.S.-Japan Security Treaty should be maintained and reinforced. It should serve as a link between two goals: the pursuit of engagement and the commitment to security. Such a new role may be a burden for the treaty, which was designed for a cold war contingency, but no other reliable bilateral framework exists. The U.S.-Japan Security Treaty is, by default, the starting point for policy coordination.

AN AGENDA FOR CLOSER COORDINATION

The following is an outline for policy coordination over the short, medium, and long term. The short-term agenda includes interim measures for the next two to three years. That for the medium term involves policy orientation for the years around 2002, when both China and Taiwan will probably have a new set of leaders. The long-term agenda looks beyond that period.

SHORT-TERM AGENDA

- Revision of the defense guidelines. The revision passed the Diet in May 1999. The United States may regard the revision as too little, too late, but the United States should show understanding of Japanese domestic politics.
- Involvement of the Okinawa prefectural government in Japan-U.S. security talks. Any policy coordination between Japan and the United States on the Taiwan issue would affect Okinawa. The Okinawa government can influence Japan's posture in national defense, as has been seen in the past. Its voice must be heard.
- Comprehensive review of the 1996 Taiwan Strait Crisis. The crisis had as much impact on the Japan-U.S. security arrangement as it did on Taiwan. However, disclosure of information concerning what really occurred has been limited. Unless all the details of the crisis are revealed, not necessarily to the general public but to policy experts, the lessons of the crisis are likely to remain murky and uncertain.
- Unofficial trilateral talks about Taiwan among a wide range of policy experts. Communication among Taiwan experts in the United States and in Japan is wanting. Most of the research done by Japanese scholars on Taiwan remains unpublished in English. This must be corrected.
- Greater transparency in a burden-sharing scheme. The Japanese public, like its American counterpart, is in no mood to advocate unlimited spending for defense. The Japanese Defense Agency is facing

fierce public criticism for corruption, as a result of which the defense budget will be under strict governmental scrutiny, and the burden sharing will be no exception.

- A feasibility study of TMD. Japan should assess the cost-effectiveness and political consequences of implementing TMD. The United States is responsible for explaining to Taiwan that TMD is not necessarily an effective deterrent to aggression. The United States should leave the decision regarding whether to introduce TMD to Taiwan, which may have other priorities in defense spending and may want to avoid inviting a violent reaction from China.

- Promotion of cross-strait talks and economic transactions. Cross-strait economic transactions have been growing rapidly. It should be noted that the 1996 Taiwan Strait Crisis had little, if any, deleterious effect on these transactions. China and Taiwan are engaged in a win-win game.

- Support of Chinese and Taiwanese economic contributions to the Asia Pacific economy. Both China and Taiwan displayed resilience during the 1997 Asian financial crisis. Taiwan's economy suffered little and showed healthy growth in both 1997 and 1998. Both nation's economies slowed down in 1998, but are in much better shape than those of their neighbors.

- Support of regional arrangements. The APEC forum, which in 1991 China and Taiwan together joined as Chinese-Taipei, has the potential to become a forum where China and Taiwan, as well as Japan and the United States, can meet and talk. The Asian Monetary Fund, which was aborted right before the Asian financial crisis, should be revived.

- Support of the joint entry of China and Taiwan to the World Trade Organization (WTO). U.S. resistance to China's reentry to the WTO makes little sense in terms of engagement. It is the responsibility of the United States to come through with the pledge of support it has made on several occasions. The delay in admitting China also delays the entry of Taiwan.

The November 1999 WTO agreement between China and the United States was a step in the right direction. The fiasco of the December 1999 Seattle WTO meeting, however, seemed to have offset this move forward. Now, the WTO, the United States, the European Union, and Japan must work hard to realize the next round of WTO talks. The process is not likely to begin until the U.S. presidential race is over and the new president is settled in the White House.

China may be able to enter the WTO soon. The U.S.-China Permanent Normal Trade Relations agreement and the WTO agreement with the European Union in May 2000 are encouraging signs. The United States needs to show leadership in trade liberalization in a timely manner. Otherwise, China is likely to only feel proud of itself and be less likely to reform its trade system.

MEDIUM-TERM AGENDA

- Clarification of Japan's interests in protecting safe passage of its vessels through the Taiwan Strait. Japan must explain to China that this clarification is based on international law and regulations, and has nothing to do with Japan's territorial ambitions or military expansion. The United States should support Japan's stance.
- Revision of the present burden-sharing scheme. Japan needs to replace its economic commitment to defense with greater direct commitment, starting with UN peacekeeping operations (PKOs). Japan has realized, thanks to the Gulf War, that simply paying for security does not suffice.
- Revitalizing Okinawa. Okinawa's economic dependence on U.S. bases, which account for about one-third of its local revenues, is a concern. Okinawa residents feel isolated and subject to discrimination. Taiwan is seeking to become an economic center in Asia and has local industries eager to set up operations overseas. Taiwan-Okinawa economic ties have potential.
- Periodic roundtable discussions about the future of Asia Pacific. Such discussions can bypass the bureaucratic demarcations of Japan and the United States. The rapidly changing political and economic situation in Asia demands such engagement.

LONG-TERM AGENDA

- Clarification of joint support for democracy in Taiwan. Taiwan's freewheeling local politics exemplify democracy in its primitive stages. Japan and the United States should contribute more economic and cultural support for the democratic transition occurring in Taiwanese society.
- Clarification of our handling of the China threat argument. Both sides need to give a cautious reception to the argument that China presents a threat to regional security. The idealpolitik policy orientation of the United States is particularly susceptible to such simplistic statements

(Huntington 1993; Bernstein and Munro 1997). Japan, on the other hand, should avoid justifying behavior as being in accordance with the Asian way, since this approach tends to emphasize conformity and racism.

■ Consideration of flexible security cooperation. The two nations need to be flexible in their security cooperation. As Robert Zoellick predicted in a recent lecture, in ten to fifteen years the defense posture of the U.S. armed forces in Asia Pacific could change drastically. By that time, the importance of maintaining forward bases is likely to decline, while cooperation in information and intelligence will become crucial.

■ Consideration of an integrated system for security cooperation in Asia Pacific. A regional arrangement, with multiple participants, would be more effective in offsetting unpredictable and changing threats to regional security. Japan and the United States need to expand their security cooperation with South Korea in such areas as counterterrorism and counterespionage activities, and to control the impact of massive illegal immigration and other social phenomena.

The list is already very long. It may not be possible to transcend the communication gap regarding Taiwan that has widened between Japan and the United States over the past few years. But we must begin somewhere, and this study, it is hoped, represents a small step forward.

An abridged version of this chapter was published as "Turbulence Threatens" in the Chatham House monthly *The World Today*, vol. 55 (January–December 1999), p. 16.

NOTES

1. These are contributing factors to ending many alliances. See Walt (1997).

2. One of the missiles fired on March 8 landed in the sea lanes between Taiwan and Japan, only 60 kilometers from Yonakuni Island in Okinawa (Funabashi 1997).

3. A Chinese researcher summarized the evidence of the "United States' toying with the Taiwan card" as follows: (1) President Bush's decision to sell 150 F-16 jet fighters to Taiwan in September 1992; (2) U.S. support of Taiwan's diplomatic activities seeking international recognition, including renewed membership in the United Nations; (3) President Clinton's decision to elevate U.S. contact with Taiwan in the "Taiwan Policy Adjustments" announced in September 1994; and

(4) President Clinton's decision to award an entry visa to Lee Teng-hui on May 22, 1995 (Si 1998, 805–809).

4. The prefectural government of Okinawa monitors movement on the U.S. bases. Their records show unusually heavy activity in February and March 1996. Prefectural officials were concerned not about Taiwan but about noise in areas surrounding the bases and the possibility of an increase in military-related crime. An official of the prefectural government remarked: "We do not know where those U.S. soldiers are heading. We do not care. We just want the U.S. bases to get out of Okinawa." Interview with author, July 1998.

5. It was a somewhat symbolic gesture of protest. Yen grants accounted for about 6 percent of the total of Japanese loans to China. The suspension was lifted in March 1997, eight months after China declared its adherence to the CTBT.

6. Author's interview with U.S. government officials and military officers in Okinawa in July 1998 and in Hawaii in November 1998.

7. Governor of Okinawa Ōta Masahide was the most outspoken advocate of the return of the U.S. bases. He succeeded in getting a great deal of national attention for the Okinawa problem but failed to come up with realistic political options. He was defeated in the January 1999 election. See Uesugi and Amiko (1999).

8. On these subjects, refer to Wakabayashi (1992). The question of to whom Japan surrendered sovereignty over Taiwan remains controversial. The recent Japanese view suggests it should belong to China. See Okabe (1998, 61). Okabe is the chairperson of the China-Japan 21st Century Committee, a semigovernmental forum.

9. Cross-strait trade surpassed US$1 billion in 1993, up 38 percent over the previous year. Direct investment by Taiwan in the mainland reached US$1.14 billion in 1993, or 4.6 times the 1992 figure (Department of Statistics 1998; Investment Commission 1998).

10. In August 1996, China agreed with the United States on an on-site inspection procedure for the CTBT. Secretary of State Warren Christopher's visit to Beijing in November confirmed that the presidents of both countries would pay reciprocal visits and China would join the comprehensive export ban on nuclear-related materials. In December 1996, Chinese Defense Minister Chi Haotian, whose previous travel plans had been twice aborted, finally visited the United States and agreed to the exchange of military missions and port calls for navy vessels.

11. A Chinese researcher told the author that the Taiwan issue accounted for about 70 percent to 80 percent of the significance of Jiang's visit.

12. State Department spokesman James Rubin said that the United States (1) does not support a one-China, one-Taiwan policy or a two-China policy, (2) does not support Taiwan independence, and (3) does not support Taiwanese membership in organizations that require members to be states. President Clinton repeated these three points during his talks in Shanghai during the June 1998 summit.

13. In the same article, Lee said, in Japanese, "The Japanese government returned Taiwan to the Republic of China. The Republic was defeated in the civil war and came to Taiwan. It lost everything but Taiwan. The Chinese Communist Party claims Taiwan is a province of China. What a strange dream" (Shiba 1994).

14. That task was assigned to former Ambassador to the United States Matsunaga Nobuo, who visited both Taiwan and China as a private citizen.

15. A source close to President Lee described his stance as "seeking peace without unification." The Chinese argued that President Lee was "seeking independence behind the scenes."

16. This expression was used by Robert Zoellick, director of the Center for Strategic and International Studies (CSIS), in a lecture at the Tokyo American Center (30 March 1999).

17. One Chinese diplomat told the author how shocked he was to see this evidence of Japan's direct involvement in the crisis.

18. Lee declared in July 1995, right after his visit to the United States, that Taiwan would upgrade its defense capability and indicated that it might develop nuclear weapons.

19. Another event that China considered a provocation occurred when the U.S. aircraft carrier *Nimitz* navigated across the Taiwan Strait in August 1995.

20. The landslide victory in the Tokyo gubernatorial race won by Ishihara Shintarō, the renowned nationalist and politician who wrote *The Japan That Can Say No,* is an indication of the degree of popularity an anti-U.S. stance enjoys among Tokyo voters.

21. Recent public polls show the majority of the Japanese voters feel some need to amend the constitution. Revision, however, would be extremely difficult. A two-thirds majority in both Lower and Upper Houses of the Diet is required, plus a national referendum.

22. Idealpolitik is foreign policy based on a set of ideals, like freedom and democracy. "The United States is uniquely and self-consciously a country founded on a set of ideas, and ideals, applicable to people everywhere" (Talbott 1996, 49).

BIBLIOGRAPHY

Akiyama Masahiro et al. 1996. "21-seiki no anzen hoshō o kataru" (Discussion on security in the 21st century). *Gaikō Fōramu.* Special edition: 24–39.

Bernstein, Richard, and Ross H. Munro. 1997. *The Coming Conflict with China.* New York: Knopf.

Chinese Association for Eurasian Studies. 1999. *Eurasian Studies Newsletter* (October). Taipei: Chinese Association for Eurasian Studies.

Chūgoku sōran 1998 (China almanac 1998). 1999. Tokyo: Kazankai.

Department of Defense, Office of International Security Affairs, United States.

1998. *The United States Security Strategy for the East Asia–Pacific Region 1998.* Washington, D.C.: Department of Defense.

Department of Statistics, Ministry of Finance, Japan. 1998. *Monthly Statistics of Exports and Imports of Taiwan Area, the Republic of China.* Tokyo: Government of Japan.

Funabashi Yōichi. 1997. *Dōmei hyōryū* (Alliance adrift). Tokyo: Iwanami Shoten.

Gellman, Barton. 1998. "The Missiles of March." *International Herald Tribune* (22 June 1998).

Hiramatsu Shigeo. 1997. *Zoku Chūgoku no kaiyō senryaku* (China's maritime strategy II). Tokyo: Keisō Shobō.

———. 1998. "Chūgoku no kokubō hakusho o bunseki suru" (Analysis of the Chinese defense white paper). *Tōa,* no. 376 (October): 15–22.

———. 1999. *Chūgoku no gunjiryoku* (China's military power). Tokyo: Bungei Shunjū.

Hosokawa Morihiro. 1998. "Are U.S. Troops in Japan Needed?" *Foreign Affairs* 77 (4): 2–5.

Huntington, Samuel. 1993. "The Clash of Civilizations?" *Foreign Affairs* 72 (3): 22–49.

Ihara Kichinosuke. 1998. "Bei-Chū sekkin to Nichi-Tai no tachiba" (Closer U.S.-Chinese ties and the positions of Japan-Taiwan). *Seiron* (September): 138–144.

Investment Commission, Ministry of Economic Affairs, Republic of China. 1998. *Statistics on Overseas Chinese and Foreign Investment.* Taipei Ministry of Economic Affairs.

Kuriyama Takakazu. 1997. *Nichibei dōmei: Hyōryū kara no dakkyaku* (The U.S.-Japan alliance: Managing a drifting relationship). Tokyo: Nihon Keizai Shinbunsha.

Lin Bizhao. 1999. "Taiwan's Comprehensive Security." *Journal of Strategic and International Studies* 1 (1): 1–12.

Liu Ji. 1998. "Zhongmei guanxi de xuanze" (Choices of U.S.-Chinese relations). *Xinhua Wenzhai* (January): 9–11.

Okabe Tatsumi. 1998. "Nihon gaikō no yukue" (The prospect of Japanese diplomacy). *Tōa,* no. 378 (December).

Quansheng Zhao. 1996. *Interpreting Chinese Foreign Policy: The Micro-Macro Linkage Approach.* Hong Kong: Oxford University Press.

Shiba Ryōtarō. 1994. "Taiwan kikō" (Taiwan travelogue) *Shūkan Asahi* (6–13 May): 42–49.

Shibuya Tsukasa. 1996. "Taiwan sōtō senkyo to chūtai no kinchō" (The presidential election in Taiwan and Sino-Taiwan tension). *Kaigai Jijyō* 44 (6): 55–56.

Si Ge. 1998. *Meiguo Duihua Zhengce yu Taiwan wenti* (American China policy and the Taiwan issue). Beijing: Shijie Zhishi Chubanshe.

Talbott, Strobe. 1996. "Democracy and the National Interest." *Foreign Affairs* 75 (6): 47–63.

Tsuru Shigeto. 1996. *Nichibei anpo kaishō e no michi* (The road to the dissolution of the Japan-U.S. Security Treaty). Tokyo: Iwanami Shoten.

Uesugi Yūji and Nobori Amiko. 1999. "'Okinawa mondai' no kōzō—mittsu no reberu to funsō kaiketsu no shikaku kara no bunseki" (Structure of the "Okinawa Problem": Analysis of three aspects and from the perspective of conflict resolution). *Kokusai Seiji,* no. 120 (February): 170–194.

Umbach, Frank. 1998. "Financial crisis slows but fails to halt East Asian arms race." *Jane's Intelligence Review* (August–September).

Wakabayashi Masahiro. 1992. *Taiwan: Bunretsu kokka to minshuka* (Taiwan: A divided nation and democratization). Tokyo: Tokyo Daigaku Shuppankai.

Walt, Stephen. 1997. "Why Alliances Endure or Collapse." *Survival* 39 (1): 156–179.

Watari Yō. 1998. "Taiwan mondai o kangaeru" (Thoughts about Taiwan). *Tōa,* no. 378 (December): 91–104.

Yamauchi Toshihiro, ed. 1999. *Nichibei shin gaidorain to shūhen jitai hō* (The New Japan-U.S. Defense Guidelines and Neighboring Situation Law). Kyoto: Hōritsu Bunkasha.

Toward a Japan-U.S.-ASEAN Nexus

Sudō Sueo

4

T HE Asian financial crisis of 1997–1998 was so pervasive that many argue that the nations in the region have lost confidence in the so-called Asian Miracle. Certainly, the prolonged economic crisis has important political and security ramifications. While Southeast Asian countries have largely based their political legitimacy on promoting rapid economic growth, the effects of the financial crisis on the security environment of Southeast Asia have been seen in the collapse of authoritarian states, slower defense modernization, a divided Association of Southeast Asian Nations (ASEAN), and the retreat of ASEAN's multilateralism. Pessimists may claim that ASEAN no longer works.[1]

The nations of Myanmar (Burma), Cambodia, and Indonesia are another source of major uncertainty in Southeast Asia. Should critical events like those in Indonesia occur, Southeast Asia could become politically unstable, with the sea lanes, economic activities, and other geopolitical interests of Japan and the United States jeopardized. Moreover, there exists a more salient question of policy coordination between Japan and the United States as regards the region, since post–cold war Asia has presented the two nations with different opportunities. As scholar Stuart Harris put it: "The greater risk is that, as a result of different policy goals of the two countries, it [the Japan-U.S. relationship] will continue to operate, but at a level of diminishing relevance to the new needs of global and regional order" (Harris 1997, 182).

Given their shared strategic interests—but different approaches—in Southeast Asia, it is imperative that Japan and the United States coordinate their Southeast Asian policies more substantially in order to bring about political stability in the region.[2] Based on this urgent necessity, the purpose of this chapter is to clarify major sources of instability in the region, discuss the issues that threaten to divide the Japan-U.S. alliance, and propose the formation of a Japan-U.S.-ASEAN nexus through which to invigorate and widen the Japan-U.S. alliance.

MAJOR SOURCES OF INSTABILITY
IN SOUTHEAST ASIA

THE DECLINING U.S. POSITION IN THE REGION

Northeast and Southeast Asia have long been an integral part of the United States' cold war containment strategy. During the 1950s and 1960s, this strategy was characterized by a set of bilateral defense agreements in support of forward-deployed military bases. In Southeast Asia, the containment doctrine obligated the United States to offer support to South Vietnam, especially after the Geneva Agreement of 1954, which led to the establishment of the anti-Communist Southeast Asia Treaty Organization (SEATO). Accordingly, the United States was involved in a major war in Indochina that lasted until 1973.[3]

The American domino theory containment policy was applied in both Southeast Asia and Northeast Asia. The use of American bases in Okinawa from which to attack North Vietnam further underscored the important linkage between the U.S.-Japan Security Treaty and the security of Southeast Asia. No less critical were the sea lanes—especially the Taiwan Strait, the South China Sea, and the Strait of Malacca—which were basic to the security considerations of both Japan and the United States simply because of Tokyo's dependence on oil from the Middle East.

When the unification of Vietnam finally occurred in April 1975, however, the United States was already pursuing détente on a broader level with the former Soviet Union and China, while reworking its cold war strategy. In particular, the Guam Doctrine of 1969 proposed that in future the United States would avoid direct involvement in major Asian wars, and that Southeast Asian countries would instead assume a greater responsibility for peace and security in the region. This posture has become more salient in the post–Vietnam War period, which has seen an incremental reduction in the American presence in Southeast Asia.

For instance, after the United States withdrew from Thailand in 1975, Subic Bay and Clark Air Field in the Philippines became the symbols of the American presence in Southeast Asia. It was this symbolic presence that sustained a regional balance even after the former Soviet Union obtained access to the Cam Ranh Bay bases in Vietnam. Despite implicit requests by the Singaporean government for its continued presence, however, the United States announced its pullout from the Philippines—and all of Southeast Asia—by 1992. Naturally, some Southeast Asian countries began to contemplate alternative security measures. As the Philippines and the United States began negotiations for a new base agreement in May 1990, Singapore also started talking to Washington, offering its military facilities. These talks led to an agreement in November 1991 that has enabled U.S. naval vessels to use Sembawang Dockyard for repairs, and U.S. aircraft to use Paya Lebar Airport for training missions (Department of Defense 1998).

This arrangement, however, seems far from adequate. As one study suggested, "Many regional specialists questioned the relevance of the U.S. military presence for Asian security conflicts in the post–cold war era. Many predicted that America's domestic priorities and budget problems would lead to additional downsizing of its Pacific forces over the next several years" (Simon and Ellings 1996, 223). Southeast Asian countries have specific reasons to fear the declining U.S. position, especially in light of conflicting territorial claims. A case in point is a territorial dispute that has pitted China and the Philippines against each other, and was sparked when China in 1995 occupied Mischief Reef, which is a part of the Spratly Islands. Thus, the U.S. withdrawal of its forces from Southeast Asia has been deemed by some analysts as having contributed to instability in the region.

CHINA AS A GREAT POWER

Given its population, land mass, geographic proximity, and ethnic outreach, China poses a major challenge to the security calculations of countries in Southeast Asia. The rapid growth of China's economy and its adventurous missile exercises intensify concern, for as part of China's proclaimed Four Modernizations plan, the country has poured resources into a military buildup. To be sure, the Chinese claim repeatedly that they would never seek hegemony, nor aim to intimidate smaller countries, but the history of Chinese relations with its Southeast Asian neighbors suggests a different story.

Whether China likes it or not, the China threat does exist in the minds of Southeast Asians. This threat is perceived in the context of four related factors: China's strengthening of its military, especially naval capability; its use of force in settling domestic and regional problems; its steady expansion of de facto control over contested territories in the South China Sea; and its growing influence in Myanmar.[4] Especially noteworthy are the recent experiences of Vietnam, Myanmar, and the Philippines (see Guan 1998; Seekins 1997; and Storey 1999). Vietnam, for instance, has been strengthening its diplomatic and security relations with the Philippines in an attempt to deal with China's growing presence in the region. China has also become an important security issue for ASEAN, with some analysts reportedly concerned that if Myanmar and Laos stay outside ASEAN, they will drift farther into China's sphere (see Hiramatsu 1999).

In a nutshell, it is the rapid rise of China as a great power that has contributed most to long-range apprehensions in Japan and Southeast Asia. For China is unpredictable, and it is uncertain whether China will become a benign power or seek to dominate its neighbors.

ECONOMIC TURMOIL AND POLITICAL CRISIS

In July 1997, a financial crisis struck Thailand, soon engulfing Northeast Asia and other Southeast Asian nations as well. It turned out to be the most serious financial crisis experienced by Southeast Asian countries in the postwar period (see particularly Wanandi 1998). Although Thailand immediately entered into an agreement with the International Monetary Fund (IMF) for emergency standby credit in exchange for the adoption of stringent fiscal austerity measures and a range of structural reforms, other countries responded differently. Malaysia, for instance, totally rejected the IMF's offer, while Indonesia, until its political crisis in June 1998, was torn between the IMF prescription and an independent course.

A financial crisis often has the effect of distracting the nations in a region, making them inward-looking and less cohesive, so it is not surprising that its effect on ASEAN has been profound. Already, as mentioned earlier, the crisis has led to the collapse of authoritarian states, to slower defense modernization, to a divided ASEAN, and to the retreat of ASEAN multilateralism.[5] In particular, the fall of the Suharto regime in Indonesia exemplified the political problems experienced by all Southeast Asian countries. The crisis has had yet another implication: The economic turmoil in the region has served to assist China in its ambitions to become the leading regional power.

In the face of these uncertainties, Southeast Asian countries have failed to generate any coordinated policies to deal with the crisis. As one study explains: "The failure of the region's multilateral institutions—APEC [Asia-Pacific Economic Cooperation], the ARF [ASEAN Regional Forum], ASEAN—to play any kind of leading role in addressing the crisis suggests that regional stability still depends heavily on the policies and institutions of major individual players" (Dibb et al. 1998, 24). Although the worst scenario, envisioning a regional conflict, still appears far-fetched, Southeast Asians have worried that China might seek to exploit the current inward-looking focus of Southeast Asian countries, many of which have postponed military modernization programs, to seize territory in the contested Spratly Islands. Nevertheless, thus far, according to Cronin (1998, 20), China has not used the crisis as an opportunity for aggrandizement, but as a chance to show support and regional leadership (see also Richardson 1999).

The financial crisis and the shifting influence of China and the United States in the region shows just how important a stable and prosperous Southeast Asia is for American and Japanese foreign policies and the Japan-U.S. alliance. According to the fourth (1998) in the East Asia Strategy Report (EASR) series, "The intention of the United States is to help dampen the sources of instability by maintaining a policy of robust engagement, overseas presence and strengthened alliances, while searching for new opportunities to increase confidence and a spirit of common security" (Department of Defense 1998, 7). This statement would signify that Japan and the United States share vital interests in Southeast Asia. And because ASEAN is the only regional body able to promote a regional identity, consensus on critical issues, and regional cooperation on economic, political, and security issues through its annual Post-Ministerial Conference (PMC) and the ARF, the Japan-U.S. alliance needs to work with ASEAN more extensively.

The dawn of the post–cold war era as a result of the 1989 Malta Summit was followed by the political settlement of the thirteen-year-old Cambodian conflict in September 1991, and the eventual diffusion of the polarization that had gripped Southeast Asia. Even so, the loss of cold war fears led many to wonder if ASEAN had also lost a major centripetal force in its political underpinning. To dispel this view, ASEAN convened a summit in January 1992 that achieved significant progress. In particular, the ASEAN heads of government agreed to move to a higher plane of political and economic cooperation to secure regional peace and security; to seek to safeguard ASEAN's collective interests in response to the formation of large and powerful economic groupings; to seek new avenues to engage member states in cooperation on security matters; and to forge closer relations based on friendship and cooperation with the Indochinese countries, following the settlement of the Cambodian conflict. Accordingly, since its fourth summit, ASEAN has emphasized an expansive, "deepening and widening" policy in order to play a greater stabilizing role in the region.[6]

ASEAN has shown remarkable resilience as a regional organization of developing countries in its thirty years of existence. It has acquired its organizational expertise through a gradual process of institutionalization, including an ASEAN way of managing regional affairs. Simply put, the ASEAN way can be defined as a unique diplomatic style of managing regional affairs that includes (1) noninterference in other members' internal affairs, (2) consultation and consensus, (3) amicable resolution of regional conflict, and (4) a dialogue partnership.[7] By adhering to these norms, ASEAN has achieved a special status in the region. As Paul Dibb has suggested, "The ASEAN group, which acts together as a united bloc on key issues, has already accrued to itself significant political influence out of all proportion to any objective measure of its economic, military or political power" (1995, 41). However, as ASEAN continues to be plagued by the financial crisis and concomitant uncertainty, there is a rising need for external assistance for the region.

ECONOMIC, POLITICAL, AND SECURITY ISSUES FOR THE JAPAN-U.S. ALLIANCE

JAPAN-U.S. ECONOMIC COORDINATION

The most exigent issue for Southeast Asian security is how to revitalize the region's devastated economies, a necessary condition if there is to be political and security stability. The Japanese Ministry of Finance, fearing that the Thai currency crisis of July 1997 might trigger a chain reaction in neighboring economies, immediately began discussions with key Asian countries sharing the same concern. Japan was determined to play a leading role in mobilizing international support for a rescue package, even without American participation. The Tokyo meeting in August 1997 was significant for the fact that it was the first time since World War II that Tokyo has taken the lead and laid down a new framework for regional economic cooperation.

Furthermore, through their joint efforts toward resolving the financial crisis, Japan and ASEAN countries came up with a proposal for setting up an Asian Monetary Fund (AMF). The idea was to establish a US$100 billion Asian bailout fund, consisting of money to be pooled by Japan and the ASEAN countries, given their common view that the IMF's austerity measures alone were insufficient.

The AMF proposal—and the discussions themselves—proved to be quite significant in terms of Japan's leadership role. As one observer cogently noted: "Japan's political leadership seems to have been considering moving beyond 'leadership from behind' prior to the birth of the AMF proposal. During a number of visits to other Asian capitals, Mr. Hashimoto has spoken of the need for a more vigorous Japanese foreign policy toward Asia. Some analysts interpreted Mr. Sakakibara's promotion earlier this year to the powerful position of vice finance minister for international affairs as reflecting the prime minister's desire to craft a series of more ambitious foreign economic policy initiatives" (Altbach 1997, 8; see also Yamazawa 1998).

The idea of an AMF, however, was strongly opposed by the United States, which saw it as a direct challenge to the function of the IMF. In particular, U.S. officials worried that an independent regional fund for international bailouts would not impose the stringent austerity conditions demanded by the IMF. Due to this opposition, representatives from Asia Pacific countries at a financial deputy ministers' meeting in Manila in November 1997 decided instead to seek a looser arrangement that would pool resources at a time of crisis, rather than setting up a permanent fund.[8]

In October 1998, with the financial crisis worsening, the Japanese government announced the so-called Miyazawa plan, including a US$30 billion aid package for ailing Asian economies. Finance Minister Miyazawa Kiichi explained that half of the funds were intended to meet needs for short-term capital, such as trade finance, in the course of economic reform; the other half would be made available for medium- and long-term financial needs in assisting economic recovery in the entire region (*Nihon Keizai Shimbun* 4 October 1998; *Far Eastern Economic Review* 19 November 1998). In November, Japanese Prime Minister Obuchi Keizō and U.S. President Bill Clinton issued a joint statement, timed to coincide with the Asia Pacific summit in Kuala Lumpur, which declared that restarting economic growth was the major challenge faced in Asia Pacific. To further this effort, they said, Japan and the United States, with the support of the World Bank and Asia Development Bank, were launching the Asia Growth and Recovery Initiative.

The plan's intent was to help leverage substantial new private-sector financing and to assist banks and companies to restructure so that economies could return to a growth mode. Without doubt, these joint economic coordination efforts by Japan and the United States augur well not only for the regional economy but also for the Japan-U.S. alliance.

JAPAN-U.S. POLITICAL COORDINATION

The second major focus for joint Japan-U.S. efforts is achieving political stability in the region. Perhaps of greatest concern in this respect are the four latecomers to ASEAN, which can all be characterized as having highly authoritarian regimes. Myanmar in particular has been a disquieting factor ever since the ruling State Law and Order Restoration Council (SLORC) refused to accept the result of the general elections of 1990.

Dealing with Asian values is one of the most contentious issues between Western and Asian countries, and this is true of Japan and the United States, as well. Basically, Japan promotes democratization in Asia by applying positive sanctions, in the belief that offering a carrot will gradually improve the situation. The United States, on the other hand, employs the stick of negative sanctions to force change. The question here is whether or not Japan and the United States can overcome these differences and coordinate their policies in order to bring about meaningful changes in the matter of democratization in Asia.

In this respect, it is worthwhile examining the example of Cambodia, where Japan's supportive policy has worked without provoking major objections from the United States.

Myanmar and Indochina, comprised of Vietnam, Laos, and Cambodia, were both formerly politically sensitive areas for Japanese foreign policy. Yet since the declaration of the Fukuda Doctrine in 1977, Japan has adopted a more positive, even favorable policy toward these countries.[9] In particular, the Tokyo conference in June 1990 was regarded as a significant contribution to resolving the Cambodian conflict. As one observer put it: "Japan's involvement in the Cambodian truce is likely to serve as a point of reference for its future political initiatives. The process of securing peace in Cambodia, which eventually came to fruition in October 1991 with the signing of a settlement in Paris, was the first occasion on which Japan clearly and deliberately attempted to play a political role in Asian affairs" (Tomoda 1992, 43; see also Ikeda 1996).

Thus, it was not coincidental that Japan's very first peacekeeping operations troops were sent to Cambodia in 1992. Moreover, ever since the Cambodian conflict ended, the Japanese government has been active in convening several international forums every year to assist the reconstruction of the Cambodian economy and Indochina as a whole. Because of these good offices, Japan was able to play a leading role in resolving a political imbroglio caused by Second Prime Minister Hun Sen on July 5, 1997. With ASEAN's attempt to mediate in the crisis unsuccessful, Tokyo continued to pursue a proactive policy, inviting Hun Sen to Tokyo for talks in November. The talks brought about a rapid settlement of the conflict in January 1998, with a four-point proposal by the Japanese Ministry of Foreign Affairs.[10]

Hun Sen endorsed the proposal in February, and its four conditions were met by the end of March 1998, paving the way for elections to be held in July. Although Cambodia was not admitted to ASEAN at the sixth ASEAN summit in Hanoi, due to lingering political instability in Phnom Penh, it joined the association in April 1999.

Both before and after the elections, Western observers expressed serious doubts about Hun Sen's leadership. As one observer noted: "Cambodia can have a civilized government responsive both to its people's needs and to the security interests of its neighbors only if the Hun Sen regime is removed from power. Earlier this year, the United States could have stood firmly behind the beleaguered opposition parties and supported a boycott of the election until conditions for a genuinely free contest existed. It could now declare the election results unsatisfactory" (Morris 1998, 10).[11] Given this prevailing point of view, it was hardly surprising that the United States refrained from supporting the Hun Sen regime.

Due to domestic political upheaval, Myanmar has been facing serious problems. Myanmar's junta seized power in 1988 after soldiers killed hundreds of pro-democracy demonstrators. In 1990, the government allowed parliamentary elections to be held, but it later refused to acknowledge the unfavorable results. The ruling SLORC, now known as the State Peace and Development Council (SPDC), kept opposition leader and Nobel Peace Prize winner Aung San Suu Kyi under house arrest for six years and has kept her under detention since 1995. The United States and other Western nations have used economic and other sanctions in an attempt to nudge the ruling junta toward democracy. ASEAN has approached the issue differently, pursuing a policy of constructive engagement. ASEAN has contended that isolating Myanmar does not work and would be counterproductive. It has also rejected Western criticism of human rights abuses as an attempt to impose Western values on an Asian culture.

Their recent difficulties notwithstanding, in late May 1994 government officials and academics from all the Southeast Asian countries met in Manila to draw up a "vision for a Southeast Asian Community"—which was almost achieved when Laos and Myanmar joined ASEAN in July 1997. Understandably, the United States and the European Union expressed their objection to ASEAN's inclusion of Myanmar because of its oppressive and undemocratic regime. According to an American Department of Defense document, "Now that Burma has become an ASEAN member, we look to ASEAN to shoulder greater responsibility for producing progress by prodding the State Peace and Development Council to halt its repression of the democratic opposition, move to meaningful political dialogue with the National League for Democracy under Aung San Suu Kyi and with the ethnic minorities, and take effective action against the narcotics trade" (Department of Defense 1998, 37). Japan subsequently announced its intention to resume foreign aid to Myanmar, which may necessitate closer policy coordination between Japan and the United States.

Japan's behavior vis-à-vis Myanmar is instructive. When the United States decided not to take direct action to engage Myanmar due to public pressure regarding the country's human rights abuses and undemocratic practices, Japan was able to pursue its policy for helping to resolve ASEAN's internal problems with Washington's tacit support. Of course, Myanmar may present the most difficult case for Japan and the United States. Yet, from Japan's point of view, Myanmar needs to be nurtured first as a member of ASEAN. It will take time before both Japan and the United States can arrive at an optimal policy that will be acceptable to ASEAN.[12]

The viability and capacity of Japan-U.S. political coordination will be put to the test soon. Indonesia's role as the leader of ASEAN is now in doubt, given the prospects for political and social upheaval occurring there. The independence of East Timor could set off a chain of reactions that could lead to the disintegration of Indonesia. In order to prevent this, Japan and the United States should coordinate their policies and take such actions as necessary to help stabilize the country. Doing so will also help invigorate the Japan-U.S. alliance.[13]

JAPAN-U.S. SECURITY COORDINATION

The third issue for joint Japan-U.S. efforts is the security cooperation required to deal with the precarious conditions in Southeast Asia. Soon after the U.S. announced the withdrawal of its troops from Philippine bases, some ASEAN members, such as Singapore and Malaysia, stepped up to offer their military facilities in order to maintain an American military presence in the region. Given China's expanding role, however, a limited U.S. presence is no longer a sufficient guarantee of security. Nor is it appropriate for settling territorial disputes, discouraging weapons buildups, or calming ethnic tensions. There is a need to strengthen regional military cooperation in the following three areas.

STRENGTHENING THE ARF   Faced with a rapidly changing security environment in the region, ASEAN members pondered proposals made by

Canada, Australia, and Russia and finally agreed to establish a regional body in July 1993, formally called the ASEAN Regional Forum. The use of ASEAN rather than Asian suggests that ASEAN was intended to be the backbone of future security discussions, with its PMC acting as a central body to which the United States, Russia, China, and Japan give their support. This decision was a major step for ASEAN, because the ARF may be able to generate its own momentum toward multilateralism and become the focus of all matters relating to political and security issues in the region.

Furthermore, the ASEAN Institutes for Strategic and International Studies (ASEAN-ISIS) has come to play a prominent role in the track-two process. In May 1991, for instance, to support the ASEAN PMC process, it organized a "senior officials meeting," which consisted of senior officials of the ASEAN countries and dialogue partners. ASEAN-ISIS, together with other regional think tanks, has also established the Council for Security Cooperation in the Asia-Pacific (CSCAP) to provide a forum for nongovernmental dialogue and to give direction and research support to the ARF, in the same manner that the Pacific Economic Cooperation Conference (PECC) formerly functioned for the Asia-Pacific Economic Cooperation (APEC) organization. Without doubt, the establishment of the CSCAP is an important milestone in the development of institutionalized dialogue and cooperation concerning security matters in the region. The resulting nucleus of the CSCAP, PMC, and ARF could well serve as a basic security network in Asia Pacific.[14]

The first ARF was held in July 1994 in Bangkok with six member nations of ASEAN, seven dialogue partners (the United States, Japan, Australia, New Zealand, Canada, South Korea, and the European Union), and five guest observers (Russia, China, Vietnam, Laos, and Papua New Guinea) in attendance. This broad representation implicitly underscored the centrality of ASEAN. After a three-hour discussion of such Asian security issues as the South China Sea, confidence-building measures (CBMs), and aspects of preventive diplomacy, the chairman issued a brief statement stressing that "the ARF would be in a position to make significant contributions to efforts toward confidence-building and preventive diplomacy" as well as peaceful settlement of disputes in the region.

Since it was an inaugural meeting, the eighteen participants simply agreed to two future actions: to convene the ARF on an annual basis with the next meeting in Brunei Darussalam in 1995, and to endorse the purposes and principles of ASEAN's Treaty of Amity and Cooperation in

Southeast Asia. This treaty would serve as a code of conduct governing relations between member states and a unique diplomatic instrument for regional confidence-building, preventive diplomacy, and political and security cooperation. Even more importantly, having secured China's and Russia's participation in this meeting constituted a major breakthrough, bringing together for the first time all the major powers in the Asia Pacific region. With the birth of the ARF, a multilayered structure has been established for channels of dialogue for Asia Pacific regional security, centered on the ASEAN-PMC framework and track-two dialogue.[15]

Yet, many observers have begun to question the role and viability of the ARF. For instance, Shaun Narine argues that "the political, economic, and strategic considerations that have made ASEAN a success within Southeast Asia do not necessarily apply to the more powerful states of the Asia-Pacific region. Therefore, ASEAN is an inappropriate model for the ARF" (1997, 962). In view of the ARF's main goal of engaging China, moreover, Robyn Lim argues that the ARF has a serious problem because "China's constant strategic pressure in the South China Sea has ASEAN in disarray. The ARF is doing little more than giving China opportunities to divide and rule" (1998, 115).

Given these concerns, it is clear that Japan and the United States can play a role in consolidating the security networks in the region, if they coordinate their policies. But in trying to strengthen the ARF, Japan and the United States need to help resolve its three main defects: the structural anomaly of small to medium-size states aspiring to major strategic goals covering all of East Asia, the inapplicability of ASEAN's procedures, and the misguided notion of basing the ARF on cooperative security (Yuen 1997). The first problem could be dealt with if the ARF relinquished some of its burdens—such as Taiwan and the Korean peninsula—and concentrated on the security of Southeast Asia. In this respect, the establishment of a Northeast Asian security forum should be broached by the Northeast Asian countries.[16] The second problem could be resolved if ASEAN agreed to modify its noninterference principle so as to deal promptly and effectively with regional security issues.[17] The third defect could be handled if the ARF recognized critical elements of the balance of power. That is to say, the Japan-U.S. alliance, anchored on the concept of regional partnership, may well be the best vehicle to balance competing political, economic, and security interests in the region. In order to allow it to do so, ASEAN must include the United States more extensively and find functional linkages with the Japan-U.S. alliance.[18] Accordingly, ASEAN should exercise more caution in promoting its Nuclear-Weapon-Free Zone so as not to preclude the right to free navigation in international waters.

DEALING WITH THE SOUTH CHINA SEA CONFLICT   The process of resolving the South China Sea conflict will be long and tedious because of China's substantial involvement. As one scholar wrote: "Beijing's Spratly expansion clearly demonstrates that it was willing to risk good relations with ASEAN in order to stake its South China Sea claims more firmly" (Simon 1998, 68).[19]

Can Japan play any role in mediating the conflict? Japan's limited but positive role first became evident in February 1995 when the Philippines, while asking for Japan's security assistance, also requested that Tokyo persuade Beijing to end the Chinese occupation of Mischief Reef in the Spratlys. Concomitantly, the ASEAN states seem to have adopted a much softer attitude toward Japan playing a security role in Southeast Asia. Two Southeast Asian security specialists, Mak and Hamzah, have argued that Southeast Asian nations could hope to use Japan as a countervailing power to China's military might. Thus, such countries as Malaysia, Indonesia, and even Singapore might not be hostile toward a Japanese military presence in the region (Mak and Hamzah 1996, 130).

Despite these voices for Japan's greater role, Japan's security role is quite limited, due partly to its constitution and domestic politics. Given the inherent weakness of both the ARF and Japan's security role, ASEAN would need a larger counterbalancing force to keep China in check. As one Southeast Asian official explained, "In the immediate future, only the U.S. and Japan are powerful enough to influence China's political evolution. Their security relationships will dictate the security framework of the smaller East Asian states in the new century. The U.S.-Japan relationship is the key relationship in East Asia, and one in which all bystanders have vested interests" (Almonte 1997–1998, 84–85).[20]

Japan, in meeting these challenges, needs to understand the implications of the revised Guidelines for U.S.-Japan Defense Cooperation and to implement them promptly. The guidelines set forth a more definitive role for Japan in responding to situations in areas surrounding Japan that affect its peace and security. For instance, the revised guidelines specify Japan's rear-area support for U.S. forces responding to a regional contingency. This support may include providing access to airports, ports, transportation, logistics, and medical assistance. Japan would also be able to cooperate and coordinate with U.S. forces on such functions as minesweeping, search and rescue, surveillance, and inspection of ships to enforce UN sanctions (Department of Defense 1998).[21] In other words, Japan's Self-Defense Forces could, and should, render rear-area support for American strategic involvement in the South China Sea.

MILITARY COORDINATION   Japan's security policies toward Southeast Asia have begun to shift since the advent of the post–cold war period, especially since the Gulf War in 1991. In light of the responsibilities assumed by its security alliance with the United States, many both within and outside the country have called upon Japan to play a greater security role rather than merely practicing checkbook diplomacy. One result is the adoption of PKO legislation, which enabled Japan to send its first PKO mission to Cambodia in 1992. The Japanese government reaffirmed its commitments to the alliance in the form of the new National Defense Program Outline (NDPO) in November 1995, the Hashimoto-Clinton joint declaration in April 1996, and the new Guidelines for U.S.-Japan Defense Cooperation in September 1997.[22]

Through these redefining efforts Japan has made commitments to further relations in other parts of East Asia, including cooperating with China with the aim of encouraging China to play a positive and constructive role in the region; encouraging Russia's ongoing progress of reform, and reaffirming full normalization of Japan-Russia relations as important to regional peace and stability; continuing efforts to achieve stability on the Korean peninsula in cooperation with South Korea; and developing multilateral regional security dialogues and cooperation mechanisms, such as the ARF. Eventually, Japan hopes to implement security dialogues regarding Northeast Asia. The most contentious aspect of the former Security Treaty was its Far East clause, which has been replaced in the new guidelines with the words "areas surrounding Japan." These areas have been interpreted to include the Korean peninsula, the South China Sea, and the Strait of Malacca (*Yomiuri Shimbun* 18 April 1996).[23]

One form of military cooperation could be through the Rim of the Pacific (RIMPAC) exercises. These joint military exercises are the largest conducted by the United States and its Pacific allies, an expression of their bilateral links. There have been major changes in these joint exercises, although the details have not been fully disclosed. During RIMPAC '98, held in July 1998, for example, the U.S. navy carried out joint exercises with Canadian, Japanese, South Korean, and Australian navies, with coordinated efforts in command, control, interoperability, and logistics (*Yomiuri Shimbun* 28 July 1998). Should the ASEAN countries desire functional linkages with the Japan-U.S. alliance, these naval exercises could be integrated more substantially.

As a means of strengthening regional military cooperation, the Japanese Defense Agency has begun to widen its security consultations with ASEAN countries. In January 1998, the director-general of the Defense Agency, Kyūma Fumio, visited Vietnam for the first time and agreed to hold regular security consultations with the agency's counterpart in Hanoi (*Yomiuri Shimbun* 11 July 1998). Kyūma proposed a friendship visit by Maritime Self-Defense Force vessels to Vietnam, the presence of a Vietnamese military attaché in Japan by the end of 1998, and sending Vietnamese students to Japan's National Defense Academy. It is also reported that the Defense Agency will seek to strengthen security ties with the Philippines, Thailand, and other Southeast Asian nations.

CONCLUSION

Ever since its pledge in January 1992 to move the association toward a higher plane, ASEAN has been asserting its point of view in the wider Asia Pacific region. It has introduced a new level of multilateral interactions and cooperation, and its networking efforts have led to ASEANization of the region, that is, in dealing more confidently as an organization with the post–cold war conditions that are unfolding. The ASEAN-sponsored Asia-Europe Meeting, the ARF, and the principle of one Southeast Asia are a few examples of the organization's growing initiative. An analysis of current security issues, however, suggests that ASEAN countries, economically devastated by the recent financial crisis, still require substantial external assistance, and that to strengthen ASEAN, the Japan-U.S. alliance will need to play an enhanced role in the region.

In the aftermath of the financial crisis it is clear that, although America's military forward deployment and its corresponding political and economic roles have helped keep Southeast Asia peaceful, stable, and prosperous, the cessation of economic growth, the underpinning of regional cohesion up to now, marks the beginning of the second phase of the post–cold war regional strategic order. It is likely that, as Dibb wrote, "[t]he new phase will be more uncertain and changeable than the previous period, from 1989–97" (Dibb et al. 1998, 6).

Now that the Japan-U.S. alliance has placed its emphasis on contributions to regional security, formulating and strengthening a Japan-U.S.-ASEAN nexus during the second phase would help assure the security of Southeast Asia. Prospects for Southeast Asian security hinge on how swiftly Japan and the United States can incorporate ASEAN into their common alliance agenda.

NOTES

1. Hadi Soesastro writes thus about public perceptions of ASEAN during the crisis: "The public has been largely disappointed with ASEAN. Its perception is that of a helpless ASEAN, an ASEAN that cannot move decisively, an ASEAN that is trapped under its organizational and bureaucratic weight, and an ASEAN that fails to respond to real, current problems and challenges" (1998, 373).

2. The analysis of the problems and possibilities of the Japan-U.S. alliance is partly based on discussions with Nishimura Mutsuyoshi, director-general of the European and Oceanian Affairs Bureau, Ministry of Foreign Affairs (19 December 1998) and Kent E. Calder, special advisor to the ambassador, American Embassy (23 January 1999).

3. For more about the critical role of the United States in East and Southeast Asia, see especially McDougall (1997) and McGrew (1998).

4. On the China threat issue, see especially Roy (1998) and Satō (1998).

5. On these points, see the *Far Eastern Economic Review* (5 February 1998, 22–23; 17 December 1998, 26–27).

6. For an overview of ASEAN, see Dosch and Mols (1998).

7. On the ASEAN way, see Chalmers (1996, especially chapter 2); Mak (1997); and Almonte (1997–1998).

8. This was later called the Manila Framework. See *Nihon Keizai Shimbun* (24 November 1997, 8).

9. According to the three points of the Fukuda Doctrine, Japan will never again become a military superpower; will seek to develop a heart-to-heart relationship with its Asian neighbors; and will support the economic development and stability of the entire region, including both Indochina and ASEAN.

10. The four points are (1) the termination of relations between Ranariddh and the Pol Pot faction, (2) an immediate truce between the government and Ranariddh's army, (3) an early return of Ranariddh and the offer of a royal pardon, and (4) the safe return of Ranariddh and his guaranteed participation in the coming election (*Yomiuri Shimbun* 19 February 1998). For an intriguing interview of Hun Sen on his "coup," see Ogura (1997).

11. More about the U.S. "failure" in Cambodia can be found in Kevin (1998).

12. On ASEAN's effort, see Almonte (1998).

13. Particularly, the two nations need to coordinate efforts toward establishing an assistance consortium, as Japan and the United States did for the Suharto regime in 1966.

14. For a superb analysis of the ARF, see Leifer (1996).

15. For information on the ARF, see the *Japan Times* (28 July 1998).

16. On this point, see Hernandez (1998).

17. A private think tank, the Japan Forum on International Relations, has proposed a North Pacific Cooperation Organization (*Japan Times* 20 April 1999, 1).

18. Nishihara Masashi suggests that "the Guidelines are intended to provide an indirect support for the ARF" (1997, 40).

19. For recent developments, see the *Far Eastern Economic Review* (9 December 1999, 24–25).

20. Philippine President Joseph Estrada advocates the ratification of the Visiting Forces Agreement and a strong American presence in Southeast Asia. For his interview, see *Nihon Keizai Shimbun* (17 April 1999, 7).

21. It is thus a welcome sign that the United States has decided to play a role in resolving the South China Sea conflict (*Nihon Keizai Shimbun* 10 July 1999, 6).

22. On the renewed Japan-U.S. alliance, see especially Mochizuki (1997) and Hosoya and Shinoda (1998).

23. On the four commitments, see *Gaikō Fōramu* (Special issue 1996, 162).

BIBLIOGRAPHY

Almonte, Jose. 1998. "The East Asian Crisis and the Effort to Engage Myanmar in Southeast Asia." Paper prepared for the ISDS/Konrad Adenauer Stiftung Conference. Metro Manila, the Philippines (28 November).

———. 1997–1998. "Ensuring Security the 'ASEAN Way'." *Survival* 39(4): 80–92.

Altbach, Eric. 1997. *The Asian Monetary Fund Proposal: A Case Study of Japanese Regional Leadership.* JEI Report (19 December). Washington, D.C.: Japan Economic Institute.

Chalmers, Malcolm. 1996. *Confidence-Building in South-East Asia.* Boulder: Westview Press.

Cronin, Richard. 1998. *Asian Financial Crisis: An Analysis of U.S. Foreign Policy Interests and Options.* Washington, D.C.: Congressional Research Service, Library of Congress (23 April).

Department of Defense. 1998. *The United States Security Strategy for the East Asia-Pacific Region.* Washington, D.C.: Department of Defense.

Dibb, Paul. 1995. *Towards a New Balance of Power in Asia.* Adelphi Paper No. 295. London: Oxford University Press.

Dibb, Paul et al. 1998. "The Strategic Implications of Asia's Economic Crisis." *Survival* 40(2): 5–26.

Dosch, Jörn, and Manfred Mols. 1998. "Thirty Years of ASEAN: Achievements and Challenges." *The Pacific Review* 11(2): 167–182.

Guan Ang Cheng. 1998. "Vietnam-China Relations since the End of the Cold War." *Asian Survey* 38(12): 1122–1141.

Harris, Stuart. 1997. "U.S.-Japan Relations in the New Asia-Pacific Order." In Chan Heng Chee, ed. *The New Asia-Pacific Order.* Singapore: Institute of Southeast Asian Studies.

Hernandez, Carolina. 1998. "Towards Re-Examining the Non-Intervention Principle in ASEAN Political Co-Operation." *Indonesian Quarterly* (Third Quarter): 164–170.

Hiramatsu Shigeo. 1999. *Chūgoku no gunjiryoku* (Chinese military power). Tokyo: Bungei Shunjū.

Hosoya Chihiro and Shinoda Nobuto, eds. 1998. *Redefining the Partnership.* Lanham: University Press of America.

Ikeda Tadashi. 1996. *Cambozia wahei e no michi* (The path toward the Cambodian peace). Tokyo: Toshishuppan.

Kevin, Tony. 1998. "U.S. Errs in Cambodia Policy." *Far Eastern Economic Review* (21 May): 37.

Leifer, Michael. 1996. *The ASEAN Regional Forum.* Adelphi Paper No. 302. London: Oxford University Press.

Lim, Robyn. 1998. "The ASEAN Regional Forum: Building on Sand." *Contemporary Southeast Asia* (August): 115–136.

Mak, J. N. 1997. "The 'ASEAN Way' and Transparency in South-East Asia." In Gill Bates and J. N. Mak, eds. *Arms, Transparency and Security in South-East Asia.* Oxford: Oxford University Press.

Mak, J. N., and B. A. Hamzah. 1996. "The External Marine Dimension of ASEAN Security." In Desmond Ball, ed. *The Transformation of Security in the Asia/Pacific Region.* London: Frank Cass.

McDougall, Derek. 1997. *The International Politics of the New Asia Pacific.* Boulder: Lynne Rienner.

McGrew, Anthony. 1998. "Restructuring Foreign and Defence Policy: the USA." In A. McGrew and Christopher Brook, eds. *Asia-Pacific in the New World Order.* London: Routledge.

Mochizuki, Mike, ed. 1997. *Toward a True Alliance: Restructuring U.S.-Japan Security Relations.* Washington, D.C.: Brookings Institution Press.

Morris, Stephen J. 1998. "Brutocray Wins." *Daily Yomiuri* (14 August): 10.

Narine, Shaun. 1997. "ASEAN and the ARF: The Limits of the ASEAN Way." *Asian Survey* 37(10): 961–978.

Nishihara Masashi. 1997. "Chiiki anzenhoshō no atarashii chitsujo wo meza-shite" (In search of a new regional security order). *Gaikō Fōramu* (November): 35–40.

Ogura Sadao. 1997. "Kanbozia seihen to kumēru rūju" (Cambodian political change and the Khmer Rouge). *Sekai* (November): 110–124.

Richardson, Michael. 1999. "ASEAN Struggles to Change Its Reputation as Weak, Helpless and Divided." *International Herald Tribune* (22 April): 4.

Roy, Denny. 1998. *China's Foreign Relations*. London: Macmillan.

Satō Hideo. 1998. "Japan's China Perceptions and its Policies in the Alliance with the United States." Discussion Papers. Stanford: Institute for International Studies, Stanford University.

Seekins, Donald. 1997. "Burma-China Relations: Playing with Fire." *Asian Survey* 37(6): 525–539.

Simon, Sheldon. 1998. "The Limits of Defense in Southeast Asia." *Journal of Asia and African Studies* (February): 62–75.

Simon, Sheldon, and Richard Ellings. 1996. "A Postscript on U.S. Policy." In R. Ellings and S. Simon, eds. *Southeast Asian Security in the New Millennium*. Armonk: M. E. Sharpe.

Soesastro, Hadi. 1998. "ASEAN during the Crisis." *ASEAN Economic Bulletin* (December): 373–381.

Storey, Ian. 1999. "Creeping Assertiveness: China, the Philippines and the South China Sea Dispute." *Contemporary Southeast Asia* (April): 95–118.

Tomoda Seki. 1992. "Japan's Search for a Political Role in Asia." *Japan Review of International Affairs* (Spring): 43–60.

Wanandi, Jusuf. 1998. "The Strategic Implications of the Economic Crisis in East Asia." *The Indonesian Quarterly* (First Quarter): 2–6.

Yamazawa Ippei. 1998. "The Asian Economic Crisis and Japan." *Developing Economies* (September): 332–351.

Yuen Foong Khong. 1997. "Making Bricks without Straw in the Asia Pacific?" *Pacific Review* 10(2): 289–300.

Economic Sanctions against Myanmar

Hoshino Eiichi

T HE United States is the first donor government to link foreign aid and human rights—especially political rights—in its foreign policy. The human rights diplomacy of the administration of U.S. President Jimmy Carter was emulated by the Netherlands, Norway, and Canada; Japan refrained from going with the tide until 1988, when it first attached political conditions to its assistance to Burma (renamed Myanmar in 1989). Tokyo did likewise with Beijing. In 1989, after having extended Overseas Development Assistance (ODA) and invested in China to support Deng Xiaoping's open policy and economic strategy of market reforms since the early 1980s, Japan applied negative sanctions in response to the June 4, 1989, Tiananmen Square crackdown. The sanctions were later adopted as policy under pressure from other Group of Seven (G-7) countries. When Japan lifted the sanctions against China a year later, it was among the first G-7 countries to do so.

The United States has tended to use negative sanctions, such as threats and punishment, in its human rights policies, while Japan prefers positive sanctions, such as reward and inducement.[1] The United States tends to isolate the targeted country, while Japan prefers to keep the door open. The U.S. approach can be called a North wind policy, and that of Japan a sunshine policy.

Japanese and U.S. policy differences are clear with regard to Myanmar. In mid-1996, as the U.S. Congress was discussing new sanctions against the Myanmar government in response to its arrest of opposition party members, Japan's Ministry of Foreign Affairs (MOFA) wanted to emphasize positive rather than negative sanctions. According to a spokesman: "A gradual democratization is what we can hope for. Full democratic institutionalization is too much to ask of Myanmar right now. . . . We have some doubts about the efficacy of Western human rights diplomacy, since Asian countries are at different levels of economic development. . . . The Burmese military government will bring democratization to the country after it achieves economic development. . . . Straightforward sanctions could deepen the antagonism between the government and the democracy movement" (*Asahi Shimbun* 17 July 1996, morning edition).[2]

This chapter examines the differences in the policies of Japan and the United States by comparing their use of sanctions against Myanmar, which provides an interesting case study for several reasons. First, it is an outstanding example of the gross violation of human rights. Bishop Desmond Tutu has called Myanmar "the South Africa of the nineties" (Larsen 1998, 3), and the condemnation of its military government by no less than seven Nobel Prize winners further complicates the way the world does business with Myanmar. Second, pursuit of the current Japanese and U.S. policies as regards Myanmar has the potential to create serious problems for the Japan-U.S. alliance. If Myanmar continues to stagnate economically, ASEAN countries with which Japan and the United States seek closer ties will not remain unaffected. An isolated Myanmar might lean toward China, perhaps allowing it direct passage to the Indian Ocean, and this could destabilize the regional security framework. Third, Myanmar could be a test case for other potential problem areas in the region, such as North Korea and China.

In April 1991, then-Prime Minister Kaifu Toshiki announced four major ODA policy principles that the Japanese government would henceforth consider when deciding whether to extend ODA: the recipient country's military spending; its arms exports and imports; its development and production of such weapons of mass destruction as nuclear missiles; and its efforts to promote democratization, ensure human rights, and move toward a market-oriented economy. These principles are the first example of Japan's post–cold war proactive foreign policy.[3]

Of the four factors, the fourth was seen as the new battleground for East-West confrontation in the post–cold war world. The winner of the cold war had declared that democracy and human rights were universal principles. In May 1990, the European Bank for Reconstruction and Development (EBRD), in stating the purpose of its establishment, attached the political conditions of promoting multiparty democracy, pluralism, and a market economy when extending economic assistance. The political communiqué of the G-7 countries at the 1990 Houston summit meeting expressed a similar commitment to supporting development through democratization, human rights, and a market-oriented economy.

Despite the worldwide trend toward democratization and increasing support for political conditionality, Japan and the United States have shown widely diverging stances on proffering and withholding aid. Inada Jūichi (1995) has explained these tendencies by suggesting that at issue are different national interests (political, economic, strategic, and regional), different cultural approaches (direct versus indirect, that is, negative as opposed to positive sanctions), and different domestic politics (interest groups and legislative concerns). These differences exist even as the United States and Japan share value systems and interests and are working toward a global partnership.

Similarly, when the MOFA press secretary was asked at a news conference what impact these differences had on the Japan-U.S. alliance, he replied: "Japan and the U.S. share the same value systems in terms of democracy and human rights. It is true that Japanese and U.S. policies toward Myanmar are not exactly the same, but the U.S. government understands the reason why Japan is pursuing its policies" (Ministry of Foreign Affairs 1998a).

The MOFA press secretary's confidence notwithstanding, there are signs of conflict between the United States and Japan on this issue. In 1996, the state of Massachusetts enacted the Myanmar sanctions bill, barring state agencies from making contracts with any U.S. or foreign company doing business in Myanmar. The European Union and Japan, both of which had business interests in Myanmar, appealed to the State Department and the World Trade Organization (WTO). U.S. business groups also filed a lawsuit challenging the legality of state and local sanctions on international trade (Greenberger 1998).

Given the various pressures from within and without, what policies can Japan and the United States adopt regarding Myanmar that will help keep the alliance healthy?

ECONOMIC SANCTIONS AND THE JAPAN-U.S. ALLIANCE

IMPACT OF POLICY DIFFERENCES ON THE ALLIANCE

Governments utilize a variety of tools to influence the policies of other governments. These tools, in order of increasing severity, include diplomatic persuasion, public appeals, noneconomic sanctions, economic sanctions, and military action. They may be applied either unilaterally or in conjunction with other countries through the United Nations or other international organizations.

As regards economic sanctions, Baldwin has used the term "economic statecraft" to refer to "influence attempts relying primarily on resources which have a reasonable semblance of a market price in terms of money" (1985, 13–14). Economic sanctions can be either positive or negative, such as increasing or limiting trade with a country, tariff reduction or discrimination, providing or suspending aid, allowing or restricting investment, and granting or withdrawal of most favored nation (MFN) treatment.

As regards Myanmar, the objectives of sanctions are critical when considering their impact on the Japan-U.S. alliance. Sanctions are employed for a wide range of purposes: to discourage the proliferation of weapons of mass destruction, discourage armed aggression, end support for terrorism, replace governments, promote human rights and democracy, stop drug trafficking, protect the environment, ensure market access, or ensure compliance with trade arrangements (Haass 1998).

On May 20, 1997, U.S. President Bill Clinton announced a ban on new investments in Myanmar. He cited two reasons: the continuing refusal by the ruling military junta, the State Law and Order Restoration Council (SLORC), to recognize the victory of the opposition party, the National League for Democracy (NLD), in the May 1990 general election, and the junta's confinement of opposition leader and Nobel Peace Prize winner Aung San Suu Kyi under house arrest for six years. This is a typical example of promoting democracy and human rights, whereby the United States is seeking to replace a current government with a more democratic one or, at least, have current policies made more democratic.

Historically, however, economic sanctions have a poor track record (Hufbauer, Schott, and Elliott 1990a). Between 1914 and 1990, various countries imposed economic sanctions in 116 cases. In 66 percent of these, the stated objectives were not achieved; in the remainder, the sanctions at best only partly succeeded in achieving their aims. Since 1973, the success rate for economic sanctions has fallen precipitously to 24 percent in all cases. When the stated objectives of the sanctions were a modest change in policy, such as settlement of an expropriation dispute or limited improvement in human rights, the success rate was 31 percent. When the stated objectives of the sanctions involved a major policy change, such as the United Nations (UN) campaign against South Africa to end apartheid, the success rate was only 25 percent.

Given this poor record, one may wonder why governments resort to economic sanctions so frequently. For example, one report notes that during President Clinton's first term, U.S. laws and executive orders imposed new unilateral economic sanctions sixty-one times on a total of thirty-five countries. The countries were home to 2.3 billion people, or 42 percent of the world's population, and they purchased exports of US$790 billion, or 19 percent of the global export market as of 1997 (National Association of Manufacturers 1997). The simple answer is that the sanctions must involve hidden or unstated goals. Miyagawa (1992) attempts to categorize these as follows: the rule-making effect, the demonstration effect, satisfying (or placating) domestic public opinion, satisfying international public opinion, the lifting of sanctions as a bargaining tactic, and undermining the target's strategic position.

With the rule-making effect, Miyagawa writes, the imposer of sanctions informs the world of the principles it believes others must observe. The demonstration effect means that by imposing the sanction, a government displays its firmness of conviction to the world. With the lifting of sanctions as a bargaining tactic, a government achieves its hidden objective by offering to lift the sanctions it has imposed if the targeted country refrains from certain behavior.

The different objectives by the two partners would obviously have an effect on the Japan-U.S. alliance.

Walt (1997) provides a useful framework for assessing factors that influence alliances. He says that an alliance can end for three reasons: changing perceptions of a threat, declining credibility of the alliance, and domestic political reasons. In terms of domestic political reasons, he specifies four factors: demographic and social trends that have weakened common bonds, domestic opposition, change of regime, and ideological differences. In turn an alliance endures, according to Walt, for four reasons: the strongest member of the alliance is willing to bear a burden to maintain it; the alliance is seen as a symbol of credibility; the self-interest of elite groups works to maintain it; and it has become institutionalized as a result of which there is bureaucratic inertia.

The different policies of Japan and the United States on economic sanctions could negatively affect the alliance directly or indirectly. The impact of practicing different policies may be weak when the alliance is faring well in most aspects of bilateral relations, but it is of serious concern when the cultural basis of nontariff barriers is considered a cause of trade conflicts. This is especially so in the post–cold war years, when the common enemy, the Soviet Union, has vanished and the alliance no longer serves as a fire-wall to prevent bilateral relations from deteriorating.

Policy differences due to differing values and objectives among policy-makers could have a direct effect on the alliance by triggering the loss of support for the alliance on one side, in this case among U.S. policymakers. Direct effects might also be seen in domestic opposition due to a perceived difference in values and objectives, thus bringing into question the cred-ibility of the alliance. The U.S. public and human rights lobbies might la-bel Japan as not abiding by their standards, which could lead to a loss of support for the alliance itself.

Indirectly, the alliance can be affected when the results of the policy or sanctions become problems for the alliance. For example, the credibility of the alliance may decline as a result of conflicting interests—strategically, economically, or ideologically.

If economic sanctions are harsh and there is room to maneuver, the tar-geted country might shift its stance away from the sanction-imposing gov-ernment and begin to favor that government's enemy. This shift in strategic configuration could affect the alliance partners differently, causing their strategic interests to conflict and thereby eroding the basis of the alliance.

The same is true for differing economic and ideological interests. Each alliance partner has its own economic relations with the targeted coun-try: While one partner might rely on the targeted country for imports of strategic resources, the other may hardly have any economic relations with it. Each alliance member must also take into account its own domestic po-litical situation: One might face strong interest groups or a legislative body that favors negative sanctions, while another might lack the domestic pres-sure necessary to support the imposition of such sanctions.

TWO STRATEGIES FOR ECONOMIC SANCTIONS

Lavin (1996) categorizes economic sanctions as either asphyxiation or oxygen strategy. Oxygen strategy relies on positive sanctions to influence a country's behavior, while asphyxiation strategy favors the use of negative sanctions.[4]

The oxygen strategy is supported by several arguments. The most com-mon holds that fast economic growth has the power to change whole so-cieties for the better. Growth improves the traditional order by creating diversity. "Thus neither highly centralized rule nor self-sufficient localism is any longer adequate; authority must be divided and shared in complex ways" (Lavin 1996, 101). Prosperity also creates a middle class that seeks greater political freedom. And economic and political development ends a country's isolation from other nations.

Lavin sees other arguments to support the oxygen approach: Economic development will put an end to a government monopoly, so that people no longer need to follow a party line or a government's dictates. Economic activity is a confidence-building measure, in that economic progress will induce authoritarian governments to behave better. Such strategies are more humane, leading to improved living conditions in the targeted country.

The asphyxiation strategy, on the other hand, attaches an economic cost to bad behavior and thus acts as a disincentive. The economic cost of sanctions can limit the targeted government's capacity to engage in the offending practices. At an extreme, economic sanctions could even result in a government being overthrown due to mass discontent or unhappiness within a leadership faction, thereby ending the intolerable behavior.

Negative sanctions can operate on a symbolic level as well. If a country wishes to demonstrate its objection to certain unacceptable behavior, then asphyxiation strategy fits the bill, since it is an active gesture while oxygen strategy is more or less passive. Negative sanctions send a clear political message. Even if they are economically toothless, they can suggest more serious moves to come.

In order for the asphyxiation strategy to work, Lavin wrote, four criteria need to be met: sufficiency, economics, confluence, and proportionality.

Sufficiency refers to the impact of economic sanctions on the targeted country. In this regard, the geography of the targeted country and the solidarity of the imposing nations are key factors. A country with few neighbors is more vulnerable to sanctions, and multilateral sanctions by solidly aligned nations have more impact than sanctions without solidarity. In any case, "the most important requirements for successful sanctions are largely outside the control of policy makers" (Lavin 1996, 103).

Economics—the targeted country's vulnerability to sanctions, and the imposer's economic relations with the targeted country—play an important role in this dynamic. The more the targeted country is dependent on, for example, inflows of fuel, hard currency, or high-technology weaponry, the more it is vulnerable to economic sanctions. Since economic sanctions have an equal and opposite effect on the imposer, the economy of the targeted country relative to that of the imposing country must be factored in.

The need for confluence implies that an asphyxiation strategy could raise the cost of unacceptable behavior, but it is rarely successful by itself. One key to success, therefore, is to target a country that is already burdened by other problems, such as a lack of popular support or engagement in a costly counterinsurgency.

Proportionality refers to the degree of results of the sanctions. That is, if other aspects, as described above, are not in order, economic sanctions will not fulfill serious foreign policy goals such as winning a war, toppling a government, or encouraging an administration to change core policies. Sanctions will be successful for only modest goals.

When, then, would it be wise to apply the oxygen strategy? Lavin's one critical criterion is that the targeted country have enough openness to allow economic benefits to flow broadly to the general population. An oxygen strategy is not simply the opposite of an asphyxiation strategy. It may be difficult to disrupt the targeted country's economy by negative sanctions, but it is still easier than stimulating it by positive sanctions. An asphyxiation strategy needs time to make its impact felt, but an oxygen strategy may need even longer. The growth of a middle class or the buildup of democratic pressure to relax an authoritarian political structure will not happen overnight.

It may perhaps appear a little simplistic to characterize the U.S. approach as an asphyxiation strategy and that of Japan as an oxygen strategy, since one can find cases in which both countries have practiced the other approach. Moreover, globally minded liberals and human rights organizations are often supporters of the asphyxiation strategy, while the business community is a paramount supporter of the oxygen approach. And, during the cold war with Iran, Nicaragua, the Philippines, South Korea, and Chile, among other countries, "Washington . . . show[ed] as great an indifference to democracy and human rights as Tokyo" (Seekins 1992, 368). With these variations in mind, we can set forth four courses for coordinating sanctions policies between Japan and the United States (table 1).[5]

Examples can be found of partial engagement policies, in which one party applies an oxygen strategy and the other imposes sanctions, as well

Table 1. Four Alternatives for Coordinating Sanctions Policies

	Japan	
	Asphyxiation	*Oxygen*
U.S.		
Asphyxiation	Disengagement	Partial Engagement (Japan as sunshine)
Oxygen	Partial Engagement (U.S. as sunshine)	Engagement

as cases in which both parties adopt similar strategies. The response of both Japan and the United States just after the nuclear bomb tests by India and Pakistan constituted a typical case of disengagement, while their recent relations with China are a typical display of engagement. The Korean peninsula presents a rare example of partial engagement, with the United States adopting an oxygen strategy: The United States is trying to induce North Korean cooperation through the offer of economic assistance and diplomatic channels, yet Japan is unwilling to follow suit. Myanmar, however, is a more typical example of partial engagement, with Japan following an oxygen strategy.

THE LAST TEN YEARS

SANCTIONS AGAINST MYANMAR IN 1990

In March 1988, police mismanagement of a minor incident in Rangoon resulted in the death of forty-two students. Prodemocracy demonstrations broke out all over the country, fueled by widely felt frustration about the military government's mismanagement of the economy. The government responded with a brutal crackdown on demonstrators, imposed a curfew in major cities, detained hundreds of protesters, and closed down universities.[6]

In July 1988, General Ne Win, de facto leader of Burma since 1962, resigned as the chairman of the ruling Burma Socialist Programme Party (BSPP). He was succeeded by General Sein Lwin, who had been responsible for suppressing the earlier protests as head of the security police. Thousands marched through Rangoon and other cities demanding the removal of President Sein Lwin, the release of those detained earlier, the establishment of a multiparty political system, and free elections. Security forces fired on these unarmed demonstrators, killing at least 3,000 in Rangoon alone, according to estimates by diplomats. The U.S. Senate unanimously passed a resolution condemning the Burmese government for its brutality and called for the restoration of democracy.

In August, Sein Lwin resigned as BSPP chairman and was replaced by former Attorney General Maung Maung. Prodemocracy protests resumed, although with less violence. West Germany, the second largest foreign donor to Burma, suspended all economic assistance. Japan, the largest donor, also suspended aid "until Burma attains liberty and democracy" (*Far Eastern Economic Review* 22 September 1988, quoted in Hufbauer, Schott, and Elliott 1990b, 611).

On September 18, President Maung Maung was replaced by General Saw Maung, the chairman of the newly established SLORC. He announced that elections would be held but only after law and order were restored. Washington suspended all foreign assistance, with the exception of humanitarian aid, and cancelled the scheduled delivery of already purchased ammunition to the Burmese Army.

In late September, the Japanese ambassador to Burma met with Burmese foreign ministry officials and confirmed that economic aid was in a "state of suspension." He urged the government to avoid further bloodshed and to pursue a "democratic political settlement reflecting the general consensus of the Burmese people" (Hufbauer, Schott, and Elliott 1990b, 611). In January 1989, Japan formally suspended indefinitely all aid to Burma. This represented the first Japanese use of negative sanctions.

In mid-February of 1989, President Saw Maung announced that elections would be held in May 1990. In response, Japan recognized Saw Maung's government, but stipulated that recognition should not be construed as conveying moral support for the regime. Japan defended its action by claiming that recognition granted Japan access to higher levels of the Burmese government, which would allow it to press the case for free elections and economic reform. Disbursement of aid previously approved was resumed on a case-by-case basis where "individual circumstances allow," but no new aid programs were instituted (*Far Eastern Economic Review* 16 March 1989, quoted in Hufbauer, Schott, and Elliott 1990b, 612).

In June, opposition leader Aung San Suu Kyi was quoted in the *Bangkok Post* as calling on foreign countries to impose a complete economic boycott on Burma, including a trade embargo, until the regime followed through on its promise to hold elections. In July, the military government placed Aung San Suu Kyi and U Tin Oo, another NLD leader, under house arrest. Mistreatment of political prisoners, including torture, was reported to be widespread. U Tin Oo was later convicted of subversion and sentenced to three years of hard labor.

The Burmese government responded to international criticism by "simply deny[ing] that it [was] violating human rights. On 22 November 1989, President Saw Maung accused unnamed foreign powers of attempting to bring about the 'disintegration of the state under a new form of colonialism'" (*Far Eastern Economic Review* 21 December 1989, 22, quoted in Hufbauer, Schott, and Elliott 1990b, 614).

In January 1990, U Nu, a former prime minister (1948–1962) and now an opposition leader, was placed under house arrest, and Aung San Suu

Kyi was barred from participating in the elections in May. Japan's MOFA responded with a statement expressing its "disappointment" over the decision. In the spring, the U.S. Senate voted 92–0 to ban imports from Myanmar, and the House of Representatives soon approved the measure. The *Financial Times* reported in May that there were calls for the European Community to take similar action (25 May 1990, quoted in Hufbauer, Schott, and Elliott 1990b, 613).

In May, despite the widespread detention of demonstrators, house arrest of opposition leaders, and harassment of opposition supporters, the NLD won a large majority of seats in the National Assembly. At that point, however, the military government announced that it could not turn over power until the Assembly completed a new constitution, which could take years. General Saw Maung stressed that, even after the new government took power, the military would not back away from its "basic duties: preventing disintegration of the nation and national solidarity, and defending national independence and sovereignty" (*Washington Post* 29 May 1990; *Financial Times* 21 June 1990, quoted in Hufbauer, Schott, and Elliott 1990b, 613). The military government remains in power today, having in November 1997 been renamed the State Peace and Development Council (SPDC).

After examining the impact of economic sanctions against Myanmar, Hufbauer, Schott, and Elliott (1990b, 617) quoted two assessments from the *Far Eastern Economic Review*: "There seems to be a general feeling among other diplomats in Rangoon that Japan's and Australia's decisions to reestablish relations with Rangoon were premature, undermining the efforts of other democratic countries to bring pressure on the military regime to institute political and economic reforms. . . . Their critics say the early resumption of aid has let the regime off the hook and made it even less likely that free and fair elections will be held" (19 October 1989, 19).

An unnamed Western diplomat in Myanmar noted: "External pressure is . . . believed to have played an important role in forcing the [regime] to make sure the polls were not fraudulent. . . . Every time a foreign government condemns human-rights abuses in Burma, the regime loses face in front of its own population, and that's very important" (*Far Eastern Economic Review* 7 June 1990, 11).

MYANMAR POLICIES DURING THE 1990S

In October 1991, Aung San Suu Kyi was awarded the Nobel Peace Prize, which focused world attention on the repressive policies of the SLORC and triggered a wave of domestic demonstrations on behalf of the imprisoned opposition leader. The government responded by shutting down universities in the capital, arresting protesters, and mounting a dry-season campaign against dissident minorities, especially Karen insurgents along the Thai border.[7]

By spring 1994, the Clinton administration had begun a diplomatic campaign to further isolate the military regime in Myanmar and was considering economic sanctions aimed at forcing the government to improve its human rights record. The U.S. administration asked several countries, including China, to cease arms sales to Myanmar, and asked United Nations Secretary General Boutros Boutros-Ghali to make a personal appeal to the government of Yangon (the new name adopted for Rangoon in 1994) to free Aung San Suu Kyi. Since 1990, when the military government refused to honor the results of the national elections, Congress had pressed for a tougher policy toward Myanmar. The actions by the Clinton administration stopped short of the severity of the measures advocated by Congress, such as a ban on imports of gems and timber, but they went further than the steps taken by the preceding administration of President George Bush (Lippman 1994).

Japan had recognized the new government of Myanmar five months after the military coup and before the national election planned for 1990, and then resumed suspended projects that had been begun before 1988. Disbursements after the suspension was lifted reportedly included monies for these projects, emergency humanitarian aid, and grant aid for debt relief, which was based on a 1978 resolution by the United Nations Conference on Trade and Development (UNCTAD).

In early 1994, however, Japan decided to refreeze its economic assistance to Myanmar, although it was willing to initiate small grants, amounting to several million yen per project. This grass-roots ODA was aimed at helping local nongovernmental organizations (NGOs), not the Myanmar government. A MOFA official explained that this kind of ODA would directly assist the many Burmese people who were suffering economically. The ministry's decision was also reported to the U.S. government (*Kyōdō Tsūshin* 17 February 1994).

During 1994, senior Myanmar government officials in a change of strategy met twice with Aung San Suu Kyi. A highly publicized ninety-minute meeting on September 20 yielded little more, however, than a number of photographs that were displayed on television. Details were similarly lacking of a three-hour session on October 28 between Aung San Suu Kyi and a delegation headed by the SLORC first secretary.

In November, Deputy Assistant Secretary of State Thomas Hubbard, who had been a member of a U.S. delegation to Myanmar, noted in a speech to members of "The Friends of Burma at Harvard" that the United States would be observing the situation in Myanmar carefully over the next few months. Hubbard said, "We hope that a substantive dialogue will result between Aung San Suu Kyi and the SLORC, and that Aung San Suu Kyi will be released, the sooner the better. We also urge that all the other political prisoners in Burma be released" (1994).

The Japanese response was more forbearing. There would be no new loans to Myanmar for airports or electrical power stations until Aung San Suu Kyi was released and the government democratized, but Japan was still planning to offer a nearly ¥1 billion grant in emergency and humanitarian aid, including medical supplies and aid to hospitals in Yangon. Among Japanese business circles, however, there were expectations that the government would refreeze ODA. The United States was also reportedly seeking dialogue with the Myanmar government at this time (*Kyōdō Tsūshin* 8 November 1994).

It was not until July 10, 1995, nearly six years after her confinement, that the world's most celebrated prisoner of conscience was given her freedom. Following her release from house arrest, Aung San Suu Kyi called for reconciliation between the democracy movement and the SLORC leadership, but the NLD delegation pulled out of the national convention in November, insisting that the body had displayed scant interest in democratic reform.

At the end of July 1995, Japanese Foreign Minister Kōno Yōhei met with Myanmar's Foreign Minister Ohn Gyaw at the Brunei International Airport. Kōno described the release of Aung San Suu Kyi as a brave decision and requested further democratization and improvement of human rights conditions by the Myanmar regime. At the same time, he officially announced that Japan would gradually resume the yen loan projects that had been frozen since 1988 (*Kyōdō Tsūshin* 31 July 1995).

In response, an official from the U.S. State Department, meeting with the House Subcommittee on the Asian-Pacific Region in September, stated that the United States opposed Japan's decision on the gradual resumption of loan projects in Myanmar. The U.S. government, he stated, did not support Japan's constructive engagement policy and would not improve diplomatic relations with Myanmar until there was evidence of further democratization. However, the official also opposed the Republican suggestion that more severe sanctions should be imposed, arguing that to do so would be counterproductive (*Kyōdō Tsūshin* 8 September 1995).

In May 1996, in advance of a planned NLD congress, some 260 party members were arrested, reducing the number of attendees to eighteen. In September, between 500 and 800 NLD supporters were reportedly arrested when they attempted to hold another congress at Aung San Suu Kyi's house.

In June 1996, special envoys who had been dispatched to Asia Pacific earlier in the month reported to the White House that Association of Southeast Asian (ASEAN) members and Japan shared the United States' fundamental concerns about Myanmar. They also shared the U.S. view that peace and stability could only come about through dialogue between the ruling authorities and the democratic opposition, led by Aung San Suu Kyi. In a statement issued on June 20, the White House (1996) stated that the envoys believed their mission to have enhanced the basis for productive discussions on the link between political dialogue, stability in Myanmar, and Myanmar's successful integration into the region. Nevertheless, this statement did not mean that Japanese and U.S. policies toward Myanmar were coordinated, or that ASEAN nations agreed with U.S. policies on economic sanctions.

According to Hirose (1996), leaders of ASEAN countries disagreed with the U.S. human rights diplomacy and the isolation policy it had applied to Myanmar. They preferred to support Myanmar's economic development, to seek further improvement in the standard of living, and to try to encourage the military regime to soften its stance. ASEAN leaders expressed the belief that isolating Myanmar would cause instability in the region and that Myanmar's domestic stability required maintaining the current military government. Myanmar's Minister of Finance and Revenue Win Tin told the press that U.S. sanctions would be in vain and would have no impact on the country's economy.

Still, the U.S. stance was clear. In December 1996, U.S. Ambassador to the United Nations Madeleine Albright addressed the United Nations General Assembly, calling on Myanmar to stop its abuse of human rights, release political prisoners, and start talks with democratic leaders. Unless Myanmar stopped the repression of its people, she said, the international community would continue to speak out against the government. On April 22, 1997, President Clinton announced a ban on new U.S. investment in Myanmar.

The Japanese stance was one of neither isolation nor full engagement. The government decided not to emulate the U.S. sanction prohibiting new investment, but announced it would retain its previous plan of not issuing new yen loans. The government also announced that Prime Minister Hashimoto Ryūtarō's support for Myanmar's membership in ASEAN was unchanged. A MOFA official said it was important to pursue dialogue with both SLORC and the NLD, and that Japan would encourage Myanmar's democratization through constructive engagement rather than merely applying sanctions (*Yomiuri Shimbun* 4 May 1997).

In March 1998, the Japanese government decided to release ¥2.5 billion out of a frozen ¥27 billion loan for the Rangoon International Airport.

In October 1998, President Clinton sent Congress a required report on conditions in Myanmar and U.S. policy toward Myanmar for the period from March 28 to September 28, 1998. "The people of Burma continue to live under a highly repressive, authoritarian military regime that is widely condemned for its serious human rights abuses," the report notes. "The reorganization and renaming of Burma's ruling military junta in November 1997 through which the . . . SLORC . . . became the State Peace and Development Council (SPDC) did not herald significant policy changes" (Clinton 1998).

The report goes on to say that the Myanmar economy was deteriorating due to "SPDC economic mismanagement, combined with spill-over effects from the Asian financial crisis. . . . As a result of sanctions and the ongoing financial crisis in much of the rest of Southeast Asia, approvals of new foreign direct investment in Burma fell by 65 percent in fiscal year 97/98, contributing to the financial collapse of the Burmese economy. U.S. and European investors continue to pull out of Burma due to the unfavorable political situation. While the government's own mismanagement contributes to the problem, the SPDC is unlikely to find a way out of the crisis unless political developments in Burma permit an easing of restrictions on lending by international financial institutions" (Clinton 1998). The United States remains engaged in multilateral diplomacy to encourage ASEAN, Japan, Korea, China, the European Union (EU), and other nations to also take steps to encourage the SPDC to reform.

THE SANCTIONS DEBATE

U.S. sanctions and Japanese engagement were both the targets of criticism by observers. Auerbach wrote in *The Washington Post*: "They [the U.S. sanctions] sound tough, but in practice they often end up helping the very people who are supposed to be punished. . . . Yet in the post–cold war world, with the United States the dominant superpower and crisis breaking out around the globe, economic sanctions have become the weapon of choice. 'What else do you do?' asked a frustrated U.S. diplomat. 'Sanctions are better than war and they are easier to get through the United Nations than permission to . . . use military force'" (1993).

Unocal Corp., a California-based firm that was building a natural gas pipeline from Myanmar to Thailand, weighed in as well. "Economic engagement, not isolation, is the best way to promote positive change," said a spokesman for the company, the largest U.S. investor in Burma (Mintier 1997). Unocal Chairman Roger Beach, who was in Thailand when the sanctions were announced, stated flatly that unilateral sanctions don't work, and he declared that the big losers in this case would be U.S. companies, not the government in Yangon.

In an editorial in the *Washington Post*, Rodman complained of a double standard. "The Clinton administration's economic sanctions against Burma have been criticized as a cop-out by human-rights advocates for whom China is the target most deserving of challenge. Burma is a tiny country, and its heavy-handed military junta, the SLORC, has no defenders. Therefore it was an easier target to go after. China got a pass" (1997).

Moreover, Rodman went on, "Burma, as the West isolates it, is rapidly developing closer ties with China. Political, economic, military and intelligence links between the two are expanding. China is wooing Burma, with a likely aim of achieving naval access to the Bay of Bengal and Indian Ocean—a quantum leap in China's strategic position in Asia" (1997).[8]

Rodman's point, in fact, is a major reason that ASEAN leaders disagree with the U.S. policy of isolating Myanmar and are eager to recruit Myanmar to ASEAN: They want to counter the Chinese attempt to suborn Myanmar as a military ally. Rodman concluded, "The West's sanctions on Burma are thus a great strategic boon to China. The law of unintended consequences is at work here, as in so many other instances where Americans seek moral ends without all that much care as to the practical effects" (1997).

Leon Hadar, adjunct scholar at the Cato Institute, agreed with Unocal Chairman Beach: "The U.S. policy of imposing unilateral trade and investment sanctions against Burma has proven to be a failure on all fronts. By forcing U.S. firms to disengage from Burma, that policy has harmed American economic interests and done nothing to improve the living conditions or human rights of the people of Burma" (1998).

Hadar added: "Unilateral sanctions have alienated our allies in the region and strengthened the hand of China but achieved none of the stated foreign policy aims. If Washington had allowed the Association of Southeast

Asian Nations to take the lead in setting policy toward Burma, the United States could have enjoyed a 'win-win' situation—better relations with our allies and more influence over the regime in Rangoon" (1998).

As for Japan's policy, some have argued that it was based largely on economic considerations. They say that just as economic interests in Myanmar, which is rich in human and natural resources, lie behind ASEAN's constructive engagement policy, the basis for Japan's oxygen policy is the opportunism of Japanese business, which is looking to invest in Vietnam as well as Myanmar. For example, Japan's recognition of the Burmese government in February 1989, some contend, was strongly influenced by the lobbying of the Japan-Burma Association (as it was then known), which had asked MOFA in January that year to resume aid projects so that related Japanese businesses would not have to stockpile goods and supplies for shipment to Myanmar (Mainichi Shimbunsha Shakaibu 1990).

A point repeatedly heard is that positive measures only help the military regime. NGO activists concerned with human rights have declared that Aung San Suu Kyi has been under de facto house arrest since October 1997 and that human rights conditions in Myanmar have been deteriorating since July 1995 (*Weekly Burma Today*, special edition, 10 April 1998). ASEAN's policy of constructive engagement has failed, they say. In an interview with *Business Week*, Aung San Suu Kyi herself called for keeping economic sanctions against Myanmar intact, claiming that investment would not help the people but would give moral support to the military regime (*Weekly Burma Today*, no. 12, 26 March 1998).

Finally, there were calls in the media for Japan to apply greater pressure to convince SLORC to initiate a dialogue with the NLD. Some commented that since constructive engagement had not been effective, Japan needed to persuade ASEAN that this approach should be abandoned (Ōno 1996).

NO ROOM FOR PARTNERSHIP?

A COMMON AGENDA

The June 1996 statement of the Japan-U.S. Common Agenda includes civil society and democratization as global issues that the two countries of the partnership should pursue. This was a specific reference to giving support to newly democratic countries in their preparations for elections and a new system of law. But is such a partnership possible for promoting democratization in Myanmar?

When in March 1998 the Japanese government reactivated that part of the frozen yen loan projects earmarked for Rangoon International Airport, the United States made its stance clear. The U.S. government, State Department spokesman James Foley declared, would not support the restart of any large-scale economic assistance to Myanmar until its record on human rights and drug trafficking improved. Japan's reopening of its ODA channel, Secretary of State Albright asserted, would send the wrong signal to the military government (*Yomiuri Shimbun* 28 February 1998).

In response to Foley's statement, a MOFA spokesman explained that Japan was defreezing the yen loan only as a measure to prevent serious accidents from occurring at the airport in the near future, and that the Japanese government believed the United States understood Japan's stance. The spokesman added that Foley had not said specifically that the United States opposed Tokyo's decision; when questioned again on this, he repeated that Foley had simply used the words "do not support" with regard to the U.S. stance (Ministry of Foreign Affairs 1998b).

It is clear that the sanction policies of these global partners were not coordinated. According to Yamada (1998) of the *Mainichi Shimbun*, some MOFA officials were frustrated by the U.S. double standard, saying that Washington was harsh on Myanmar but soft on Israel and China, where national interests were involved. Yamada added that some LDP members argued that Japan needed to officially state that the national interests of the two countries were not identical.

In 1998, Japan's stance appeared to waver. In May, Prime Minister Hashimoto sent a letter to the Myanmar government calling for greater democratization (*Kyōdō Tsūshin* 28 May 1988), at the same time that the *Yomiuri Shimbun* reported that Tokyo had mapped out a course to start new yen loans for humanitarian assistance and public welfare (20 July 1998). This would have constituted the most significant change in Myanmar policy since 1988. Within a week, however, a MOFA official clarified Japan's position, stating no new yen loans would be offered to Myanmar until the country cleared a path to democratization. Japan's restarting a small-scale humanitarian grant in 1995 and unfreezing a part of its frozen yen loan in March clearly did not constitute a real change in Japan's ODA policy toward Myanmar (*Yomiuri Shimbun* 24 July 1998).

A few months later, the partners seemed to be back on the same track. In July in Manila, Kōmura Masahiko, then a MOFA vice minister, criticized the Yangon government's rejection of Japanese and U.S. requests for a meeting with Aung San Suu Kyi (*Yomiuri Shimbun* 30 July 1998). In September in New York, Kōmura, now the minister of foreign affairs, indicated to

Secretary of State Albright that Japan would not offer any more financial support to Myanmar (*Weekly Burma Today*, no. 37, 1 October 1998).

REASONS FOR ENGAGEMENT AND SANCTIONS

The Japanese tendency to give and the U.S. tendency to hold back can be considered in three contexts: national interests (ideological, economic, and strategic), approaches (sunshine versus the North wind), and domestic politics (legislative bodies, business circles, and human rights NGOs). These can be better understood by looking at three corresponding types of criticism often levied against Japan's ODA Charter. Advocates of the separation of politics from economics argue that, as for the first context, national interests should not play a role in foreign aid programs (Murai 1996). With regard to engagement versus the sanctions approach, the second context, advocates of Asian values and critics of U.S. double standards often argue that Western values are not necessarily Japanese values, and that Japan does not have to follow the American way in formulating its foreign aid policies. As for the third context, advocates of human rights and democracy, who are themselves players in domestic politics, often say that either Japan is not serious about these principles, or it has a hidden agenda (Hoshino 1999).

Ideology constitutes an important part of U.S. national interests. As Senator Jesse Helms wrote: "The price tag for U.S. economic sanctions comes to a whopping US$3.77 per American. . . . That is a small price to pay for a moral foreign policy—and a price most Americans are willing to bear. . . . Americans do not need to sell their souls or their national security to create jobs and economic prosperity" (1999, 7). It is clear that such a stance involves much more than just influential lobbies or playing to opinion polls.

Inada (1995) maintains that the United States and Japan share value systems and interests, and are working toward a global partnership. The MOFA press secretary essentially said the same when questioned about possible conflict with the United States with regard to Myanmar: Japan and the United States share the same value system in terms of democracy and human rights and, while U.S. and Japanese policies toward Myanmar are not exactly the same, U.S. officials understand Japan's intentions because of Tokyo's continuing efforts to communicate them (Ministry of Foreign Affairs 1998a).

How about economic interests? U.S. trade with Myanmar was largely inactive during the eighties and nineties (fig. 1). In 1996, U.S. exports to Asia

Figure 1. Japan and U.S. Trade with Myanmar

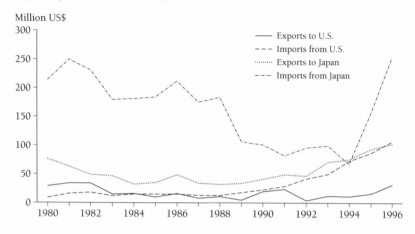

totaled US$144 billion, while exports to Myanmar came to only US$32 million. While total U.S. imports from Asia were US$213 billion, imports from Myanmar came to just US$107 million. Trade with Myanmar constitutes less than 1 percent of total trade in Asia for the United States.[9] Japan, however, has closer economic ties with Myanmar. In 1996, it imported US$102 million in goods from that country and exported to it US$254 million worth of goods.

American investment in Myanmar has been limited. In 1997, the United States was only the fourth-largest overseas investor in the country, with US$582 million committed to sixteen projects in the gas and oil sector (Mintier 1997). Japanese investment in Myanmar has been even more limited, with US$33 million in total at the end of fiscal year 1996. Most foreign investment in Myanmar comes from European or other Asian countries. By the end of October 1998, foreign direct investment in Myanmar had reached around US$7 billion, from twenty-three sources for 303 projects. Singapore, the United Kingdom, Thailand, and Malaysia have the largest investments there (*Weekly Burma Today*, no. 6, 11 February 1999).

Because of the size of its investments in Myanmar, the U.S. ban on new investment was mainly symbolic, but it could have greater meaning now. With the Asian financial crisis, foreign investment in Myanmar dropped by more than half to US$1.2 billion in fiscal year 1997 (*Weekly Burma Today*, no. 22, 11 June 1998). The Merchant International Group of London ranked Myanmar the fifth most risky country in the world, citing its political risks as well as bureaucratic corruption, inequitable markets, radical

Figure 2. Japanese and U.S. ODA to Myanmar

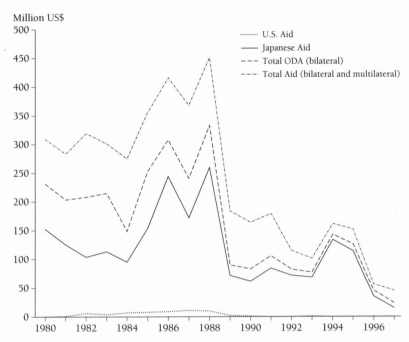

Million US$

Legend:
- U.S. Aid
- Japanese Aid
- Total ODA (bilateral)
- Total Aid (bilateral and multilateral)

opposition, and a poor communications infrastructure (*Weekly Burma To-day*, no. 19, 21 May 1998).

Japan has been the largest donor of development aid to Myanmar (fig. 2). U.S. aid to Myanmar, on the other hand, has been negligible. Over the last ten to fifteen years, Japan's ODA has represented between 70 percent and 90 percent of the nation's total bilateral aid flow, and about 60 percent of its total aid flow. Japan delivered ¥512 billion worth of development assistance (¥403 billion in loans and ¥109 billion in grants) to Myanmar between 1968 and 1988. Weissink suggests that Japan had a say in the BSPP's decision in July 1988 to pursue economic liberalization. "Just before the SLORC took over in 1988, Japan warned the former regime that it would reconsider its economic relations with Burma if economic reforms were not undertaken" (Weissink 1997). Weissink argues, therefore, that Japan could have much more leverage over policymaking in today's Myanmar.

Myanmar was one of the ten largest recipients of Japanese ODA before 1989. It was the fourth-largest recipient in 1980, fifth in 1986, eighth in

1987, and seventh in 1988. Seekins suggests that "such generosity was as much a recognition of the country's future potential as it was domestic pressures to create porkbarrel projects . . . which would benefit Japanese companies" (Seekins 1992, 372). Others would point out that a "special relationship" has existed between Japan and Myanmar since World War II. "Myanmar was the first Asian country to sign a reparations and peace agreement with Japan. [It] was also the first to allow the Japanese government access to the country to search for, and retrieve, the remains of their soldiers killed in action" (Dobbs-Higginson 1996).

A strategic factor here is China, which is probably the main reason ASEAN maintains its policy of constructive engagement.[10] As Weissink quoted from the *Far Eastern Economic Review*'s *Asia 1996 Yearbook*, "Officials readily admit privately that Burma's political system is not the issue: fear of Chinese expansion south, through weak countries such as Burma, is. . . . Rather than attempting to promote democracy in Burma, ASEAN wants to 'constructively engage' the present government in Rangoon to wean it away from too dependent a relationship with Beijing" (*Asia 1996 Yearbook*, quoted in Weissink 1997).

Not only ASEAN but also Japan—and probably India, too—would have serious reason to feel threatened if China gained a foothold in the Strait of Malacca. Mutō Kabun, former Japanese foreign affairs minister, has spoken of China's intention to go south to the Indian Ocean, and argued the need for a balancing act by assisting Myanmar together with ASEAN (*Yomiuri Shimbun* 24 March 1998). According to Weissink, "China has been helping develop naval facilities, including a base at Hajinggy Island and upgrading existing naval bases at Sittwe (Akyab), Mergui, and an intelligence signal's station (SIGINT) on Great Coco Island" (1997).[11]

MOFA officials communicated their strategic analysis to their U.S. counterparts, according to Sasajima (1998). When Japan supported ASEAN's decision to welcome Myanmar as a member, MOFA officials did not openly link the Japanese stance with their concerns about China, for obvious reasons. Washington, on the other hand, was not greatly worried about China's strong ties with the military government in Yangon, and it, therefore, along with the EU, opposed ASEAN's constructive engagement policy. Steinberg (1998) argues that Washington could afford a moral foreign policy in the case of Myanmar because there is little at stake in terms of national interests.

The ODA White Paper of 1996 further delineates the Japanese approach when it explains how the principles of the ODA Charter are applied.[12] In general, the principles are not automatically applied to every instance. Credibility is important, but the rigid application of rules can have drawbacks. Differences in national interests can easily lead to conflict in economic sanction policies. If partners, on the other hand, agree on serious common interests, the terms of the dialogue as well as the outcome of sanction policies would be improved.

Asphyxiation versus oxygen, the North wind versus sunshine, or crafting democracy through direct assistance versus facilitating democratization through economic assistance—these are the differences in approach between the United States and Japan. Behind these different approaches are different understandings of the dynamic process of democratization: the classical modernization thesis, the relatively new crafting democracy thesis, and the Asian way thesis (Hoshino 1997, 2–3).

The mainstream scholarship of the sixties and seventies focused on necessary conditions for the emergence of a stable democracy: modernization and wealth ("the more well-to-do a nation, the greater the chances that it will sustain democracy"), political culture, and social structure ("no bourgeois, no democracy") (Hoshino 1997, 2–3).

When a MOFA official said that full democratic institutionalization would be too much to ask of Myanmar and that SLORC would bring democratization to the country after its economy developed, we heard echoes of the classical modernization thesis. The military regime would agree with the tone of such arguments and assert that, given Myanmar's immaturity as a state, it cannot under current circumstances accept democracy and liberalization, as Aung San Suu Kyi requests. In other words, democracy and human rights are luxuries that only a developed society can afford.

The crafting democracy thesis can be seen in "the widespread sense of optimism that [democracy] can be crafted and promoted in all sorts of places, including those where structural and cultural qualities are deemed unfavorable or even hostile" (Shin 1994, 161). Huntington's *The Third Wave* (1991) is a typical example of "crafting democracy" literature. Of particular interest is his "Guidelines for Democratizers," or steps for reforming and overthrowing authoritarian regimes.

Huntington (1991) cites two international factors that have worked for so-called third wave democracies: democratic pressures from other countries and assistance from international organizations, as well as diffusion (an international snowballing effect). The latter occurs because countries seem to face similar problems, because democratization seems like a cure for internal problems, and because a democratized country is viewed as a political and cultural model. In general, however, large, socially cohesive countries with strong economies are much less susceptible to international pressure than are small and socioeconomically weak countries. The strong countries are likely to assign higher priority to other goals, such as security and economic interests (Sorensen 1993).

The Asian way thesis, which posits the uniqueness of the Asian tradition and cultural mores, is voiced by many leaders of East Asian and Southeast Asian countries, who accuse the U.S. and other Western governments of trying to impose Western mores on them. At the World Conference on Human Rights meeting held in Bangkok in March 1993, Asian leaders criticized "any attempt to use human rights as a conditionality for extending development assistance."[13]

Inoguchi (1997) warns there are two straw men in this debate: one is ultra-Orientalism, the other ultra-universalism. Inoguchi dismisses both views as extreme and suggests that Asian values be looked at in the context of political economy. The Japanese government tends to understand the Asian way arguments, but does not join the ultra-Orientalism school.[14]

Another way of considering the divergent approaches between the United States and Japan to aid and sanctions is to look at democratization in terms of two dimensions: the cultural dimension (universality versus pluralism) and the economic-development-toward-democratization dimension (preconditions of democracy versus crafting democracy). Japan would seem to favor pluralism and the preconditions of democracy, while the United States tends more toward believing in universality and a country's ability to craft democracy.[15]

There is another important factor to consider: domestic politics. In Japan, human rights NGOs (like Amnesty International) and Diet members —some of whom belong to the International Network of Political Leaders Promoting Democracy in Burma (PD Burma)—have stridently opposed assistance to the SLORC, and subsequently SPDC, regimes.[16] However, there has also been support for assistance, in particular among business groups, like the Japan Myanmar Association, which are working to reactivate ODA to Myanmar. Neither side, however, is strong enough to spur active public debate among policymakers, academics, or the media. Seekins points out that the significant difference between Japan and the United States is "the lack of powerful domestic constituencies in Japan who actively pressure the government on human rights issues" (1992, 368). More than 75 percent of the respondents to a national poll in October 1996 voiced positive views about the current ODA policy, so the government has continued in the same direction.

Seekins speculates that, under this calm surface, a good deal of jockeying for position is going on. In trying to explain Japan's generosity to Myanmar, he writes that a "truncated pyramid" with no "peak" or "institutional incoherence in Japan may have made the system particularly vulnerable to determined lobbying by Ne Win and his cronies through dedicated 'friends' of Burma" (1992, 373). This argument is reminiscent of Bonner's description (1987) of U.S. aid to Marcos's Philippines.

In the United States, the Congress and human rights NGOs such as BurmaNet have urged a firm stance against the SPDC, while business groups, like USA*Engage, have pushed for engagement.[17] The government finds itself in the middle of the sanctions debate. According to Steinberg, hardliners dominate the silent majority in Congress. "Most Congress members are not supporting economic sanctions against Myanmar, but they cannot vote against the bill, because they do not want to be labeled supporters of the military regime" (Steinberg 1998). Dobbs-Higginson is harsh in his judgment of public opinion: "For everyone in the United States, Myanmar is a soft, risk-free, human rights target, which, irrespective of the facts, people from all walks of life, from politicians to students, can abuse with a great sense of both righteousness and that they are making a positive contribution" (1996).

Yet, state and local legislation could well derive from moral considerations and ethics-driven public opinion. By the end of 1996, one state and eight cities in the United States had adopted measures seeking to penalize business entities trading or investing in Myanmar (Schmahmann and Finch 1997). The Massachusetts sanctions bill, also known as the Massachusetts Burma Law, bars Massachusetts state agencies from buying goods or services from companies doing business in Burma. As Schmahmann and Finch note, "The fact that serious questions remain about the constitutionality of these local forays into foreign affairs may largely be due to the significant political disincentives to challenging their constitutionality. Few corporations would have been bold enough to challenge a community's censure of apartheid, and not many more will want to be perceived as supporting the SLORC regime in remote Burma" (1997).

Japan and the EU were bold enough to challenge these state and local laws. In October 1998, they called for a WTO dispute panel on the Massachusetts Burma Law. Rita Hayes, deputy U.S. trade representative and U.S.

representative to the WTO, noted, "The U.S. regrets and is disappointed that the EU and Japan have again taken the step of requesting a panel, given the strong interest of all three parties in improving the human rights situation in Burma. The U.S. remains concerned about the extensive abuses of human rights by the SLORC [SPDC] regime in Burma, which has been internationally condemned" (Hayes 1998).[18]

HOW TO PROCEED

FOUR POLICY ALTERNATIVES

According to Human Rights Watch, Myanmar continues to be "one of the world's pariah states" (1999). More than 1,000 people have been imprisoned as a result of the standoff between opposition leader Aung San Suu Kyi and the country's military rulers. In this climate, how should the United States and Japan proceed? Disengagement, partial engagement (with either Japan or the United States as oxygen), and engagement are, as discussed earlier, the policy alternatives.

Disengagement is asphyxiation by both alliance partners.[19] The United States has good reason to follow this policy in terms of its ideological interests and domestic political concerns. Japan, absent its fear of losing its global partnership with the United States, has much less reason.

When sanction policies are coordinated, there is no direct negative effect on the alliance, and any indirect effect is related to the outcome of the sanctions. But even were this the case for Japan and the United States, the ruling SPDC would be unlikely to loosen its control over the country, and prospects for democratization and economic development in the near future would be unlikely to improve. Should isolation make Yangon more dependent on Beijing, Tokyo would feel the need to protect its sea lanes, either alone or with the help of its alliance partner. If the United States failed to respond in a way perceived to be appropriate, tension between the two countries would grow. Thus, disengagement does not offer the alliance much gain, and there is the chance that it could bring harm.

Given ASEAN's constructive engagement policy, Weissink proposes playing the game good cop, bad cop with Myanmar (Weissink 1997). Japan, the United States, and the EU could be the bad cop and put pressure on the SPDC, while ASEAN, as the good cop, could offer the regime the option of resigning without a complete loss of face. He argues that this "concerted approach" is more realistic "as it would circumvent the [SPDC] having the feeling of being cornered and subsequently forced to jump into

China's lap while the ASEAN would not lose face by giving in to the West over its constructive engagement policy" (Weissink 1997).

Partial engagement with Japan as the oxygen is a variation of the good cop, bad cop ploy, according to which the United States and the EU play the bad cop to Japan and ASEAN's good cop. Japan has good reason to choose the oxygen policy in terms of its economic and strategic interests, while the United States would probably be content with the asphyxiation policy.

When two countries in an alliance follow different policies, the effects can be both direct and indirect. In terms of direct effects, policymakers in the respective countries would understand the differences and try not to harm the alliance. The perception, however, that Japan has chosen a path not in accordance with universal moral standards could lead to a loss of support for the alliance among the American public. Conversely, if Washington pushed Tokyo to play the role of bad cop, the result could be lower Japanese public support for the alliance.

Partial engagement could imply negative indirect effects. The United States might face being isolated from Southeast Asian countries, unless they made concerted efforts and pursued some policy coordination. In terms of outcome, this kind of partial engagement would be as realistic as Weissink's concerted approach. Thus, partial engagement with Japan as the oxygen may result in lower support for the alliance at home, but it could garner some political improvements in Myanmar.

Partial engagement with the United States as the oxygen is the most unlikely alternative of these policy alternatives. Outside of pressure from business groups, the United States has little incentive to choose an oxygen policy. Nor does Japan have much interest in pursuing an asphyxiation policy.

Engagement is the last policy alternative to be examined here. Although Japan has good reason to choose engagement in terms of economic and strategic interests, the United States has no such incentive.

When sanction policies do not differ, as in the case of the disengagement alternative above, there is no direct negative effect on the alliance, and any indirect effect is related to the outcome of the sanction. But even if both countries engage Myanmar, it would be too optimistic to expect the economic situation to improve immediately. Assuming that there are preconditions for democratization, democracy in Myanmar would be a long time coming. From the crafting democracy perspective, democratization would depend on a negotiated settlement between the government and the opposition. But given the military regime's current stability, engagement by too many good cop governments might leave the SPDC feeling that it need not make many concessions or easily cede power. Thus, while engagement would not hurt the alliance, Japan and the United States would not gain much from it either.

So which policy alternative would be most viable for these global partners to pursue? Six factors emerge as critical determinants: first, policies must be synchronized, so that there are no negative direct effects on the alliance. Second, ideological interests must be respected, even if sanctions are largely symbolic. Third, neither the United States nor Japan should be isolated from ASEAN countries. Fourth, it would be unwise to isolate Myanmar or push it into a corner. Fifth, the use of positive sanctions for building democratic institutions could be effective. Sixth, and finally, economic development and civilian pain are no less important than political gain.

CONDITIONAL ENGAGEMENT

The objectives of the sanctions were clearly stated in 1995 at the Halifax, Nova Scotia, Group of Seven summit: "We call on the Government of Myanmar to release Aung San Suu Kyi and other political prisoners, without conditions, and to engage in a dialogue of reconciliation aimed at the full and early realization of democracy and national unity" (Chairman's Statement 1995).

Unfortunately, the world is not a perfect place where individual human rights, and collective rights such as sovereignty, are respected without conflict. And no one policy can right wrongs in the face of widespread abuses of human rights and collective rights, as is the case in Myanmar. Each policy alternative comes with drawbacks.

Under such circumstances, it may be that conditional engagement is the most effective choice for the Japan-U.S. alliance to pursue. It may also be the least dangerous.[20]

An oxygen policy of conditional engagement would utilize both positive and negative sanctions. It would not be a simple sunshine orientation. The 1996 ODA White Paper (Ministry of Foreign Affairs 1996) gives examples of Japan's oxygen policy, which includes positive as well as negative sanctions. When favorable progress according to principles in the ODA Charter are observed, Japan will support the country by extending economic assistance (positive sanctions). When unfavorable events take place, Japan will try to bring about change, first through diplomatic channels, then through the freezing of ODA. If the situation still does not improve, Japan will reduce assistance (negative sanction).

Based on his interview with a MOFA official, Orr (1995) describes the three stages of Japan's negative sanctions as follows: The first is to try to influence through ODA and diplomatic channels; the second is to stop the delivery of ODA within one year if the recipient does not demonstrate respect for ODA principles; and the third is to reduce the aid commitment from the next year if there is no change. The third stage—that is to say, the reductions—will continue until the recipient complies or aid is completely eliminated. This could be an appropriate manner of giving and holding back in this conditional engagement alternative.

How can this oxygen policy be applied so that it is viable? In accordance with the six aforementioned factors for viability, it is first necessary for Japan and the United States to apply the oxygen in harmony, to avoid negative direct effects on the alliance. Acting together for the same objectives also helps to assure public support for the alliance.

Disengagement might be a warranted response, but a more modest approach may be necessary to help developed countries overcome Third World resentment of the North's imperialist past and the huge gap between the rich North and the poor South, and their criticism of the serious problems (high rates of homicide, divorce, drug problems, and other social diseases) found in Western societies. While there is no direct bearing between the right to criticize a political situation on one hand, and past immoral behavior or present flaws on the other, sensitivity is required. As Ōnuma argues, in many instances self-righteousness, double standards, and excessive aggressiveness on the part of the West have hurt the cause of human rights and democracy, and have been counterproductive. Prudent behavior in a less hypocritical and less self-righteous manner is "particularly needed in international relations, where national pride and the memory of a resentful past play a significant role" (1996, 10). Displays of modesty and an openness to self-criticism by the developed nations would help secure greater acceptance of the notions of human rights and democracy by developing countries.

Second, in order to satisfy ideological interests, a clear message should be sent to the targeted country. In some cases, this could be done by symbolic sanctions. As Van Ness (1997) notes, the power of symbolic sanctions can be magnified when the targeted government has a self-image of moral superiority, or when it is vulnerable to domestic challenges to its legitimacy. At least with Myanmar, the latter would seem to be the case.

Third, although this engagement policy differs from ASEAN's constructive engagement, it would not work to isolate Japan or the United States from ASEAN countries. Rather, Weissink (1997) proposes, if the two countries took a concerted approach, the differences could be constructive, as with a good cop, bad cop strategy. With this approach, he notes, Japan, the United States, and the ASEAN nations should meet privately to discuss their course of action and clarify their intentions.

Fourth, while an asphyxiation policy would isolate Myanmar by shutting down communication channels, an oxygen approach would keep them open. Conditional engagement is not a series of incremental concessions; it utilizes both positive and negative sanctions. Washington would need to establish an open channel with Yangon in order to effectively utilize the sanctions.

Fifth, the use of positive sanctions for building democratic institutions would be effective. Reuters reported in November 1998 that the United Nations and the World Bank had held secret talks with Yangon in which they offered financial assistance if the Myanmar government would begin a dialogue with the opposition. According to the report, diplomats conceded that "given the tough economic conditions prevailing in Myanmar, the 'dollar diplomacy' concept might be a novel way to attract the cash-strapped government's attention" (CNN 27 November 1998). If the world's two largest aid donors do not use this option at their disposal, no one can, particularly in light of the recent Asian financial crisis.

In the same Reuters report, one diplomat was quoted as saying, "Inflation is very high, the economy is in bad shape and the people are facing lots of hardships. It could be a good time and way for a meeting of minds" (CNN 27 November 1998). This raises the issue of the importance of the sixth factor, that of economic development and "civilian pain" (Weiss et al. 1997). Japan's ODA White Paper speaks of the need to consider the people in recipient countries: "In the event it decides for some reason to suspend aid to a given developing country, Japan should be flexible enough to exempt, for example, humanitarian or emergency aid, or aid given through international organizations or NGOs" (Ministry of Foreign Affairs 1997, 73). This consideration should be applied by both alliance partners in their policy toward Myanmar.

Three specific conditions should be attached to any conditional engagement policy. One is the principle of reciprocity, which allows a government to demonstrate its modesty and tolerance for self-criticism in international diplomacy. For example, several months after the Tiananmen Square uprising on June 4, 1989, when Beijing began to engage in its own "human rights diplomacy," Australia sent two delegations to China. Canberra then invited Beijing to send a human rights delegation to Australia to inspect the workings of Western democracy (Van Ness 1999). This Australian model could be an interesting addition to the terms of engagement, especially in view of Amnesty International's report of poor human rights conditions within the United States itself, the first such censure among developed countries (*Yomiuri Shimbun* 8 October 1998).

A second condition is consistency, which enhances the legitimacy of sanctions for democracy, which in turn helps local promoters of democratization gain more support within their country. It is also appreciated by other developing countries, which are critical of the double standards of Western sanctions (Ōnuma 1996). It is natural for countries not to sacrifice their national interests for the sake of promoting democracy in other nations, but it is still important to be as consistent as possible.

A third and final condition is the use of positive sanctions that directly assist democratization. In this regard, Japan should learn from the U.S. approach of helping to establish an infrastructure for democracy as part of its official assistance. The National Endowment for Democracy (NED) is another example, as it works to reform the legal system, welfare and education systems, and mass media. At Myanmar's request, technical training in these areas could also be given through NGOs.

Haass describes the alternative to straightforward economic sanctions as constructive or conditional engagement, like the policy proposed in this chapter. "Such an approach, involving a mix of narrow sanctions and limited political and economic interactions that are conditioned on specified behavioral changes, might be preferable, especially if the goal is to weaken the near-monopoly of an authoritarian leadership over a country like Cuba, Iran, or China" (Haass 1997, 85). Myanmar certainly qualifies to be on that list.

Inoguchi argues that the Japanese ODA Charter needs "a careful application, taking into account regional and cultural sensitivities" (1997, 20). If this caveat is given full consideration, it would seem that a conditional engagement policy vis-à-vis Myanmar would be a viable sanctions option for Japan and the United States.

NOTES

1. On positive and negative sanctions, see Baldwin (1985) and Van Ness (1997).
   2. Similar statements about the State Law and Order Restoration Council and

the National League for Democracy were repeated by the MOFA press secretary on March 12, 1997, and February 27, 1998.

3. On Kaifu's stipulation of the four ODA policy principles, Alan Rix wrote, "It sprang both from post-Gulf War attitudes that Japan needed to do more to contribute to the maintenance of international security, and from a desire to redress Japan's reputation for commercialism in its aid philosophy" (1993, 34).

4. The following arguments in this section rely mainly on Lavin (1996).

5. To further differentiate policies, we could classify asphyxiation policies in terms of (1) ODA and other government-government relations, and (2) trade, investment, and other market relations. This categorization has not been adopted in this chapter, however, since, in the case of Myanmar, rapid development of market relations is not likely without government support.

6. The following descriptions in this section rely on Hufbauer, Schott, and Elliott (1990b).

7. The following descriptions in this section rely mainly on Banks and Muller (1998).

8. According to Rodman: "In June 1994, Japanese sources reported that China had completed construction of radar bases on Burma's two islands in the Indian Ocean—Great Coco and Little Coco—which are on lease to China. Work was also about to begin on a port. In January 1996, SLORC Chairman General Than Shwe visited Beijing, where he and Chinese President Jiang Zemin had 'warm and friendly' talks reflecting their 'extensive consensus on major regional and international issues.' In April 1996, General Zhang Wannian, vice chairman of China's Central Military Commission, paid a six-day visit to Myanmar and hailed the 'good-neighborly friendship' between the two countries. In October 1996, General Zhang invited General Maung Aye, vice chairman of SLORC, for a return visit to Beijing. Premier Li Peng received him and praised the expansion of military exchanges between China and Burma" (1997, 29 May).

9. These figures do not include estimates of U.S. exports transshipped through third countries, such as Singapore. See Preeg (1999, 130).

10. Leszek Buszynski (1998) lists two other benefits of constructive engagement from the viewpoint of the Thai government: economic benefits and border security.

11. Weissink also argues, "Effective Chinese control over Myanmar would diminish the chance of the latter becoming a democratic nation" (1997).

12. First, military expenditures, democratization, and human rights are sensitive issues closely connected with a developing country's security issues and domestic politics. It is impossible to define a clear threshold for suspending or extending aid. Second, positive and negative actions may occur at the same time. In such cases it would not be appropriate to utilize some negative sanctions that assume only negative actions. Third, in order to avoid unnecessary rebuffs from the recipients, Japan's first move should be an attempt to influence through dialogue. A country's socioeconomic situation and Japan's bilateral relations should

be comprehensively considered when judging the use of negative sanctions. Japan should not use sanctions based on a given threshold or absolute criteria, but it should watch trends over time, especially in terms of military expenditure and arms transfers.

13. See, for example, Roy (1994), Mahbubani (1993), Kausikan (1993), and the Chinese Information Office of the State Council (1991).

14. Robert Orr (1995) argues that, in their different conceptions of democracy, the United States emphasizes individual rights and Japan cares more about group rights, and that the United States pursues participation and Japan prefers political stability.

15. Robert Orr (1995) says that Americans tend to believe that a democratic political system is a prerequisite for economic growth, while Japanese tend to believe social stability and an authoritarian system are the prerequisites for economic growth that will be followed by democratization.

16. See <http://www.jca.ax.apc.org/~kotetu/burma/pdburma/whats.html> for the PD Burma website.

17. See <http://burma.net> and <http://www.freeburma.org> for information on human rights NGOs, and see <http://www.usaengage.org> for USA*Engage.

18. It was surprising to read that, two weeks after its enactment, the Massachusetts Burma Law was announced unconstitutional by a U.S. Federal Court in Boston. It was not surprising, though, to learn that the plaintiff was the National Foreign Trade Conference (NFTC), a business network of more than 500 companies, including thirty that had been banned from doing business in Massachusetts (*Kyōdō Tsūshin* 6 November 1998).

19. If we differentiate asphyxiation policies into those that deal with ODA and other government-to-government relations from those that deal with trade, investment, and other market relations, one could persuasively argue that it's best to "let the market prevail." But if this argument assumes that ODA money goes directly to the military government, then it misses the point. In the case of Myanmar, the main economic actors are closely linked to generals in the government.

20. Preeg suggests a similar policy alternative, using the phrase "proactive flexible engagement" (1999, 140–142).

BIBLIOGRAPHY

Asahi Shimbun "Enjo" Shuzaihan. 1985. *Enjo tojōkoku Nippon* (Japan: The developing country in aid). Tokyo: Asahi Shimbunsha.

Auerbach, Stuart. 1993. "Are Sanctions More Harmful Than Helpful? Experts Say Embargoes Enrich Targets, Hurt Poor." *Washington Post* (28 March): H1.

Baldwin, David A. 1985. *Economic Statecraft*. Princeton, N.J.: Princeton University Press.

Banks, Arthur S., and Thomas C. Muller, eds. 1998. *Political Handbook of the World: 1998*. Binghamton, N.Y.: CSA Publications.

Bonner, Raymond. 1987. *Waltzing with a Dictator: The Marcoses and the Making of American Policy.* New York: Times Books.

Buszynski, Leszek. 1998. "Thailand and Myanmar: The perils of 'constructive engagement'." *Pacific Review* 11 (2): 290–305.

Chairman's Statement at the Halifax Summit. 1995. Halifax, Nova Scotia (17 June).

Chinese Information Office of the State Council. 1991. "Human Rights in China." *Beijing Review* 44.

Clinton, Bill. 1998. "Text: March 28 to Sept. 28, 1998 Report on Conditions in Burma (SPDC has made no progress toward democratization)." (23 November).

Dobbs-Higginson, M. S. 1996. "Myanmar: A Chance Too Good to Miss." *Japan Times* (3 July): 19.

Greenberger, Robert S. 1998. "State and Local Sanctions Trouble U.S. Trade Partners." *Wall Street Journal* (1 April). <http://www.usaengage.org/news/980401wsj.html>. (5 August 2000).

Haass, Richard N. 1997. "Sanctioning Madness." *Foreign Affairs* 76 (6): 74–85.

———. ed. 1998. *Economic Sanctions and American Diplomacy*. New York: The Council on Foreign Relations, Inc.

Hadar, Leon T. 1998. "U.S. Sanctions against Burma: A Failure on All Fronts." *Trade Policy Analysis* 1 (26 March). <http://www.freetrade.org/pubs/pas/tpa-001.html>. (5 August 2000).

Hayes, Rita. 1998. "Text: Dustr Hayes 10/20 Statement on Massachusetts Burma Law (U.S. regrets EU, Japan requesting WTO dispute panel)." (20 October).

Helms, Jesse. 1999. "What Sanctions Epidemic?: U.S. Business' Curious Crusade." *Foreign Affairs* 78 (1): 2–8.

Hirose Kinshirō. 1996. "Myanmā-no minshuka undō danatsu, Bei tokushi-no settoku fuhatsu" (Suppression of the democracy movement in Myanmar: U.S. delegate failed to persuade). *Mainichi Shimbun* (18 June).

Hoshino Eiichi. 1997. *Crafting Democracy or Promoting Democratization: U.S. Foreign Aid for Democracy*. Tokyo: FASID.

———. 1999. "Human Rights and Development Aid: Japan after the ODA Charter." In Peter Van Ness, ed. *Debating Human Rights: Critical Essays from the United States and Asia*. London: Routledge.

Hubbard, Thomas. 1994. "Hubbard: Burma Needs Changes to Improve Relations with U.S. (DAS Hubbard remarks to Harvard Burma group 11/28/94)." (28 November).

Hufbauer, Gary Clyde, Jeffrey J. Schott, and Kimberly Ann Elliott. 1990a. *Economic Sanctions Reconsidered: History and Current Policy.* Second edition. Washington, D.C.: Institute for International Economics.

———. 1990b. *Economic Sanctions Reconsidered: Supplemental Case Histories.* Second edition. Washington, D.C.: Institute for International Economics.

Human Rights Watch. 1999. *The 1999 Human Rights Watch Report.* <http://www.hrw.org/worldreport99/asia/burma.html>. (August 2000).

Huntington, Samuel P. 1991. *The Third Wave: Democratization in the Late Twentieth Century.* Norman: University of Oklahoma Press.

Inada Jūichi. 1995. "Jinken minshuka to enjo seisaku" (Human rights, democratization, and aid policy). *Kokusai Mondai,* no. 422 (May): 2–17.

Inoguchi Takashi. 1997. "Asian Values and Japanese Official Development Assistance." In Matsumae Tatsurō and Lincoln C. Chen, eds. *In Pursuit of Common Values in Asia.* Tokyo: Tokai University Press.

Kausikan, Bilahari. 1993. "Asia's Different Standard." *Foreign Policy* 92 (Fall): 24–41.

Larsen, Jenseine. 1998. "Crude Investment: The Case of the Yadana Pipeline in Burma." *Bulletin of Concerned Asian Scholars* 30 (3): 3–13.

Lavin, Franklin L. 1996. "Asphyxiation or Oxygen? The Sanctions Dilemma." In Charles W. Keglry, Jr., and Eugene R. Wittkopf, eds. 1998. *The Global Agenda: Issues and Perspectives.* Fifth edition. Boston: McGraw-Hill.

Lippman, Thomas W. 1994. "U.S. Steps Up Campaign To Isolate Burma Rulers: Relaxed Human Rights Policy Is Sought." *Washington Post* (26 March).

Mahbubani, Kishore 1993. "The Dangers of Decadence." *Foreign Affairs* 72 (4): 10–14.

Mainichi Shimbunsha Shakaibu. 1990. *Kokusai enjo bijinesu* (International aid business). Tokyo: Aki Shobō.

Mintier, Tom. 1997. "U.S. businesses criticize Burma sanctions, Some say restrictions will hurt U.S." <http://cnn.com> (24 April).

Ministry of Foreign Affairs. 1996. *Waga kuni no seifu kaihatsu enjo* (Japan's official development assistance). Tokyo: Kokusai Kyōryoku Suishin Kyōkai (APIC: Association for Promotion of International Cooperation).

———. 1997. *Waga kuni no seifu kaihatsu enjo* (Japan's official development assistance). Tokyo: Kokusai Kyōryoku Suishin Kyōkai (APIC: Association for Promotion of International Cooperation).

———. 1998a. 27 February. <http://www.mofa.go.jp/mofaj/gaiko/happyo/kaiken/kako/>. (5 August 2000).

———. 1998b. 3 March. <http://www.mofa.go.jp/mofaj/gaiko/happyo/kaiken/kako/>. (5 August 2000).

Miyagawa Makio. 1992. *Do Economic Sanctions Work?* New York: St. Martin's Press.

Murai Yoshinori. 1996. "The New Choice for Japan in the Age of 'Sustainable Development.'" *Heiwa Kenkyū,* 21 (November).

National Association of Manufacturers. 1997. *A Catalog of New U.S. Unilateral Economic Sanctions for Foreign Policy Purposes, 1993–96.* Washington, D.C.: National Association of Manufacturers.

Ōno Shun. 1996. "Myanmā eno Nihon no seisaku, 'Taiyō rosen' no minaoshi-wo" (Japan's policy toward Myanmar: Reconsider the 'Sunshine Policy'). *Mainichi Shimbun* (12 June).

Ōnuma Yasuaki. 1996. "In Quest of Intercivilizational Human Rights." Occasional Paper No. 2. Tokyo: Center for Asian Pacific Affairs, Asia Foundation.

Orr, Robert M., Jr. 1995. "Taigai enjo to nichibei kan no seijiteki kadai (Foreign aid and political issues for the United States and Japan). Ichikawa Hiroya, ed. *Posuto reisen jidai no kaihatsu enjo to nichibei kyōryoku* (Common vision, different paths). Tokyo: Kokusai Kaihatsu Jahnarusha.

Preeg, Ernest H. 1999. *Feeling Good or Doing Good with Sanctions: Unilateral Economic Sanctions and the U.S. National Interest.* Washington, D.C.: Center for Strategic and International Studies.

Rix, Alan. 1993. *Japan's Foreign Aid Challenge: Policy Reform and Aid Leadership.* New York: Routledge.

Rodman, Peter W. 1997. "The Burma Dilemma." Editorial, *Washington Post* (29 May).

Roy, Denny. 1994. "Singapore, China, and the 'Soft Authoritarian' Challenge." *Asian Survey* 34 (3): 231–242.

Sasajima Masahiko. 1998. "Myanmā-e en-shakkan saikai, Chūgoku-no sekkin keikai, paipu kakuho nerau" (Resuming yen loans to Myanmar: Cautious about approaching China, hoping to keep high-level contact). *Yomiuri Shimbun* (6 March).

Schmahmann, David, and James Finch. 1997. "The Unconstitutionality of State and Local Enactments in the United States Restricting Business Ties with Burma (Myanmar)." *Vanderbilt Journal of Transnational Law* 30 (2) (May): <http://www.vanderbilt.edu/Law/journal/home.html>. (5 August 2000).

Seekins, Donald M. 1992. "Burma's Relations with Japan: Some Preliminary Observations." *Ryudai Law Review* 48: 459–478.

Shin, D. C. 1994. "On the Third Wave of Democratization." *World Politics* 47: 135–170.

Sorensen, G. 1993. *Democracy and Democratization.* Boulder, Colo.: Westview Press.

Steinberg, David I. 1998. "Tairitsu-tōron, Myanmā shien" (Opposing opinions: Aid to Myanmar). *Yomiuri Shimbun* (24 March).

Van Ness, Peter. 1997. "Understanding Japan's ODA as International Sanctions: The Case of Sino-Japanese Relations." Matsumae Tatsurō and Lincoln C. Chen, eds. *In Pursuit of Common Values in Asia.* Tokyo: Tōkai University Press.

———. 1999. "Conclusion." In Peter Van Ness, ed. *Debating Human Rights: Critical Essays from the United States and Asia.* London: Routledge.

Walt, Stephen. 1997. "Why Alliances Endure or Collapse." *Survival* 39 (1).

Weiss, Thomas G., David Cartright, George A. Lopez, and Larry Minear, eds. 1997. *Political Gain and Civilian Pain: Humanitarian Impacts of Economic Sanctions.* Lanham: Rowman & Littlefield.

Weissink, Alexander. 1997. "A Concerted Approach towards Myanmar." *IIAS Newsletter* 11 (Winter). <http://iias.leidenuniv.nl/kreenft/IIASNONLINE/Newsletters/Newsletter11/Regional/11CDEA01.html>. (5 August 2000).

White House. 1996. "Japan, ASEAN Countries Share U.S. Views on Burma (Text: White House statement on Burma envoys' return)." (20 June).

Yamada Ken. 1998. "Myanmā eno en shakkan saikai, Bei no 'nijū kijun' ni hanpatsu" (Resuming yen loans to Myanmar: Opposing the U.S. "double standard"). *Mainichi Shimbun* (8 March).

Combating Arms Proliferation

Miyasaka Naofumi

T HE purpose of this chapter is to analyze the asymmetrical responses of the United States and Japan to arms proliferation by nonstate actors and to propose a cooperative policy on this issue in order to strengthen the Japan-U.S. alliance.

The end of the cold war and the breakup of the Soviet Union have produced a new international security environment with new dangers. Among these hazards are what the U.S. government terms transnational threats[1]—perils that stem from activities of such nonstate actors as terrorists, drug traffickers, and criminal organizations, or from situations involving uncontrolled refugee migrations, illicit arms trafficking, or environmental pollution. The threats are seen by the administration of U.S. President Bill Clinton as posing a possible challenge to U.S. national interests in the immediate or long term. This expanded notion of security is derived partly from the U.S. role as the world's sole superpower. In the U.S. national security community, transnational threats or, as they are often called, nontraditional threats, have provoked a great deal of controversy (Stares 1998).

It is obvious that Japan, like the United States, is not immune to threat, particularly if we focus on arms proliferation by violent nonstate actors. Japan has been attacked by two of the world's most notorious terrorist organizations, namely, the Japanese Red Army and Aum Shinrikyō. Asian criminal organizations have penetrated Japanese society, and the smuggling of weapons and drugs is an everyday occurrence. Analysts often point out that Japan is unprotected against unconventional warfare. Japan has repeatedly shown a national vulnerability in the face of terrorist attacks, not only because of legal restraints and lack of political leadership, but also due to poor information-gathering and the lack of a system for response. In addition, Japan is surrounded by totalitarian North Korea, communist China, isolated Taiwan, unstable Russia, and its "distant" neighbor, South Korea. The power structures and mutual histories of relations with these countries have caused Japan to concentrate on a state-to-state or traditional national security framework. In particular, this has meant aiming to deter warfare through the alliance with the United States and that country's military power, and promoting confidence-building measures (CBMs) among states.

It is a mistake to believe that transnational threats should be excluded from consideration when assessing national security issues. Some may say that it is necessary to distinguish between domestic public safety and national security, but reality blurs the concept of security, because nonstate actors transcend national borders and choose weapons freely. Whether they threaten public safety or national security is of no concern to them.

On a broader level, Japan should utilize transnational threats to help craft a more flexible and robust Japan-U.S. alliance for the twenty-first century. If we underestimate the threats, Japan-U.S. relations will deteriorate. Even now, in responding to specific threats, the alliance has experienced undercurrents of dissatisfaction, frustration, and misunderstanding. It is imperative that both governments coordinate and integrate their respective policies in order to respond more effectively to the threats and avoid friction.

The Japan-U.S. alliance, in contrast to other U.S. alliances, has not yet taken measures to prevent and counter arms proliferation by nonstate actors. Since the current Japanese Constitution allows such cooperation, to do more in this area would serve the national interests of both countries.

This chapter explores the question of alliance-based cooperation by examining four related themes. First, it reviews the changing nature of arms proliferation in the post–cold war world. Second, it examines the policies and perceptions of the United States and Japan toward the proliferation of weapons of mass destruction (WMD), and third, it considers their policies concerning the proliferation of small arms by nonstate actors. Finally, with reference to current bilateral treaties between the United States and its allies, it provides the basic components of a comprehensive strategy for combating arms proliferation by nonstate actors.

PROLIFERATION BY NONSTATE ACTORS

In the post–cold war security environment, the nature of arms proliferation has changed considerably. Nations retain large arsenals, but the cast of actors in armed conflicts has gradually changed from nations to nonstate actors. In fact, over the past ten years, interstate conflicts like the Gulf War and the Peru-Ecuador border hostilities have been the exception. As many studies indicate, most armed conflicts in the 1990s were intrastate wars involving nonstate actors.

The comprehensive term nonstate actor can be used to refer to all kinds of illegitimate armed groups and individuals, including terrorist organizations, paramilitary guerrilla groups, cults or fanatic organizations, crime syndicates, drug cartels, mercenaries, individuals, pirates, armed refugees, and breakaway units of a state's military, intelligence, or police services (Falkenrath 1998). Some have solid organizational structures, while others are linked loosely, if at all. The usual practice is to clearly label each actor according to one of the above descriptions and, in fact, at United Nations (UN) conferences, terrorism, organized crime, drug trafficking, and mercenaries are addressed separately. The reality, however, is that the ways and means employed by these actors overlap at many points. A common feature is that actors often operate across borders and threaten the lives of ordinary people regardless of their objectives. But whatever they are called, what is important for our purposes is not the objective or ideology but, rather, the actors' choice of weapons.

Nonstate actors tend to use either weapons of mass destruction—nuclear, radioactive, biological, and chemical—or small arms and light weapons.[2] The latter category is the more common but, as past records demonstrate, the possibility that WMD may be used cannot be ignored. Between the two categories are the so-called conventional weapons, such as tanks, ships, and aircraft, as categorized in the United Nations Register of Conventional Arms and the Conventional Armed Forces in Europe (CFE) convention. For financial and technical reasons, conventional weapons tend not to be used by illegitimate nonstate actors.

The international community has already established nonproliferation schemes and total bans on WMD at the state level, including the Nonproliferation Treaty (NPT) and the Comprehensive Test Ban Treaty (CTBT) for nuclear weapons, the Chemical Weapons Conventions (CWC), and the Biological Weapons Conventions (BWC). But the United States is clearly not only concerned about regional powers such as India, Pakistan, and Israel, and the so-called rogue states such as North Korea, Iraq, and Iran, but also about the above-mentioned illegitimate nonstate actors. Samuel Burger (1999), assistant to the U.S. president for national security affairs, has pointed to the likelihood of rogue states supplying terrorist organizations with WMD. Sophisticated WMD with delivery systems may still be confined to a small number of states, but rudimentary chemical and biological weapons are increasingly common choices for nonstate actors. The technological knowledge required to produce and use these weapons is no longer difficult to obtain, as the basic science underlying their production has become more readily available. The Internet contains a vast amount of information relevant to WMD. In addition, it has been relatively easy to gain access to, and hide, biological and chemical agents.

The proliferation of small arms and light weapons is also of concern because such weapons have been used in almost all the conflicts of the post–cold war era. They are portable, durable, inexpensive to maintain, and easy to manufacture and manipulate. Even a child can use an automatic rifle. In today's intrastate armed conflicts, small arms are the weapons of choice. The use of small arms and light weapons, while not the primary cause of conflicts, is a decisive factor in prolonging intrastate wars. Nevertheless, little effort has been made until recently to prevent and curb their proliferation. The UN and other international organizations have studied the impact of proliferation on conflicts and society with the objective of drafting international agreements and mechanisms to prevent it. But the complicating factor here is that, because every nation's military and police forces have a legitimate need for small arms, it is virtually impossible to ban the weapons. Yet once government authority breaks down as a result of a civil war or revolution, weapon caches are often stolen or smuggled to nonstate actors.

The violent activities of nonstate actors challenge the governability of individual states. And over the long term these actors may present a ubiquitous, sustained threat that will destabilize the world's nation-state system. Armed nonstate actors are a worldwide phenomenon promoted by the internationalization of arms sales and production, which is now so extensive that even small groups have acquired a sophisticated range of weaponry, enabling them to openly challenge a government's monopoly of force (Olson 1994). This can lead, in extreme cases, to a collapse of the government or anarchy. The result is that a new type of state-versus-nonstate-actor conflict is now emerging, in which armed nonstate actors threaten all states to a greater or lesser degree.

While we should not overestimate the dangers here, since nonstate actors cannot easily topple major democratic powers like the United States and Japan, it is, nevertheless, clear that they can certainly damage relations between nations. Since the incidence of armed nonstate actors will grow in our increasingly interdependent world, it is imperative that we strengthen international cooperation. To this end, Japan-U.S. relations must be improved.

RESPONSES TO WMD PROLIFERATION

THE UNITED STATES

Because WMD pose the greatest threat to regional and national security, preventing and curbing their proliferation has become a top strategic priority for the United States. Washington has expressed concern about nuclear weapons development in the Asia Pacific region by India, Pakistan, North Korea, and China (Department of Defense 1998). On the domestic front, the Clinton administration has tried to establish a nationwide civil defense system to counter WMD terrorism.

Concern about the use of WMD by terrorists is not new. The use of toxins for political assassination can be traced back to ancient times and, in the mid-1970s, many politicians and academics publicly voiced fears about the use of nuclear materials by nonstate actors (Loehmer 1993). Nevertheless, at no other time has either the government or the private sector been as concerned about the issue as they are today. In 1998, it was reported that President Clinton had read Richard Preston's bioterrorist novel, *The Cobra Event*, and had ordered the government to investigate the plausibility of such a scenario occurring.[3] The prevailing opinion regarding WMD terrorism was neatly summed up by Defense Secretary William Cohen when he said that the question is not whether it will occur, but when and where (Sprinzak 1998). For those who are unconcerned about terrorism, this view may seem exaggerated. But there are three compelling reasons for top officials and specialists to be obsessed with WMD terrorism, especially with biological and chemical weapons (Betts 1998; Falkenrath 1998).

First, the United States recently experienced incidents of terrorism on a scale previously unknown. On February 26, 1993, Ramzi Ahmed Yousef and Islamic fundamentalist accomplices bombed the B-2 level of the parking garage at the New York World Trade Center, killing six people and injuring thousands. Other members of Al-Gama's Al-Islamiyya, an Egyptian-based terrorist organization led by Shaykh Omar Abdel Rahman, attempted to bomb the United Nations Building, the FBI, and the Lincoln Tunnel in New York City. In April 1995, a truck bomb completely destroyed the Alfred P. Murrah Federal building in Oklahoma City, Oklahoma, killing

168 and injuring hundreds. The principal offenders in this incident, Timothy McVeigh and Terry Nichols, were linked to a survivalist organization, the Michigan Militia, and were apparently influenced by the group's fanatically antigovernment conspiracy theories.

These incidents, which occurred in the first half of the 1990s, were seen by specialists as reflecting the advent of a new type of terrorist, the pseudo-religious fanatic who differs from the traditional political terrorist in that the latter will hesitate to commit mass murder because of a desire to gain public sympathy and support (Laqueur 1998; Hoffman 1994). The new terrorists, it seems, are driven by the urge to destroy something hateful, but lack a concrete political motive. It is, thus, hardly far-fetched to imagine that, were these terrorists to acquire WMD, they would use them without hesitation.

Second, events over the past few decades suggest that the United States is not immune to WMD terrorism. According to the Center for Nonproliferation Studies of the Monterey Institute of International Studies, six of the fifty-five instances in which WMD were used in the United States between 1960 and December 1998 resulted in injuries or fatalities, with the first of these instances occurring in 1973 and the remaining five occurring between 1980 and 1998 (Monterey Institute of International Studies 1999). In 1984, for example, followers of the religious cult Bhagwan Shree Rajneesh sprinkled homemade salmonella bacteria at the salad bars of restaurants in Oregon in an attempt to influence a local election; 751 people were hospitalized as a result. In 1985, The Covenant, the Sword and the Arm of the Lord, a fundamentalist Christian-linked group, was stopped before its members could dispense sodium cyanide in the water supplies of several cities. More recently, the Minnesota Patriot's Council, a group opposing government taxation, was discovered to have manufactured the biological agent ricin with the intention of killing federal law enforcement officers. The amount they produced was enough to kill more than 100 people. Judging from the documented increase in activity by the right-wing militia movement, it seems reasonable to suppose the presence of other WMD terrorists in the United States.

Third, many experts believe that the case of Aum Shinrikyō is neither exceptional nor particular to Japan, but a harbinger of future global terrorist activities. The use of the nerve gas sarin by the cult on Japanese civilians is seen as the first time that a nonstate actor has crossed the threshold between conventional weapons and WMD.

No government supplied Aum with its armaments, but it is important to acknowledge the cult's connections with high Russian officials like Oleg Lobov, then security council secretary, and Alexandro Rutskoi, then vice president. Without such connections, Aum could not have purchased the AK-74 rifle which it then tried to mass produce, acquired a military helicopter to disperse the sarin, or viewed plans for a factory that some of its members envisioned would produce two tons of sarin per day.[4]

Given these outside links, many American experts saw the Aum incident as a model case study of WMD proliferation among nonstate actors (Senate Permanent Subcommittee 1995; Kaplan and Marshall 1996; Campbell 1997; Falkenrath, Newman, and Thayer 1998). Their study of Aum's 1995 attack on the Tokyo subway system helped officials from the United States and other countries formulate ways to handle similar situations, including dealing with public panic and alarm.

In June 1995, the Clinton administration promulgated Presidential Decision Directive 39 (PDD-39), which established a policy framework for deterring, defeating, and responding to terrorism, including WMD. According to PDD-39, specific agencies are responsible for particular concerns: the Federal Bureau of Investigations (FBI) for domestic terrorism, the Department of State for international terrorism, and the Federal Emergency Management Agency (FEMA) for consequence management. The directive clearly demonstrates the high degree of concern in the United States about the possibility of WMD terrorism.

In July 1996, Congress passed the Defense against Weapons of Mass Destruction Act, commonly known as the Nunn-Lugar-Domenici Act. The act designated the Department of Defense as the lead agency for the Domestic Preparedness Program, which has been implemented by 120 cities to train firefighters, hazardous materials technicians, emergency medical service personnel, law enforcement personnel, hospital personnel, and dispatchers to handle a WMD crisis (General Accounting Office 1998).

JAPAN

Japan and the United States differ in their perceptions of, and approaches to, WMD terrorism. The Japanese government is yet to devote much public discussion to its concerns about WMD terrorism. The Ministry of Foreign Affairs states in its blue paper that, due to the danger of WMD proliferation, the international community needs to promote disarmament and arms control, and strengthen nonproliferation agreements. While Japan has ratified the four key nonproliferation conventions—the CWC, BWC, NPT, and CTBT—the ministry's statement seems to betray a lack of strategic thinking on the part of Japan with regard to its national interests and the specific problems it faces.

In its recent responses to terrorism, the Japanese government has seemingly displayed a tough stance, yet the country lacks an official definition of terrorism, and the National Police Agency (NPA) does not distinguish terrorism from guerrilla activities. Consequently, there is a lack of consensus regarding whether Aum is a terrorist organization. Bizarrely, Japanese academics, a majority of whom are leftist in orientation, disdain the study of terrorism because it is government-oriented. Thus it is that international relations researchers, who focus on nonstate actors, be they armed or not, are often viewed as nonrealists, while realists, to whom the state is the most important unit, consider Aum a public safety concern rather than a national security issue. This helps explain why most Japanese international politics scholars failed to regard the Aum incidents in the context of WMD proliferation. In fact, one can find few academic books or articles written by Japanese experts in modern terrorism.

The Tokyo Metropolitan Government has deprived Aum of its status as a religious corporation, which had provided it with preferential tax treatment, yet the organization not only survives, but has gradually expanded its power base.[5] The Japanese government has the right to disband politically dangerous groups or individuals in accordance with the Antisubversive Activities Law (Hakai Katsudō Bōshihō), but the law has yet to be invoked due to strenuous opposition by members of the Japan Federation of Bar Associations. These lawyers, many of whom are strongly antigovernment, claim that the law violates the constitution, which guarantees freedom of association and fundamental human rights. Aum has played this card well with the mass media and legal community, and has succeeded in thwarting implementation of the law.

Clearly, the perceptions of the Japanese and U.S. governments regarding the threat of WMD terrorism are asymmetric. The United States views WMD proliferation as a possible danger to its own society, while Japan appears unable to imagine that it might again be attacked by WMD terrorists. As will be seen later in this chapter, these differences have been a cause of bilateral friction.

RESPONSES TO SMALL-ARMS PROLIFERATION

Small arms and light weapons circulate out of war-torn countries and are passed from soldiers to civilians to children. Terrorists, organized crime syndicates, and other nonstate actors tend to choose either small arms —machine guns, submachine guns, and assault rifles—or light weapons— hand-launched missiles, mortars, grenades, and truck bombs.

The UN has been the leading organization in confronting the issue of small-arms proliferation since the end of the cold war (Miyasaka 1999). General Assembly Resolution 50/70 B, passed on December 12, 1995, requests that the secretary general, with the Panel of Governmental Experts on Small Arms, investigate the types of small arms and light weapons frequently used in conflicts, study the nature and causes of proliferation, and make recommendations on ways and means to prevent and reduce proliferation. Representatives from sixteen countries, including Japan and the United States, were appointed to the panel, which held three sessions over two years and adopted a final report in July 1997 that recommends seven measures for the reduction, and thirteen for the prevention, of small-arms proliferation. The report was adopted by the UN General Assembly in December 1997. Since 1998, the panel has been reorganized as the Group of Governmental Experts on Small Arms, with a membership representing twenty-three countries.

There is a wide divergence in the Japanese and U.S. perceptions concerning, and approaches to, small-arms proliferation. However, in examining these disparities, countries' societal and cultural differences must be taken into account.

THE UNITED STATES

The right to bear arms is guaranteed by the Second Amendment to the U.S. Constitution. This constitutional right is cited by the National Rifle Association (NRA), a powerful political lobby, in its efforts to oppose any arms control legislation, even though the United States suffers from a high rate of crime involving firearms. As one historian put it, it is assumed that the nation's love affair with the gun is impervious to change, since its roots are so deep in the nation's history and psyche (Bellesiles 1996).

During the cold war, the United States supported anticommunist governments and forces around the world by extending economic and military assistance. Somalia is one such example. But when the dictatorship of Said Barre was toppled in January 1991, Somalia fell into anarchy. Armed nonstate actors now divide and rule the nation. In Angola, the National Union for the Total Independence of Angola (UNITA), the country's largest guerrilla organization, continued its armed resistance against the government with support from the United States and South Africa even after the cold war ended. Southwest Africa, Southwest Asia, and Central America are now the focus of small-arms proliferation. The United States is no innocent bystander; like Russia, China, and other arms-exporting countries,[6] it bears some responsibility for this state of affairs. Its experiences are reflected in the fact that it has adopted a lower profile than the Japanese representative in both the small arms experts panel and group. One of the panel's key recommendations sought UN support for disarmament and demobilization in post-conflict societies, a matter of great sensitivity with the United States. Because of the failure of its Operation Restore Hope in Somalia, and the difficulties it experienced in Haiti with Operation Uphold Democracy, the United States understands better than Japan how difficult it is to carry out post-conflict measures related to disarmament and demobilization.

Furthermore, the United States tends to interpret the proliferation of small arms as a regional, rather than a global, problem. This thinking is evident in the Inter-American Convention Against the Illicit Manufacturing of and Trafficking in Firearms, Ammunitions, and Other Related Materials, a treaty which the United States signed with other Organization of American States (OAS) members in November 1997. The treaty, which seeks to prevent, combat, and eradicate the illicit transfer and manufacture of arms, includes practical measures, such as the tagging of weapons at the point of manufacture, the standardization of licensing procedures, and the exchange of information on these issues.

JAPAN

In Japan, citizens are strictly prohibited from owning firearms by the Firearms and Swords Control Law (Jūhō Tōkenrui Shojitō Torishimarihō) and the Ordnance Manufacturing Law (Buki-tō Seizōhō). There was a total of only 168 incidents nationwide involving firearms in 1995, 128 in 1996, 148 in 1997, and 154 in 1998. The number of fatalities resulting from gun-related injuries stood at 34 in 1995, 17 in 1996, 22 in 1997, and 19 in 1998 (National Police Agency 1999). Comparison with the United States in this regard is ludicrous, given the three-digit difference between the countries' figures. Although Japan's media and police officials have warned that Japanese society is beginning to resemble the armed society of the United States, most Japanese do not share that view. While the potential for danger exists because Chinese and Russian mobsters have accelerated their efforts to smuggle guns into Japan, and the price of guns is now so low that they have spread from organized gangs of yakuza (bōryokudan)

to those not in gangs, this can hardly be described as worrisome proliferation.

The domestic situation is, thus, relatively stable, and Japan has not ex-
ported small arms, light weapons, or other conventional weapons since the
cabinet of former Prime Minister Satō Eisaku in 1967 declared self-restraint
in line with three principles of non-arms exporting. These principles were
expanded in 1976 by the cabinet of succeeding Prime Minister Miki Ta-
keo, and have been maintained ever since. Unlike the United States, Japan
is innocent of involvement in the current global proliferation of small arms.
It is, thus, easy for Japan to adopt the moral high ground.

Against this background, the Japanese government, particularly the
Arms Control and Disarmament Division of the Foreign Ministry, has been
eager to tackle the issue of small-arms proliferation. Ambassador Dono-
waki Mitsurō, special assistant to the minister of foreign affairs, has served
as chairman of both the experts on small arms panel and of its subsequent
incarnation as the experts group. Remarkably, Japan was the only country
that offered to finance the three regional workshops held in Pretoria, San
Salvador, and Katmandu, in addition to the panel's regular sessions.

Since there is no multilateral regional alliance in East Asia, Japan has
been unable to lead initiatives to establish treaties comparable to the 1997
OAS and European Union (EU) agreements on preventing and combating
illicit arms trafficking. Japan has thus bypassed regional-level initiatives in
favor of global measures, albeit they do not relate directly to the country's
interests. What is noteworthy here is not that the approaches of the United
States and Japan have sometimes differed, but that, as with WMD, these
approaches have sometimes resulted in friction.

JAPAN-U.S. STRATEGIC COOPERATION

FROM COMMON AGENDA TO COMMON THREAT

In July 1993, Japan and the United States launched the Common Agenda,
a bilateral framework for coping with global issues such as the environment, population, AIDS, food, narcotics, and the support of women in developing countries. As then-Deputy Vice Minister for Foreign Affairs Ogura
Kazuo explained, both countries together are capable of providing the bulk
of the economic and technological wherewithal needed to solve global
problems (Ogura 1997).

Then, at an April 1996 summit meeting between President Clinton
and Prime Minister Hashimoto Ryūtarō, antiterrorism was added to the

Common Agenda. The reason for doing so was not, however, purely altruistic, but reflected the desire of both parties to ensure the safety and security of their respective governments and populations. In recent years, there have been several cases involving nonstate actors who have posed a common threat, and in which both countries have cooperated.

- Shirosaki Tsutomu, a member of the Japanese Red Army, attacked the U.S. Embassy in Jakarta in May 1986, and was taken into custody by Japan and turned over to the FBI in 1996.
- Ramzi Yousef, mastermind of the World Trade Center bombing, was indicted by the United States for detonating a plastic bomb aboard Philippine Airlines Flight 434 on December 11, 1994, killing one Japanese passenger.
- Members of Aum Shinrikyō were found to have purchased equipment and material necessary for their WMD program from some American companies, including molecular modeling software from CAChe Scientific of Beaverton, Oregon, and gas masks from a company in San Jose, California. They had also allegedly attempted to acquire a sophisticated laser from a Northern California manufacturer in March 1995, and an interferometer from a Connecticut company in 1993 (Campbell 1997).

Japan and the United States should have cooperated more closely with regard to the following:

- The sharing of information concerning Aum Shinrikyō. After the nerve gas attack in Matsumoto, Nagano prefecture, not only was Washington told nothing of what Japanese law enforcement agencies knew, but these agencies did not even themselves know what other domestic organizations had uncovered. The parties involved did not share their knowledge or expertise and so were unable to prevent the subsequent poison gas attack, which occurred with much greater devastation in the Tokyo subway system[7] (Carter, Deutsch, and Zelikow 1998).
- The August 1998 U.S. bombing of Osama Bin-Laden's training camps in Afghanistan, in retaliation for the bombing of the U.S. Embassies in Kenya and Tanzania. Immediately after the attack, the Japanese government commented that this use of force was understandable, a response that Washington considered sympathetic, but not terribly supportive. U.S. officials felt frustrated with this passive reaction from their "most important ally in the Asia-Pacific region."[8] By the time of Operation Desert Fox—the four consecutive days of

bombing of Iraq in December 1998—Japan had learned its lesson and voiced immediate, unqualified verbal support. Yet, ironically, Tokyo's seemingly automatic reaction appeared to reveal the government's continuing desire not to become involved in the conflict.

■ The Convention on the Prohibition of the Use, Stockpiling, Production, and Transfer of Anti-personnel Mines and on their Destruction. This treaty had been discussed at the Conference on Disarmament in Geneva from January 20, 1997, to September 10, 1997, in an attempt to create a consensus among participants. However, many of the nations favoring the elimination of antipersonnel land mines felt that the treaty should be signed without delay, even without a consensus, and joined a strong appeal in what came to be known as the Ottawa Process. Although Japan had at first sided with the United States in support of the Geneva bid to obtain a consensus, it suddenly changed its position in August 1997 and joined the Ottawa Process. The Japanese government saw this as a golden opportunity to make an international contribution and, spurred on by domestic and international pressure to take a stronger stand, decided to disregard U.S. claims that, for want of a suitable substitute, land mines were sometimes necessary for defense during wartime.

The Clinton administration had been emphasizing the military value of land mines, claiming that they needed exceptions to the convention for mines on the Korean peninsula, and for self-destructing land mines. The U.S. government was, thus, reportedly critical of Japan's decision to sign the convention without prior consultation. Meanwhile, the convention appears to contradict some areas of the Japan-U.S. military agreement, particularly with reference to the Japanese transportation of U.S. land mines within Japan (Ichikawa 1997).

TOWARD A COMPREHENSIVE AGREEMENT

Given the increasing need for cooperation, it is high time that both governments considered an antiproliferation strategy under the alliance framework, as has been proposed by several securities experts (Council on Foreign Relations 1998). When facing transnational threats, especially when dealing with nonstate actors whose activities are not limited to the two countries, it is widely believed that a multilateral approach is more effective. Nevertheless, the United States regularly holds bilateral consultations on transnational threats with many other governments (Revell 1991), and some of these have been formalized as part of strategic alliances. An example is the U.S.-Israel Counter-terrorism Cooperation Accord, consisting of six articles, which was signed on April 30, 1996 (Department of State 1996). The special nature of the U.S.-Israeli relationship aside, this agreement could help advance the Japan-U.S. relationship.

In May 1997, the United States and Mexico signed the Declaration of the United States-Mexico Alliance against Drugs (Office of National Drug Control Policy 1998), with a view to cooperating more closely in combating narcotics trafficking. However, one of the sixteen goals of the declaration stipulates that sources of illegal traffic in firearms are to be identified and deterred, and that an agreement outlawing illegal traffic in firearms is to be concluded in connection with the OAS firearms convention.

The above examples can be seen as precedents for treaties between the United States and its important allies. There have even been cases of cooperation in this area between the United States and China. To combat illicit drug trafficking along the border between China and Burma, the United States has established secret electronic surveillance posts in border areas and will provide funds for managing a surveillance center. This cooperation is viewed as a step toward joint operations in fighting international crime (*International Herald Tribune* 2 November 1998). Since U.S.-China relations have their share of tension and conflict, expanding these spheres of cooperation is very important to both sides.

It is time to consider developing a bilateral mechanism between Japan and the United States. The cooperation should go beyond fragmented interagency contacts and be based on a well-coordinated body with a presence in both nations. The first step would be reaching a comprehensive agreement on fighting arms proliferation by nonstate actors. In order to implement such an agreement effectively, Japan would need to establish an interagency mechanism to coordinate its policies.

The general objectives of this agreement should be preventing and curbing the proliferation of WMD by nonstate actors in the United States and Japan, and of small arms and light weapons by nonstate actors in the Asia Pacific region, as well as the encouraging of Asia Pacific countries to establish nonproliferation conventions in a regional framework. In the agreement, both governments should reaffirm that (a) all the activities of armed nonstate actors threaten national interests and regional stability; (b) both sides should mobilize all necessary means and resources to combat proliferation by nonstate actors; (c) private and commercial activities promoting proliferation should be penalized; and (d) neither side should support, directly or indirectly, armed nonstate actors in the United States, Japan, or Asia Pacific.

In addition, the agreement should stipulate five requirements. First, all information concerning terrorists and the international transfer of small arms and WMD-related materials will be shared, as the exchange of information is vital to bilateral cooperation.

Second, personnel from both countries will maintain close contact, extending beyond interagency relations, exchanges of experts, and training programs. Meetings of top officials should be held regularly, including programs involving government officials and private researchers.

Third, joint research and development projects are to be set up, especially in the areas of antiterrorism weapons and surveillance systems to prevent the illegal transfer of weapons at sea or in ports. For example, Japan could help fund the U.S. State Department's Counter-Terrorism Research and Development Program, which has recently sponsored projects in such areas as developing detectors for nuclear materials, the decontamination of chemical and biological weapons, law enforcement and intelligence database software, and surveillance technology (Perl 1998). Japan could also provide decontamination data from the Tokyo subway poison gas attack.

Fourth, future joint military operations other than wars are to be studied. While such cooperation is certain to touch a nerve with some, it should not be forgotten that the U.S. military presence in Japan can serve multiple purposes, and Japanese forces have expanded their role from national defense to peacekeeping operations and humanitarian assistance around the world. In this context, it is not inconceivable that joint U.S. operations with the Maritime Safety Agency (MSA) or the Self-Defense Forces (SDF) might be held to stop the illegal transfer of arms in the West Pacific. Not only is security in the area vital for maintaining sea lines of communication, but this is also where the greatest number of pirate attacks in the world occur (National Defense University 1998). Piracy is not a matter that usually concerns the national security communities of the United States and Japan, but it is not improbable that pirates will choose more sophisticated and destructive weapons in the future, in which case military force may be required.

Fifth, close contact and joint operations are to be effected where international terrorism involves U.S. or Japanese citizens in third countries.

The above points cover concerns that directly threaten the national interests of Japan and the United States. In addition, both governments should act aggressively to prevent and contain future potential threats worldwide in the interests of promoting a global partnership. To this end, Tokyo and Washington would be wise to bear in mind further considerations.

First, a Japan-U.S. fund should be set up to help nations combat terrorism and arms proliferation in Asia Pacific. China and East Asia are not immune to the threats of armed nonstate actors (Chalk 1998) and the recent political, economic, and social changes in the region may fuel discontent and frustration that could lead to violence and terrorism. The stability of the region serves the national interests of both the United States and Japan. In that regard, it is interesting to note that, in 1998, the United States established a counter-terrorism fund for the Middle East Peace Process, to which Japan and other countries provided funding.

Second, the partners should sponsor conferences and joint initiatives in the United Nations and other international organizations. Underestimating the need for this kind of cooperation has resulted in unwarranted discord, as with the land mine treaty. Such cooperation could be a step toward a firearms agreement covering East and Southeast Asian countries similar to the OAS convention. Another area for cooperation would be in proposing a treaty outlawing WMD terrorism, a needed addition to the eleven international treaties on terrorism already signed. Both governments could take the lead in preparing such a treaty for submission to the United Nations.

Third, the two nations absolutely must provide joint surveillance of, and support for, Russia. As the conflicts in Chechnya and the cases of unaccounted-for nuclear materials have shown (Stern 1999), Russia may very well turn out to be the main source of arms proliferation in Asia Pacific and around the world. Russia's huge but unmanageable arsenal and human resources are attractive to nonstate actors as well as rogue states. Offering economic and technological support to Russia helps the country save face, while guaranteeing vital national interests for Japan, the United States, and Asia Pacific. Japan has provided US$65 million to Russia since 1993 to assist dismantling its nuclear weapons. This support should be coordinated with the United States and expanded to include fighting organized crime activities and weapons proliferation.

Fourth, both governments must conduct regular consultations before adopting counter-proliferation and counter-terrorism policies. In the future, the United States will probably expand its use of force against these threats around the world. While Japan may choose not to fight militarily alongside the United States, there are many areas before and after military operations in which cooperation is possible.

In order to accomplish the above, Tokyo and Washington should consider establishing a counter-proliferation center, under the control of the prime minister and president, respectively. The center would have the authority to coordinate interagency efforts related to transnational threats, and its members could also include researchers from universities and think tanks.

CONCLUSION

In the post–cold war era, there are many areas involving transnational threats in which Japan could play an active role. However, because Japan is eager to enhance its international reputation and achieve a seat as a permanent member of the UN Security Council, it has chosen to regard the issues as global, rather than national or bilateral, and has, thus, neglected to use them as a means of forging a stronger alliance with the United States.

It is important for great powers to establish a national image among members of the international community. Japan has tried to replace its former image as a country that merely provides funds with that of one that is a contributor to international causes. This has been the guiding philosophy behind the nation's post–cold war foreign policy. While Japan's contributions appear to be wholly altruistic, a philosophy that does not allow a government to assign priorities in its foreign policy, as defined by its national interests, can be counterproductive. No government can help the entire world avert tragedy, and priorities must be decided.

Japan remains the second-largest economy in the world, but it has long been struggling with a recession, so now may not be the best time to assume permanent membership in the UN Security Council. Tokyo should stop defining proliferation as a global issue and reinterpret it from the perspective of national interest; it should seek to enhance the safety and security of the Japanese people and promote peace and security in Asia Pacific through the Japan-U.S. alliance. Looking at transnational threats from the perspective of national interest has proved beneficial to the United States, particularly as it has continued to expand its cooperation with allies in fighting arms proliferation by nonstate actors. The Japanese government needs to behave more positively in this regard, and link the elimination of transnational threats to the Japan-U.S. alliance. To do so would keep the relations between the two countries vital and important.

NOTES

1. The National Security Council established an office to address transnational threats under the direction of the Special Assistant to the President and National Coordinator for Infrastructure Protection and Counterterrorism. See also the White House (1998, 15–16).

2. The internationally accepted definition of small arms and light weapons can be found in United Nations General Assembly documents (1997, 11–12).

3. Richard Preston was called before the Senate Judiciary Subcommittee on Technology, Terrorism and Government Information and the Senate Select Committee on Intelligence about biological weapons threats on April 22, 1998 (Preston 1998).

4. In September 1998, the mass media were allowed to enter Aum's nerve gas factory, which the cult called Dainana Satian (Satian No. 7), in Kamikuishiki village, Yamanashi prefecture, just before it was dismantled in accordance with procedures of the Chemical Weapons Convention. According to one newspaper (*Asahi Shimbun* 16 September 1998), Dr. Inoue Naohide, a neurologist at Kyushu University, said: "It may be the largest facility for producing sarin ever built."

5. The Public Security Investigation Agency released the following information in February 1999 about the present Aum Shinrikyō. The cult at the time had a membership of 1,500, operated over thirty facilities, and 1998 sales of personal computers by related firms had amounted to US$58 million. Since a series of arrests in 1995, Aum had not been involved in any criminal activities, but the presence of cult members caused problems and conflicts with residents near Aum facilities and with local governments. Aum members had retained their original way of thinking and continued to believe in their absolute leader, Asahara Shōkō, who was in jail.

6. Since data for the global trade in small arms and light weapons is not issued by, for example, the Stockholm International Peace Research Institute, the International Institute for Strategic Studies (IISS), or the Arms Control and Disarmament Agency (ACDA), and such weapons are excluded from the UN Register of Conventional Arms, only fragmentary information is available.

7. John Sopko, deputy chief counsel to Senator Sam Nunn on the Permanent Subcommittee on Investigations, pointed out the lack of coordination in the United States: "The FBI viewed Aum as a CIA problem; the CIA viewed it as a domestic police problem for the Japanese; and within the CIA, bureaucratic divisions slowed progress. The subcommittee learned that the CIA's Counter Proliferation Center viewed Aum as a terrorist problem to be handled by the CIA Counter Terrorism Center. The Counter Terrorism Center, however, classified it as a proliferation or

regional problem falling under the purview of the agency's regional desks. The regional desks, in turn, shifted the responsibility to others. Meanwhile, no one in the CIA was focusing on Aum and their WMD development program until after Tokyo" (Sopko 1996–1997, 16–17).

8. A government official in charge of Japan made these off-the-record comments at a briefing and interview in September 1998 in Washington, D.C.

BIBLIOGRAPHY

Bellesiles, Michael A. 1996. "The Origins of Gun Culture in the United States 1760–1865." *The Journal of American History* 83 (2): 425–455.

Betts, Richard K. 1998. "The New Threat of Mass Destruction." *Foreign Affairs* 77 (1): 26–41.

Burger, Samuel R. 1999. Remarks to the Carnegie International Non-Proliferation Conference, Washington Marriott Hotel. Washington, D.C. 12 January 1999) <http://www.whitehouse.gov/WH/EOP/NSC/html/speeches/1990112.html> (30 January 1999).

Campbell, James K. 1997. "Excerpts from the Research Study 'Weapons of Mass Destruction and Terrorism: Proliferation by Non-state Actors'." *Terrorism and Political Violence* 9 (2): 24–50.

Carter, Ashton, John Deutsch, and Philip Zelikow. 1998. "Catastrophic Terrorism: Tackling the New Danger." *Foreign Affairs* 77 (6): 80–94.

Chalk, Peter. 1998. "Political Terrorism in South East Asia." *Terrorism and Political Violence* 10 (2): 118–134.

Council on Foreign Relations, Study Group on the U.S.-Japan Security Alliance. 1998. "The Tests of War and the Strains of Peace." Translation in Ronza 37 (May): 296–325.

Department of Defense, Office of International Security Affairs, United States. 1998. *The United States Security Strategy for the East Asia–Pacific Region 1998.* (23 November). <http://www.defenselink.mil/pubs/easr98/> (30 January 1999).

Department of State. 1996. "U.S., Israel Sign Counter-Terrorism Cooperation Accord—President Clinton, Israeli Prime Minister Peres, Text of Counter Terrorism Cooperation Accord, Joint Statement." *Dispatch* 7 (19): 225–227.

Falkenrath, Richard A. 1998. "Confronting Nuclear, Biological and Chemical Terrorism." *Survival* 40 (3): 43–65.

Falkenrath, Richard A, Robert D. Newman, and Bradley A. Thayer. 1998. *America's Achilles' Heel: Nuclear, Biological, and Chemical Terrorism and Covert Attack.* Cambridge, Mass.: The MIT Press.

General Accounting Office. "Combating Terrorism: Opportunities to Improve Domestic Preparedness Program Focus and Efficiency." 1998. Letter report, no. 12 (GAO/NSIAD-99-3): 1–52.

Hoffman, Bruce. 1994. "Responding to Terrorism Across the Technological Spectrum." *Terrorism and Political Violence* 6 (3): 366–390.

Ichikawa Fumitaka. 1997. "Chīsana jirai ga Nichibei anpotaisei wo yurugasu?" (Is the U.S.-Japan security alliance shaken by small land mines?). *Sekai Shūhō* (16 December): 10–13.

Kaplan, David E., and Andrew Marshall. 1996. *The Cult at the End of the World: The Terrifying Story of the Aum Doomsday Cult, from the Subways of Tokyo to the Nuclear Arsenals of Russia.* New York: Crown Publishers, Inc.

Laqueur, Walter. 1998. "The New Face of Terrorism." *The Washington Quarterly* 21 (4): 169–178.

Loehmer, Andrew. 1993. "The Nuclear Dimension." In Paul Wilkinson, ed. *Technology and Terrorism.* London: Frank Cass.

Miyasaka Naofumi. 1999. "Kokusaiteki na shōkaki no kakusan to Nihon no taiō" (Small arms proliferation and Japan's response). *Chianfōramu* 5 (6): 61–68.

Monterey Institute of International Studies. 1999. "Chemical and Biological Weapons Resource Page." <http.//cns.miis.edu/research/cbw/incid> (25 February 99).

National Defense University. 1998. *1998 Strategic Assessment: Engaging Power for Peace.* Washington, D.C.: U.S. Government Printing Office.

National Police Agency, Japan. 1999. *Heisei 11 nen-do keisatsu hakusho* (National Police Agency white paper).

Office of National Drug Control Policy. 1998. *United States/Mexico Bi-National Drug Strategy.* Washington, D.C.: U.S. Government Printing Office.

Ogura Kazuo. 1997. "Komon ajenda towa nanika?" (What is the common agenda?). *Gaikō Fōramu* (January): 58–60.

Olson, William J. 1994. "The Crisis of Governance: Present and Future Challenges." *Terrorism and Political Violence* 6 (2): 146–162.

Perl, Raphael F. 1998. "Terrorism, the Future, and U.S. Foreign Policy." CRS Issue Brief 95112.

Preston, Richard. 1998. "Chemical and Biological Weapons Threats to America: Are We Prepared?" Statement before the Senate Judiciary Subcommittee on Technology, Terrorism and Government Information and the Senate Select Committee on Intelligence (22 April). <http://www.senate.gov/~judiciary/preston.htm> (February 28).

Revell, Oliver B. 1991. "Structure of Counterterrorism Planning and Operations in the United States." *Terrorism* 14: 135–144.

Senate Permanent Subcommittee on Investigations, Committee on Governmental Affairs. 1995. "Hearing on Global Proliferation of Weapons of Mass Destruction." Staff Statement of 31 October.

Sopko, John F. 1996–1997. "The Changing Proliferation Threat." *Foreign Policy* 105 (Winter): 3–20.

Sprinzak, Ehud. 1998. "The Great Superterrorism Scare." Foreign Policy 112 (Fall): 110–124.

Stares, Paul B., ed. 1998. *The New Security Agenda: A Global Survey.* Tokyo: Japan Center for International Exchange.

Stern, Jessica. 1999. *The Ultimate Terrorists.* Cambridge, Mass.: Harvard University Press.

United Nations General Assembly documents, A/52/298. 1997. *General and Complete Disarmament: Small Arms.* (22 August): 11–12.

White House. 1998. "A National Security Strategy for a New Century." (October).

About the Contributors

NISHIHARA MASASHI is President of the National Defense Academy, where he taught as Professor of International Relations for 23 years until March 2000. He graduated from the Department of Law, Kyoto University (1962), and received his M.A. and Ph.D. in political science from the University of Michigan. He was associated with the Kyoto University's Center for Southeast Asian Studies in Jakarta, and taught at Kyoto Sangyo University. He was a Visiting Research Fellow at the Australian National University (1979) and at the Rockefeller Foundation (1981–1992). From 1993 to 1996, he served as Director of the First Research Department of the National Institute for Defense Studies. He is currently a Research Associate at the Research Institute for Peace and Security, Tokyo, and a member of the Trilateral Commission and the Korea-Japan Forum. He is the author of many works on Japanese security issues and international relations, including: *East Asian Security and the Trilateral Countries* (1985), *Senryaku kenkyū no shikaku* (An angle on strategic studies, 1988), *UN Peacekeeping: Japanese and American Perspectives* (coeditor, 1995), *Vietnam Joins the World* (coeditor, 1996), and *The Japan-U.S. Alliance, Q & A 100* (coeditor, 1998).

HOSHINO EIICHI has been Professor of International Relations, College of Culture and Communication, Tokyo Woman's Christian University, since April 2000. He was an Associate Professor in the Faculty of Law and Letters at the National University of the Ryukyus, Okinawa, beginning in October 1993 and a visiting researcher at the Graduate School of International Studies, University of Denver, from March 1996 to March 1998. From October 1998 to March 2000, he was Professor of International Relations at the Faculty of Law and Letters, National University of the Ryukyus, Okinawa. Professor Hoshino earned an M.A. in Law and Political Science from the Graduate School of Law and Political Science at Seikei University, Tokyo, in March 1980 and obtained an M.A. in International

Studies from the Graduate School of International Studies, University of Denver, in June 1990. His publications include *Crafting Democracy or Promoting Democratization: U.S. Foreign Aid for Democracy* (research report published by Foundations for Advanced Studies on International Development, 1997); "Japanese Foreign Aid and Human Rights Conditionality," in *Ryudai Law Review* (March 1997); and "Three Models of the Foreign Economic Aid Allocation: Preliminary Analysis for the Case of China," in *Ryudai Law Review* (March 1993).

MICHISHITA NARUSHIGE is a Research Associate at the National Institute for Defense Studies of the Defense Agency of Japan. He earned a B.A. in International Relations from the College of International Relations, University of Tsukuba, in 1990 and an M.A. in International Relations (Strategic Studies) and International Economics from the Paul Nitze School of Advanced International Studies, Johns Hopkins University, in 1994. Mr. Michishita also graduated from the Korean Language Institute at Yonsei University, South Korea, in 1988. His recent publications include "War and Technology," in *Sensō: Sono tenkai to yokusei* (War: Its development and restriction, 1997); "Role of Force in North Korean Diplomacy," in *Korea and World Affairs* (Summer 1997); "Two Koreas' Negotiation Strategies Revisited: Focusing on the Nuclear Issue," in *Middle Powers in the Age of Globalization: Implications for Korean Political Economy and Unification* (coauthor, 1996); and "Weapons of Mass Destruction on the Korean Peninsula," in *Tairyōhakai heiki fukakusan-no kokusaiseijigaku* (International politics of non-proliferation of weapons of mass destruction, 2000).

MIYASAKA NAOFUMI is Associate Professor of the Graduate School of Security Studies at the National Defense Academy, Yokosuka. After graduating from the Department of Law at Keiō University, Tokyo, in 1986, Miyasaka joined N.Y.K. (Nippon Yūsen Kaisha) Line (a car carrier operation). In 1990, he entered the Waseda University graduate school where he obtained an M.A. in Political Science in 1992 and became a Ph.D. candidate in Political Science in 1993. From 1993 to 1997, he was a Research Assistant at Senshū University, Tokyo, and from 1997 to 1999 he was a Lecturer of International Politics there. His area of concentration includes U.S. foreign policy after the Vietnam War, terrorism, military interventions, and small arms. His publications include "U.S. Anti-Terrorism Policy," in *Kokusai Mondai* (Japan Review of International Affairs, February 1999).

MURATA KŌJI is Associate Professor, Faculty of Law, at Dōshisha University in Kyoto. He holds a B.A. in Political Science from Dōshisha University and an M.A. and Ph.D. in Political Science from Kobe University. Dr. Murata obtained an M.Phil in Political Science from George Washington University, where he studied from 1991 to 1995 as a Fulbright student. He received the Yomiuri Merit Award for New Opinion Leadership in 1996, the Shimizu Hiroshi Award from the Japan Association for American Studies and the Suntory Academic Prize in 1999, and the Yoshida Shigeru Award in 2000. He is a member of the Research Institute for Peace and Security (RIPS), Tokyo. His areas of concentration include U.S. foreign policy, Japan's defense policy, and the Japan-U.S. security relationship. Dr. Murata is the author of *Daitōryō no zasetsu* (Downfall of a president, 1998) and *Beikoku shodai Kokubō Chōkan Foresutāru* (The first U.S. Defense Secretary Forrestal, 1999) and various papers and articles both in Japanese and English.

NAKAI YOSHIFUMI has been Senior Researcher, Area Studies Department I, at the Institute of Developing Economies since 1997. He graduated from Tohoku University with a B.L. in Politics in 1972 and from Indiana University with an M.A. in Comparative Politics in 1981. He also earned a Language Certificate (Chinese) from Beijing University in 1981. Dr. Nakai received a Ph.D. in Comparative Politics at the University of Michigan, Ann Arbor, in 2000. He was Lecturer at the Department of Asian Languages and Cultures, University of Michigan, from 1988 to 1991, Researcher at the Consulate General of Japan in Hong Kong from 1991 to 1994, and Senior Researcher, Center for Asia-Pacific Affairs at the Japan Institute of International Affairs from 1994 to 1997. His recent publications include "The Role of China in Building a New Northeast Asian System," in *The Future of China and Northeast Asia* (1997); "China, Japan and East Asia: Prospects for a Post–Cold War Security Arrangement in East Asia," in *China's International Role: Key Issues, Common Interests, Different Approaches* (1997); and "China and Regional Cooperation in the Asia-Pacific Region," in *Regionalism and Regional Cooperation* (1997).

SUDŌ SUEO is Professor of International Relations at Nanzan University, Nagoya. Prior to taking his current position, he was a researcher at the Institute of Asian Studies, Chulalongkorn University, Bangkok, and a fellow at the Institute of Southeast Asian Studies, Singapore. He is a graduate of the University of Michigan (Ph.D. in Political Science, 1987). Dr. Sudō's areas of concentration include Southeast Asian international relations and ASEAN and Japan-Southeast Asian relations. His publications include *Tōnan Ajia kokusai kankei no kōzu* (Structure of international relations in Southeast Asia, 1996), *The Fukuda Doctrine and ASEAN* (1992), and *Southeast Asia in Japanese Security Policy* (1991).

Index

Japan Center for International Exchange

FOUNDED IN 1970, the Japan Center for International Exchange (JCIE) is an independent, nonprofit, and nonpartisan organization dedicated to strengthening Japan's role in international affairs. JCIE believes that Japan faces a major challenge in augmenting its positive contributions to the international community, in keeping with its position as one of the world's largest industrial democracies. Operating in a country where policy making has traditionally been dominated by the government bureaucracy, JCIE has played an important role in broadening debate on Japan's international responsibilities by conducting international and cross-sectional programs of exchange, research, and discussion.

JCIE creates opportunities for informed policy discussions; it does not take policy positions. JCIE programs are carried out with the collaboration and cosponsorship of many organizations. The contacts developed through these working relationships are crucial to JCIE's efforts to increase the number of Japanese from the private sector engaged in meaningful policy research and dialogue with overseas counterparts. JCIE receives no government subsidies; rather, funding comes from private foundation grants, corporate contributions, and contracts.